Swiss You Were Here
The Expat Life In Switzerland

By
Michael Thomas Spenard

For Aaron
For Lisa

Introduction

Of all the things I thought I would be doing in this personally monumental moment, chomping down on a Big Mac was the very last thing I could imagine. But here I was, 5,300 miles from where I started, inside a 400 year-old building, in my new Swiss home, glassy-eyed and exhausted to the bone, digging into god damned McDonald's fast food.

Not schnitzel, not fondue, not bratwurst. Not a beer, not a glass of wine, not an Aperol spritz. No, I was eating the single most American meal possible. We had come thousands and thousands of miles, and here I was in a stupid ass Mickey D's.

How the hell did that happen!?

I blame the FAA.

"I'm sorry, did you say we can't leave out of the Austin *International* Airport because it's too hot, and instead we have to leave out of... Houston? Because Houston is so much cooler than... Austin?"

"For your cats' safety, per FAA guidelines, they cannot fly out of Austin because they classify it as too hot. The closest approved airport is Houston."

"Where it's cooler"

"I didn't write the law, sir"

The flights that left Houston were, of course, not direct flights, like the ones we could have taken out of Austin (which astounded me considering how much bigger Houston is than Austin). Now, we would have to detour to Frankfort, Germany, for a layover.

"Yes, you will stop over in Frankfort, but the cats will have to go to Amsterdam."

"I'm sorry, what now?"

"There are no flights to Frankfort that have room for your cats. We can get them on a flight to Schiphol, and then you can all meet up in Zurich"

"Why can't we go to Amsterdam with the cats?"

"That flight is booked, people-wise"

"So we can't fly out of Austin, cannot fly to Frankfort or Amsterdam together, and cannot fly to Zurich together? Wait, wait, wait! We're not going to Zurich!"

"Yes, you must go to Zurich because that is the Swiss airport with animal customs"

"Oh, fuck me"

At this point it was too late to try and sell five house cats on the dark web. Besides, they already had their kitty passports and microchips and vaccinations and special travel carriers and hundreds of dollars wrapped up in an international pet relocation service. My wife, Lisa, informed me that, no, we couldn't just send them via FedEx. We had thought securing an international moving company, getting visas, breaking a lease, and selling half of our possessions was the hard part. That ended up being the easy part. Moving our oblivious children was proving to be the breaking point, both mentally and financially.

In the end, it would end up costing us more to fly the cats to Switzerland than it did to move all of our possessions across the Atlantic Ocean.

So now, because of all of these FAA restrictions, we had arrived in our new home of Basel, Switzerland on a Sunday evening instead of a Monday morning as originally planned. This little twelve-hour difference had actually made all the difference. Arriving on a Sunday evening meant that the whole of the city was effectively closed. It was well after 7pm by the time we had finally found our temporary studio apartment in a hidden alley of the Old Town, deposited the scared, tired, and pissed off cats, and set off to find a bite to eat. After nearly twenty-four hours of travel, we weren't hungry - we were hangry.

And everything was closed. Except for the cruelly familiar Golden Arches. Which is why our very first meal as expats in Switzerland was an American fast food value meal.

On the flip side, it was, surprisingly, the best freaking Big Mac I've ever had, and that was saying something, because I thought I had already found the elusive Perfect Mac.

I got to visit the USSR's very first McDonald's back in 1991. It had only been open for a month, and the line snaked across Moscow's Pushkin Square, down the street, and around the block. As Americans, and escorted by our government-provided *InTourist* guide (read: KGB), we were taken past the endless queue, shivering in the brutal Russian winter, to the very front of the line. A counter the length of a football field stretched out before us. There were at least thirty registers, and behind them, I found the only smiles I ever saw in my entire tour of the country. Beaming proudly, my Russian burger dealer handed me a paper menu to peruse.

After ordering my meal, she said something to me that I didn't quite understand in my rudimentary Russian. Holding up the universal finger of "just a moment", she beckoned behind her to a wall of waiting employees who I realized had just been standing there the whole time. This, I learned, was an army of interpreters. A helpful Sergei explained that I was simply being given my change and told to enjoy my meal.

And enjoy it, I did.

I grew up in the 1970s when places like McDonald's and Burger King still took pride in their product and were considered a big treat. By the time I visited the Soviet Union, in the early 90's, quality was not a word associated with burger joints. So when I took a bite of my gorgeous, steaming гамбургер, I was blown away. Beef was a luxury item in the Soviet Union, and to be served a patty with so much flavor was a big surprise. Food quality was not a Russian hallmark. I had been served a chicken with three legs on an Aeroflot flight in Uzbekistan, and this was only a few years after Chernobyl. Seriously, it literally had three legs. Here in Moscow, my burger was so good, my milkshake so silky smooth, that I kept the wrapper and the paper menu as souvenirs (matted and framed, I still have them to this day).

So sitting there, examining my Swiss Big Mac, I was amazed to find it so picture perfect, like a television ad. It was hot, and the beef patty actually tasted like beef (instead of grease, as seems to be the norm anymore). The fries were so good you just wanted to be alone with them. And the chocolate milkshake was a revelation. I didn't know milk could taste so… magical. If this kind of perfection was the norm in a place like a crappy chain burger joint, how perfect was everything else here in Switzerland going to be?

One of the less magical things, we quickly learned, was that Switzerland shuts down at sunset. This was why we were stuck with McDonald's as our only dinner option on a Sunday evening. It was August, in the throes of summer, and we fully expected to plonk down at a sidewalk cafe, calm our frayed nerves with a bock or lager, and nibble a pretzel or two. Even though the evening was beautifully attuned to al fresco dining and drinking and relaxing, there was nary a light in any shop or restaurant window. Sunday evenings were sacrosanct. Only the vulgar American fast food joint was open for business. The bars, the cafes, the kiosks, the grocery stores, all closed for the day. Sundays are the day of rest, and when the Swiss say rest, they mean rest. As we settled in, we learned just how serious the Swiss consider work-life balance. In retrospect, it seemed appropriate that our first real assimilation into Swiss culture was to not experience any at all.

Growing up, I didn't have pictures of fast cars or supermodels or pop stars on my bedroom walls (well, other than that poster of Apollonia over my bed (hubba-hubba)). Instead, I had posters of Louise Brooks and Josephine Baker and Modigliani and Sartre. My bookshelves were filled with every single thing that F Scott Fitzgerald had ever written. My dream wasn't to be a rock star or a movie star or a sports star. My dream, as weirdly dorky as it was, was to live abroad as an expat. The lives of the flappers and the romantic poets and writers of the 1920s and the glamour of leaving the mundanity of America for the exciting and exotic climes of Europe just sang to me. From the time I was a teenager, I couldn't wait to get out - out of my hometown, out of my state, out of the country. America simply held no allure. America was boredom and dullness and mundanity.

Hell, coming back to Hollywood caused F Scott's own deflated heart to utter a final, maudlin "aw, shit".

My first chance at the expat life came when Lisa got a job opportunity in Canada, and we jumped at it. Even if it was just across the border, I would be an expat at last!

And it sucked.

It sucked so very much.

We were in a tiny resort town in the middle of boo-foo British Columbia. It was four hours to Vancouver, four hours to Calgary, and there wasn't a damned thing in between. While on a beautiful lake surrounded by miniature mountains, the town was a glorified strip mall, full of Ed Hardy-clad douchebags high on meth and Daddy's oil money. It was the most isolating and depressing place I had ever lived, and we increasingly hated it there with each passing day. When the opportunity to move to Los Angeles for a job transfer became an option, we jumped on it with rabid fervor.

You would think this two-year hell-scape would have dampened, if not brutally murdered, my desire to live abroad. If anything, it only reinforced my belief that I needed to get to Europe. It wasn't America I needed to leave behind - it was North America entirely.

After years of moving across the US, we had ended up in the overhyped dumpster of Austin, Texas (though I will say that the bbq is entirely all that and more). Working her way up the corporate ladder, Lisa was eventually offered a position that would require her relocating.

"I was offered a promotion today, but it would mean moving again"

"We move all the time. No biggie"

How much had we moved? In twenty years together, we had moved from Chicago to St Pete, Florida, to Las Vegas to Portland, Oregon. It was from there that we ended up in Canada. From Canada, we went to LA (our agreed upon favorite place, it became our adopted home town), and then on to San Jose. Finally, we had spent the last two years in Austin. Moving had become second nature to us.

"Um, this move might be a little bit of a challenge"

"Oh, God, we don't have to go back to Canada, do we!?"

"Well, it is international…"

My ears perked up. Lisa had been to Europe a number of times for work trips.

"Are we moving to Switzerland!?"

"Only if you want to"

"HELL YEAH I WANNA MOVE TO SWITZERLAND!!!"

It did end up being a much more nuanced conversation than that, as the list of pros and cons ended up being enormous. This wasn't just a change of scenery. This would be a complete and total change of lifestyle, economics, culture, language, you name it. This would be a logistical nightmare. This would be extraordinarily expensive. Switzerland is considered the most expensive place on earth to live. But it is also considered the best place on earth to live. Lisa would be accepting a big promotion that would afford us lots of opportunities to travel and explore Europe.

I would finally be a real, honest-to-God expat.

The dream had been reignited earlier that year when Lisa invited me to tag along on one of her visits to Basel. This was well before she received her promotion, but given the increased amount of travel to Europe led us both to believe that if she set her sights on moving up, she could definitely make it happen. To be fair, Switzerland was never a country I considered as a place to call home. Hell, I never really ever thought about visiting there. I thought if I ever ended up living in Europe, it would be somewhere predictable like London or Paris or Berlin. Lisa had been to Basel a number of times and every time she fell for it a little more. Even before living there was a possibility, she was telling me how much she could see us there. She said she thought the city suited me. Color me intrigued. So I was thrilled to join her on a week-long sojourn in Basel.

All I knew about the city was that it hosted the Art Basel festival. I didn't know where in the country it was located (in the northwest corner where Switzerland, Germany, and France all meet at one point on the Rhine River), what to do there (it hosted a world-famous art festival, so art museums, duh!), how big it was (bigger than I thought at 170,000 people), or what the weather would be like (it was February, so cold, dumb ass). After some research, I realized what an amazing stepping off point it would be for exploring. I planned a few day trips, for when Lisa was working in the office, to Bern, to Freiburg, Germany, and Strasbourg, France. She knew I'd be content to just wander on my own. I'm a brilliant wanderer (or as they say on The Continent, *flanneur*). I had tagged along with Lisa on other work trips to London and Moscow and the majority of days, while she was working, I was left to my own devices to just wander these cities and explore. My favorite way to learn about a city isn't through tourist attractions; it's aimlessly walking the streets, poking around neighborhoods, and getting lost. So now was an opportunity to once again be in my happy place, letting my feet take me wherever they pleased, with no agenda, at my complete and total leisure.

She was right. I fell hard for Basel the moment I met her.

Small enough to be cozy and walkable, large enough to feel like a proper city with plenty to see and do, it was a Goldilocks town. I was awed by seeing one of the most famous rivers in the world cut through the middle of the city. I was gob smacked walking by houses built in the 1200s and 1300s. I was dumbfounded by standing inside a cathedral that was over one thousand years old. Even in the color-drained drabness of February, the city was brilliant and vibrant. It felt, above all, welcoming.

"I could totally see us living here"

"See, I told you"

"Man, if you could get transferred here…"

"I'm working on it, Boo. I'm working on it"

Only two months later, she made it work, and was offered the new position and the chance to live and work in Basel. While I jumped on the chance before she even finished asking if I wanted to do this, having been there once before had made my "yes" that much easier. I really did fall for Basel on that short visit. No other place had spoken so clearly and absolutely to me before, or since. It was international kismet.

Which made McDonald's as our first meal as newly minted Swiss residents so laughably stupid. After so much planning and sweating and panic, after a hellacious transatlantic journey, after so many imaginings of a new life, we began it all with the most American meal possible.

Chapter One - Becoming Swiss

In order to help us get all of our immigration and integration ducks in a row, Lisa's company had provided us with a "fixer".

"You mean like Jean Reno in *Le Femme Nikita*, the precursor to Jean Reno as Leon *The Professional*?"

"I don't think my company set us up with a hit man, sweetie"

"You owe me five francs if he shows up in a trench coat"

"It's August, dumb ass"

We met Michael in front of the Canton's offices. A short, smiling German, he looked more like a physics professor than an international man of mystery. And, no, he wasn't wearing a trench coat. He was there to get Lisa and I registered with the Canton so that we could become Residents of Switzerland.

You're probably wondering what a Canton is, just as we did when we first starting investigating the ins and outs of moving to Basel. Switzerland is a nation made up of 26 Cantons. Imagine a micro-nation and a US state had a baby. Once all independent states, countries, kingdoms, or principalities, in 1315, three of these guys came together to form a confederation (as a mutual defense pact against the Hapsburgs). Eventually, more and more of these states joined this pact, which in turn became the nation of Switzerland (so named because the original pact was signed in the Canton of Schwyz). Canton is the name given to these individual states, and Basel is one of them. Well, actually, there are two Basels - there is Basel-Stadt (or Basel City) where we would be living, and Basel Landschaft (or Basel Land) which is the city's agricultural neighbor. Basel City was the last Canton to join the confederation in 1501, making it the "newbie" on the block.

This confederation is what lends Switzerland its official name: *Confederatio Helvetica* (*Helvetica* is the Latin name given to the region by the Romans). Many people are confused, without knowing this little tidbit of information, when they learn that the abbreviation for Switzerland is CH (which makes it much easier to differentiate it from Sweden). This is also why the Swiss Franc is abbreviated as CHF. You'll see many references to the Swiss Franc throughout this story. During our tenure in Basel, the exchange rate was close to parity, with 1CHF worth about $1.10. So when you see prices in CHF, they'd be 10% more in US dollars. This will come to shock you when we get to grocery shopping. It certainly shocked us!

Cantons are much more powerful than US states. Cantons issue visas, not the federal government. This meant that we were only allowed to live in the Canton of Basel-Stadt, as that was the Canton that had issued our visa. We could not, for example, live in the neighboring Canton of Basel Landschaft, or decide to up and move to Zurich or Geneva. We were tied to Basel-Stadt because Lisa's company was in Basel-Stadt and they had sponsored her visa for work in Basel-Stadt. In the US, visas are issued by the federal government and one could live in whatever state they please. Not so in Switzerland.

So we were meeting Michael outside the Canton office in the Old Town so that he could assist us in getting registered, getting our IDs, making sure all of our immigration paperwork was completed properly, and translating for us as needed. Lisa's office had completed most of her paperwork, so I was the one who was nervous about having made a mistake of some sort that would find me deported upon arrival and forced to live with my parents in Illinois.

In a strange turn of events, we learned that the system had not finished processing the paperwork Lisa's office had submitted for her, and so she could not have her resident ID card issued to her that day. They generously provided an official stamped letter assuring whomever needed to know that she was, indeed, now a resident of the Canton. But her photo ID would need to be mailed to her in a few days. I, on the other hand, had my ID in hand as we left the office, which was a fantastic feeling. This tangible object made the whole day feel that much more real. They never even gave us resident cards in Canada. No, they just stapled a paper visa in our passports and that was it. We did have driver's licenses from British Columbia, but that was it. So having this laminated ID in hand made me feel a bit giddy.

We also received an enormous welcome packet that contained the following:

> Free tickets to every single museum in Basel
> A calendar of trash pick-up days and a map of the location of every recycling point in the city
> A certificate for German language lessons (for me, which I was obligated to take)
> Two vouchers for free iodine tablets in case of a nuclear attack

I suppose I should note how the notion of nuclear war and

Switzerland's neutrality effects everyday life. I would learn, as we house hunted and viewed apartments, that every single residential building in the country has a fallout shelter in the basement. Every apartment viewing will include a stop in the basement bunker. Yes, they have enormous vault-like doors, most with signs telling children this is not a play-space.

It made me strangely nostalgic for the Cold War. The country is both heavily fortified at the border, albeit inconspicuously, and all infrastructure is designed to be utterly destroyed in the event of an invasion. Every tunnel and bridge, every rail network and every major highway have explosives built into them so that they may be destroyed if necessary to prevent them being taken over.

The Swiss basically think "we built this, we're the only link between north and south, and if anyone tries to take it, we'd rather destroy it all". And they are serious as hell about this.

There are thousands and thousands of barns, farms, and chalets that dot the landscape that are not actually barns, farms, or chalets at all. No, these are Howitzer gun installations disguised as normal buildings, ready to shoot your ass out of the sky. As I explored the area over the course of our time there, I would regularly come across hidden bunkers and sniper hideouts along the border area, nestled deep in the woods. The Swiss will blithely stroll right past them, but for me, they were both fascinating and slightly unnerving.

Air raid siren drills are held once a month, too, which is even creepier than the tornado sirens you would hear growing up in the Midwest. After Russia invaded Ukraine in 2022, the country realized that these monthly drills were scaring the bejesus out of the Ukrainian refugees that now lived there. To minimize PTSD, fliers and television ads and radio announcements were made for a week before each test letting these poor people know this was just a test to ensure their future safety. Even to someone like me, those sirens give you the absolute creeps, acting as constant reminders of just how important neutrality is to the Swiss, and how prepared they are to defend it.

One other note about Swiss defense - military service is mandatory, and you will see reservists called up on weekends for drills. For all their infrastructural fierceness, the Swiss have the world's least intimidating military uniforms. They look like mailman uniforms, if those uniforms were designed by a high school drama department. They're adorably laughable.

Though not as laughable as the Swiss Air Force.

Why, you may be asking, is the Swiss Air Force laughable?

This is one hundred percent true (though will be changing in 2023): the Swiss Air Force is only on duty between 9am-6pm, Monday through Friday.

No, seriously.

Should an invasion occur on a weekend, or after the dinner hour, well, good luck getting a plane in the air. Yes, the Air Force follows the strict Swiss work-life balance guidelines and refuses to allow their workers to be on duty at odd hours, lest it interfere with their family life and free time. Once this anachronism made its way onto the internet, the Air Force realized that public knowledge of this lack of perpetual preparedness was detrimental
and ordered that reservists be on call from 6pm - 9am and on weekends. Sometimes the Swiss determination to give all citizens a healthy and happy lifestyle veers into the absurd.

Makes you wonder who would set off all those explosives should Switzerland be invaded at 11pm.

The importance of work-life balance was something that we had read about in our research, but did not expect it to be as serious and wide-spread in real life. Michael set us straight with this, explaining just how differently Europeans viewed day to day life than Americans. He had been born and raised behind the Iron Curtain in East Germany, moved to Detroit in his twenties, and spent the last twenty years in Basel. Having experienced a large spectrum of day to day life in a variety of cultures, he was in a good position to inform us just how different the US and Europe viewed life in general. Reading about it does not prepare you for the seriousness with which the Swiss take their leisure time.

Hearing about it is one thing. I got to experience it first hand before Lisa ever started working in the office.

Adjusting to the time change in that first week in Basel, I had been waking well before dawn. Being August, I decided I would take advantage of the warm, humid mornings and explore the Old Town in the quiet darkness, camera in hand. As the sun began to color the sky, I decided to grab myself a coffee and sit by the river and watch the city wake. I then encountered my first realization about this legendary commitment to fairness in work hours. It was 7am and I could not, for the life of me, find a single solitary place open to buy a coffee. The Starbucks was shuttered, the Migros convenience mart was closed, the McDonald's was dark.

I began to take stock of this city's awakening. The trams were running, but were virtually empty. The Kiosks, convenience counters located every 10 blocks in every corner of the city, had their metal shutters locked. There were no huddled masses of commuters waiting for the trams, no suited bankers hustling towards the business district. Other than the street sweepers and sleepy Baselers walking their dogs, the streets were empty and quiet. In any American city, this would be one of the busiest times of the day, and yet here, it was like a holiday morning, on a Sunday.

The reason for this is the Swiss idea that no one should have to work odd hours, or hours different from family members' schedules, so that everyone is home to have breakfast together, is home to have dinner together, has the same days off together. Every business in Switzerland will open no earlier than 9am, and unless it is the two weeks before Christmas, will not be open any later than 6:30pm. All businesses, including grocery stores and Starbucks and convenience marts, are all closed on Sundays. If you need to grocery shop on a Sunday, or need anything at all, your only option, true across Switzerland, is to go to the train station. Every train station in the country has either a Coop or Migros grocery store located inside, and they are the only businesses open on a Sunday. And even then, they'll only be open from 10am until 5pm.

The idea of grabbing a coffee on the way to work isn't in the vocabulary. The Swiss will, instead, take a coffee break at 9:30am, called the *z'Nüni*, where coworkers gather together and sip espresso and nosh a *gipfeli* (croissant). 9:30am is the absolute worst time of day to try and stop by a coffee shop because everyone takes their *z'Nüni* at the same time, almost as if it were a law.

The Swiss will take a full hour for lunch. You are simply not allowed to eat at your desk. This is strictly verboten and is so frowned upon that people have required plastic surgery to fix the severity of the frown they have given violators. You are expected to take your full hour, if not more should you either require it, or are simply having a good time out with your coworkers. You will dine out, usually at a sit-down restaurant or cafe, or you'll grab one of a hundred different grab-n-go sandwiches offered at every grocery store lunch counter and sit in a shaded city square or along the banks of the Rhine. You'll have a glass or two of wine, or a mug or two of beer (and you can grab a cold one at any McDonald's or Burger King, Subway or Domino's in town, too), and think nothing of it. You'll sit outside to dine, rain or shine, hot or cold. And you will be an adult and never abuse the booze or the flexibility of return-time to the office.

If you are lucky (and Lisa was), your company will provide you with a lunch card. This is a pre-loaded credit card (pre-loaded by the company, by the way) that is their way of paying for your lunch, as a perk. Lunch cards are incredibly common, seeing as business will not allow you to bring a lunch from home. To facilitate this, companies will pay for their workers' lunches via this card, which is accepted at 99% of business that serve food, be it a restaurant, cafe, take-out joint, coffee shop, or grocery store. The allowance can vary from 30CHF to 100CHF a day. Cards are automatically refilled each month. Not only does this encourage workers to have a large, hearty lunch, it also subsidizes the local food service industry. Happy, well fed workers, are productive workers.

During Covid lockdown, Lisa's company continued to load up her lunch card, even though she was working from home. In order to keep restaurants operating, companies across Switzerland continued to subsidize lunch cards for their employees. With no restrictions on what time of day you could use them, and with a 100CHF limit per day, we used her card to order in dinner many, many nights. Delivery drivers would ring the buzzer and leave our food in the lobby where we would go down and retrieve it off the bottom stair. It kept us from going out to the grocery store so often when it wasn't quite so safe to do so. In truth, we could have ordered 100CHF worth of food five days a week and had it paid for by her company, and they would have been totally fine with that because it just wasn't the Swiss way to abuse a privilege like that. We didn't abuse it, though, but we sure did appreciate it.

At 4pm, the Swiss take their *z'Vieri*, or afternoon break.

You'll step outside for another coffee, or perhaps a cold beer or a Negroni. If you had no watch, never looked at the clock on your phone, you could tell time simply by watching the office buildings empty out at *z'Nüni* or *z'Vieri*.

When 6pm arrives, you leave.

You do not stay late. You do not put in extra hours to catch up. You go home, where there will be zero emails waiting for you, as it is illegal to send work-related emails after 6pm or on weekends. When your work day is done, your work day is done. Period. Your time off the clock is your time.

Unless an *Apero* has been organized. This is an evening cocktail hour, usually set for 6-7pm, where an invitation is simply not ignored. It would be incredibly rude to decline. The American "I'll see if I can make it" is unacceptable. The Swiss are very Yoda-like when it comes to invitations. Do, or do not, there is no try. If you say you are attending, you must. The Swiss are also very conservative about inviting non-Swiss to parties, cocktail hours, or home gatherings, so should you decline, you will not be asked again. Ever.

Speaking of parties, if it is your birthday, your office will not throw you a party or buy you a cake. You must throw the party, you must invite everyone to attend, and you must provide the cake and all the refreshments. The same applies if going out to dinner. Should you go out for a celebratory birthday dinner, the birthday boy or girl is expected to be the one who foots the bill for everyone else (unlike the US where the celebrant is treated). Surprise parties, then, aren't really a thing in Switzerland.

So when 6pm rolls around, you are either going home, or going out for a cold one, and neither is negotiable.

This same principle applies to taking time off, or calling in sick. There are no set number of sick days - if you are sick, you should not come into work. It's an honor system that

works extraordinarily well. The honor
system is paramount in Switzerland. It works so perfectly, in so many ways, and every time I encountered a
scenario where honesty was the key or principle, I was blown away. Trust me, you're going to learn a lot about the Swiss honor code as we go on.

Time off is also extraordinarily important to the Swiss, and Europeans as a whole. The concept of weeks of time off is so foreign to Americans, and yet, is so ingrained in the European mind that they are more flummoxed by Americans' lack of time off as we are by their sheer number of vacation days.

Years before our move, Lisa was in Brighton, UK for business, and I tagged along. We joined her team of Brits, French, and Germans for dinner one evening and we utterly confounded these Europeans with comparisons of vacation allotment. Their minds were simply boggled to learn it could take up to a year of employment before earning, maybe, five days of paid time off. Two years might net you a week, two if you were lucky. They thought we were bullshitting them. They literally could not comprehend what we were telling them. The idea of vacation and leisure time is so totally ingrained in the European mindset, from business hours to paid time off.
Lisa had been at her job in Basel for over a year and her boss admonished her for not taking her allotted time off.

"You should take July off"

"Okay, I can take a few days off in July"

"No. Take JULY off"

And she still had enough vacation days left over to take off half of November and almost all of December, which she grudgingly did.

This was the aspect of life in Switzerland that I knew would give Lisa pause. If there was a culture she was much more suited for, it was Japan, with their insane commitment to their jobs and companies, at the expense of all other aspects of life. Just dropping things at 6pm was anathema to her work ethic. But as one of her co-workers explained it, the whole of the continent operated in this way and everything worked just fine. Businesses didn't collapse because an email wasn't sent until the next day. Businesses weren't saved because someone heroically stayed until 8pm.

In America, you are judged by how much time you put in; in Europe, you are judged by how much time you take off.

Work life balance extends to the mundane, as well. As I mentioned, everything is closed on Sunday. Traditionally, this was meant to be the day of worship, but has since evolved into the day of family time and relaxation. Relaxation means exactly that. You may not mow your yard on a Sunday. You may not vacuum or do laundry. You may not practice your musical instrument. You are not to do any glass recycling on Sundays (or during the lunch period of 11am-1pm during the week, or after dark on any day). Sunday is quiet time (though tell the hundreds of church bells in the city that). It took me half a year after moving back to the States to realize that I could vacuum, now, on a Sunday.

Should you violate the noise rules, you were going to be faced with two consequences:

The first was the *polizei*.

The second was a life-long enemy in the neighbor that called the police.

That strict neighbor is known as *Bünzli* - better known in the US as a "Karen". The Swiss will not confront you directly. They will not try and work things out in a friendly manner.

Their first and only step will be to call the police. Thankfully, the Swiss *polizei* (unlike their American counterparts) will not shoot you when they knock on your door. But they will knock on your door and tell you that your neighbors want you dead. The non-emergency line is used 1000% times more than the emergency line. This is simply a Swiss way of life. Your neighbor starts up a load of whites at 11pm, you call the police. Your neighbor accidentally drops their phone on the floor above you at 7:01pm, you call the police. Your neighbor leaves the door to the cellar open, you call the police. You inevitably become *Bünzli* because all of your neighbors are *Bünzli*. This is the way.

On the other hand, on a Sunday, most Swiss are not home anyway. They are in the myriad of wooded parks, strolling along the Rhine, or climbing up a mountain (man, the Swiss love to climb up mountains). Sunday is the day you go out, regardless of the weather, and you participate in some kind of physical activity. Playing football in the park, speed-walking through the forest, or tackling the switchback trails up the side of an alp. We very quickly learned the art of the Sunday *flanneur*, or walkabout. You'll encounter more people on a Sunday afternoon than during rush hour on a Monday. Besides, being outside on a Sunday keeps you from being called out for breathing too loud by your *Bünzli* neighbor.

After our trip to the Canton office, we were able to set up a bank account. One needed to be residents in order to do so. Michael had made an appointment for us at the only bank in Switzerland that will do business with American citizens. Because Americans must pay taxes on income, no matter their location in the world, and banks must release financial information to the IRS, it is next to impossible to find a bank in Switzerland that will do this. No Swiss bank wants to release private information to a foreign government. After all, Swiss bank accounts are famous because of their ironclad privacy. Only UBS will release information to the US, and so they were our only banking option.

China, by the way, is the only other country on the planet that forces expats to pay income tax while living outside the country. Yes, American and Chinese expats must pay double income tax - to the US/China and to the country of residence. We had to do it when we lived in Canada, and we'd have to do it again living in Switzerland. This makes tax season migraine season.

Michael had other business to attend to, so he left us to it. We made our way to the main branch of UBS, a massive Victorian palace, standing sentinel over Bankverein (loosely translated as the "confluence of banking society"), a large hub on the edge of the Old Town. We were immediately greeted by a sharply dressed Bond Girl in a navy blazer and a cloud of ethereal sultriness.

Even Lisa looked at me and mouthed "daaaaamn!"

After confirming our appointment, she led us to an elevator, pushed a button, and told us someone would be waiting for us above. As we exited the lift, we were greeted by another Bond Girl, with legs to heaven and a smile that made me forget how to speak. This time Lisa looked a bit annoyed.

"Put your tongue back in your mouth"

Alongside her was a statuesque GQ model of a man, with slicked back corn silk hair and a gleaming gold Rolex on his wrist. He guided us down a crimson-carpeted hallway to a small oak paneled room with a gleaming walnut desk and three leather chairs. We were told to take a seat and Christoph would be right with us. Would we care for any sparkling water or espresso while waited?

"Are we in a spy movie?"

"I feel like Christoph is going to walk in with a silver briefcase handcuffed to his wrist"

"And an eye patch with a scar"

"And a white cat to sit on his lap"

But Christoph came in with only a leather-bound folder and a brilliant smile. He was tall, thin, and impeccably dressed in a tailored Armani suit. Was everyone a Vogue model in this building? He greeted us warmly, in such perfect unaccented English that I had to ask if he was Swiss. We exchanged pleasantries and got down to business. Because of Lisa's company (founded by one of Basel's oldest and richest families, they owned half the city) and her high position and salary, we were afforded top tier concierge service. Thankfully, Christoph accepted the letters from the Canton office as proof of Lisa's residency, and set us up with an account that included a debit card and two different Visa credit cards - one to use in Switzerland based on Swiss francs, the other to be used throughout the EU in Euros.

We were then told that we should expect a card reader in the mail so that we could conduct online banking.

"And what is a card reader?"

"It is a reader for your card"

"Ah. I see"

I did not see.

There were many things about Swiss banking that made zero

sense, and it was the one aspect of life in Switzerland that was incredibly frustrating throughout our stay. The level of security that Swiss banks are known for also poses insane obstacles to overcome that no amount of banking in the US (or Canada) prepares you for. Indeed, back at the apartment that evening, just trying to set up our online banking account was tear-inducing. After trying to download the UBS app, we were told to enter our security PIN number. Was that our new PINs that we created or one sent to us? We had no idea. Doing this in the evening, the option of calling the help center was not an option (because of work-life balance hours). I decided that I would stop back in the bank the next day and ask what we might be doing wrong.

"Yes, you need the PIN from the card reader"

"Okay, we put in our PIN number and nothing happens"

"Do you have your card reader? I can look at it and see what is wrong"

"We don't have the card reader yet"

"Oh, then you cannot do this yet"

Apparently, every single time you want to do any kind of action, transaction, or log-in, you need to insert your debit card into the card reader and it will give you a PIN# that you put into the first part of the UBS app. This is one of two UBS apps you need to bank online. The first app is to accept your PIN# from the card reader. Once you enter that and put in your password, you are redirected to the actual UBS banking app. Without the card reader physically reading your debit card, you cannot access your online account. This was our introduction to the high level of Swiss banking security.

"So I cannot do any banking until I get the card reader?"

"You cannot do any online banking until you get the card reader. If you need access to your account right now, they can help you at the teller counter"

And so we waited for our card reader.

A few days later as I ate lunch on the balcony of our temporary apartment, the door buzzer rang. It was the postman. I booked downstairs to meet him. He had a letter and a small box in his hand, both addressed to Lisa.

"*Ja, Sie sind meine Frau*" (yes, she's my wife).

He asked my name, but when he learned my last name wasn't the same as Lisa's, he told me, in broken English, that he could not hand it to me unless my name was on the mailbox. The temporary apartment had put her name on a sticker on the mailbox, but not mine.

I borrowed his pen and scribbled my name below Lisa's.

He laughed, but told me that unless Lisa was home, he still could not give me the post until he made the main office aware that my name was on the box. Lisa was at her new office going through an orientation, and I could see that the letter was from the Canton (her ID!) and the box was from UBS (our card reader!). He told me he would be back later in the afternoon once he made the change in the office. Again, this is part of the Swiss notion of following the letter of the law, and its love of security.

Apartments do not have numbers - they simply have your name on the mailbox. Your building will have a street address, but the mailman sorts the post by last name. When we finally got our permanent flat, our address had a building number, but no apartment number, even though the building had five apartments. If your name isn't on the post box, you're not getting anything delivered. So he had to inform the main post office that my name was now on the box. Once that was made official, he could return and hand the items over to me.

Lo and behold, the buzzer rang not two hours later. The grinning postman handed over the envelope and box to me and wished me welcome. I later discovered that the post office for the Old Town was only one block away. But I realized that this helpful fellow had paused his route to go back to the office and make the change so that I might receive our items.

When we found our permanent flat, part of the contract included a fee for engraved mailbox name plates, so that they matched all the other ones (so it didn't look janky and haphazard). Our first piece of Swiss mail was, of course, a bill. This would be our yearly Television License. It is incredibly common in Europe to have to pay a fee to receive television, radio, or internet signals in your home. Then again, the majority of countries in Europe have nationalized television broadcasting and this tax subsidizes those channels. The BBC is a prime example. Our new fee was 365CHF, or 1CHF a day, to watch TV and use the internet. My mother thinks this is the most mind-blowing thing in the world.

On a side note, in regards to *Die Post*, you can put a sticker on your mailbox that tells the mailman you don't want junk mail. If they see the *"Bitte, keine Verbung!"* sticker, they will not put any fliers or extraneous mail in your box. It works perfectly, and almost every single mailbox in Switzerland has one. The Swiss love it because it helps prevent environmental waste. On the other hand, no matter how many times you sign up for "electronic correspondence only" on any website or service (like insurance or banking), the Swiss will ignore that and print out every single solitary thing they can think of and mail it to you. It completely offsets the environmental savings from the *Verbung* stickers. It's insane.

Die Post is incredibly efficient. Pharmacies will not ring the doctor up for you to renew a refill – you must call the doc yourself, who will then mail you a paper prescription for you to take in. The first time this happened, I was annoyed, until *Die Post* surprised me with their expediency. I called the doc around noon on a Monday, and when I checked my mailbox the next day at noon, when it usually arrived, there was my script. Less than twenty-four hours later and I had gotten my prescription, through the "snail" mail. Had this been the US, it would have taken over a week. Had this been through Canada Post, I'd still be waiting for it.

To be clear, *Die Post* > US Post Office > every other postal service in the known universe > The Pony Express > A one-legged sloth on Xanax with a mail bag > Canada Post.

We now had our card reader. It looks like a hand held calculator with a slot in the top to slide your card into it. Now that we had this little device, which we were told to never lose, we could finally set up our online banking account. Of course, it's almost nothing like what we have in the US. Transactions can take up to two weeks to show up on your account, so keeping daily track of expenditures via debit card is impossible. Paying a credit card bill - a credit card from the same damned bank - can take up to a month to process, if you simply pay it from your debit account. This would drive Lisa absolutely insane. She's the Chancellor of the Exchequer in our household, and every time she had to reckon the UBS accounts, it would literally leave her in tears.

Of course, receiving the card reader was not the solution to our banking problems. Tried as we might, we still could not get the damned thing to work. Back to the bank I went.

"We have our card reader, we have our cards, we have the

apps installed, and we still cannot get into our account"

"Did you receive your PIN number and decoder?"

"I'm sorry, what now?"

"Your PIN number and the decoder window?"

[Just a dumb stare at this point]

Yeah, we still had more fun things coming in the mail before we could bank with our fricking bank. We couldn't use the card reader to create our own PINs. No, we had to have a temporary PIN to be sent to us. Only once we got the PIN, we wouldn't be able to read it without a separate envelope containing a specialized polarized window to read the PIN number through because the PIN was printed behind a bunch of lines and blocks and squiggles. So now we had to wait for two different envelopes so that we could enter the temporary PIN to get into the card reader to get into the app to be able to change our PINs and start banking.

It took ten days from start to finish to be able to get into our online account and start banking.

Ten days.

Thank goodness we didn't have any immediate bills to pay. We would not be able to pay anything until the online system was finally set up. The Swiss do not send you e-bills. You will get a paper bill for everything. They are universal in appearance. Utility bills, doctor bills, insurance bills, online purchase invoices, you name it. They are always peach colored and they will always have three different eleventy-billion-digits long routing numbers plus another eleventy-billion-digits long account number and you will have to manually enter these into your card reader and it will take at least an hour to pay just one bill online and make you cry. These invoices will then take up to two weeks to process through the bank. If you pay it at the end of your grace period, the lag time may end up with you getting angry collection calls from people who speak angrier-than-usual Italian. Collection calls are always made by people speaking Italian..

It's insanely inefficient.

You then have to wait for a new bill, with a penalty attached, to arrive, which you then have to take to the bank who will contact the company to show proof of original prompt payment, and then you will wait another three to four weeks for the correction to appear on your bill and in your account. It took us nearly a year to get the system down so that we didn't get notices or have to beg the bank to fix things for us. I'm sure our bank thought we were carrot-brained Appenzeller hillbillies (it's a Swiss insult, trust me).

Every time I presented Lisa with an orange slip from the mailbox, she would drop her shoulders and mutter "fuck" and then go rock herself in the corner like an asylum patient.

Once we finally had access (or did we, it was impossible to tell at this point) to money and our ID cards, we could begin to look for a place to call our own. Even better, Lisa could now get paid! I could go grocery shopping. I could use the ATM. We could start doing all the things. First and foremost was finding a place of our own.

After our first week in Basel, we would have to move to a different temporary apartment that was to be our home for the next three months. This gave us time to start finding our way around town, learning more about our surroundings, and figuring out where we wanted our permanent place to be. If we thought establishing ourselves as residents was an ordeal, finding an apartment in a foreign land was going to be an even bigger challenge.

Chapter Two - A Haus Of Our Own

So I'm standing at the tram platform in the plaza of the main train station, studying the posted transit map when suddenly the whole wall in front of me swings open in my face. Out steps a tram conductor adjusting his belt. Behind him, inside this tiny metal kiosk of ticket machines and maps, was a tiny, airplane-sized toilet. He smiled at me, locked the door behind him, and climbed into the tram parked alongside us. Hidden conductor toilets is Swiss ingenuity at its finest.

We were getting ready to take the tram across town to find where our new temporary apartment was going to be. This, of course, meant figuring out the tram schedule, what lines went where, and how to read the station stop boards. Lisa had some familiarity with this from her previous trips to Basel. I tried to think of it as a microcosm of the London Tube system.

Trams routes have numbers (the #8 line, the #10 line, the #11 line, etc.), but multiple tram routes stop at many of the same stops, so it's important to know which tram to jump on at each stop (you have to look for the number posted above the driver's window). More importantly, you need to know which side of the street to stand on so you go the right way. There are large electric signs that show which trams are arriving at that stop, when, and in which order. It will show you that the #8 is arriving in 2 minutes, the #10 is arriving in 3 minutes, and the #2 is arriving in 6 minutes. Maps of the routes are posted on large posters at every stop, and for visual clarity, each line is given a color on the map, so you can follow it throughout its journey to see where it leads.

My dad would follow my Facebook posts about daily life in Basel and the one thing that always confounded him were the trams.

"How do you guys figure this shit out!?"

No matter how I tried to explain the system to him, he just thought it was black magic.

I took great pride when only six months later, I was able to help a couple of tourists hopelessly lost at the tram stop at Bankverein. I saw them out of the corner of my eye looking at a map in their hands, at the tram map posted at the platform, and up at the arrivals board. I could literally see smoke coming from their brains.

"You folks look lost"

"Oh, you speak English!"

"Yep. American, but I live here, so I'm happy to help you get where you need to go"

We quickly realized that they were looking for Barfüsserplatz but instead ended up in Bankverein. Two long B-names, sure, I get it. Lisa and I would always imagine how flustered my folks would be trying to decipher the myriad of alphabet soup tram stop names.

I was going to just give them directions, but realized that I had nothing to do, so I'd take them where they needed to go. We piled on the correct tram and a few stops later, disembarked at Barfüsserplatz. Before leaving them to it, I inquired what their agenda was, so I could help them find where they wanted to go next. When they told me they were looking for the Münster (Cathedral), I decided it was easier to show them how to get there by leading them myself. Once we got them to Münsterplatz, I walked them half a block in one direction to show them how to get to the Rathaus (on their list), and half a block in the other to show them how to get to the Kunstmuseum (the city's epic art museum, also on their list). Finally, I asked which hotel they were staying at so I could show them which tram to take back there. They offered me money for my trouble, but I refused. It was just nice being able to help someone find their way in my new city, and I relished in knowing how to get these folks where they needed to go.

I used to do this at Disneyland. Lisa once worked for the House of the Mouse, and we had free passes to the parks. We must have gone at least once or twice a month. I became so familiar with the layout, it became second nature, when I saw people looking at a park map, to lean over and help them find their way. So when I finally had the chance to do this in Basel, I was overjoyed. It meant that this town was now, truly, mine.

Our new temporary flat was in a neighborhood known as the Gellert, which is a quiet, leafy residential area popular with families and professionals (doctors and lawyers, not hitmen (I assume)). Most of the buildings date from the Victorian era, with rows of stately brownstone-style row houses. You can tell this part of Basel has some money because this is where the Ferrari dealership is located. Not only did it do brisk business, it expanded to a second neighboring building to accommodate their burgeoning inventory. At least twice a week we would hear the roaring engine of a supercar zooming down the tiny side streets, out for a casual test drive. Bentleys, too, were a common sight, but their showroom was on the other side of town.

Our new place was just a block from a tram stop near a small green square called Karl Barth Platz (named after a famed Swiss theologian who mailed a letter to Hitler telling him that God actually hated Nazis). A bakery and barbershop were just steps away, and three grocery stores were just three blocks away. The trip, by tram, for Lisa to get to her office would take about 15 minutes. I immediately liked this neighborhood, but we still had many other areas of town to scout and check and see if they would be worth viewing. So we set off on a warm sunny Saturday to see those parts of the city we had only read about in real estate listings.

Pharmaceuticals are Basel's claim to fame, as the city hosts the headquarters for Roche, whose twin towers on the Rhine are the tallest buildings in Switzerland. Abbey Hoffman invented LSD here. Novartis is the largest employer in Basel and the largest employer of expats. It sits in the very northern part of the city on the French border, across the river from Germany. All three countries meet at a point in the middle of the Rhine right in front of the Novartis campus (where a large silver rocket sculpture marks the spot, called the Dreiländerek). There were quite a few apartments on our list that were within blocks of the campus. We imagined that if so many expats lived in the area, it must be a vibrant, bustling area where we might have a chance of meeting people who could help us assimilate.

As we exited the tram at Voltaplatz, we just looked at each other with confused faces. We were surrounded by dilapidated 1970s brutalist housing complexes, and unending anti-Turkish, anti-Armenian, anti-Roma graffiti. The only business we saw within three blocks was a sketchy pub. If everything had been in English, you could have bet money we had been plonked down in the middle of Detroit. I knew St Louis, France, was just blocks away, but it felt like we were in St Louis, Missouri. It was a side of Basel that shocked me. Visibly drunk men staggered down the street. I checked the address of an apartment that, from the listing, looked amazing - on the inside. No matter how chic and modern this apartment interior was, and how less expensive it was than others on our list, there was no way in hell we were living in this neighborhood. Of course, we should have known that the area around a giant pharmaceutical plant would be less than stellar. But we couldn't imagine that a Swiss city could be so depressing. It just didn't occur to me that, yes, every city in the world has its seedy parts. Still, I just had trouble taking it in.

"Is this Switzerland's armpit?"

It wasn't. That would be Olten, the butt of every Swiss joke. Picture Peoria with a chocolate factory. Picture Toledo without the charm.

So we scratched nearly a third of the apartments off our list.

Michael had already warned us about getting a place on the Kleinbasel side of the river. Basel is divided between Grossbasel (or large Basel, which is the older part of town on the south/west bank of the Rhine) and Kleinbasel (Small Basel, which is a more industrial and modern part of town on the north/east side of the river, abutting the German border). I had quite a few on my list in a different area of Kleinbasel near the river, which, according to all the expat blogs I had been reading, was an "up and coming artsy area." That usually means one of two things. Either it's an old warehouse district that is undergoing gentrification, or it's a loud party area for twenty-somethings. As we made our way back towards the city, we alighted in the Matthäus district. We found it to be an area that straddled a variety of immigrant enclaves, the budget shopping district, and the

Red Light District.

Yes, Basel has a designated Red Light District. Nothing quite like the famous one in Amsterdam, this four square block area has sections of the pavement blocked off in green paint, with a streetlamp painted in the center, about 10 feet square in area. Prostitutes may station themselves within the green box to solicit their customers. Brothels are located on the same block and are the only location that they may take their customers to conduct their business. Anything outside of this controlled area was illegal.

On a walkabout in the area a few months later, I had forgotten about the Red Light District and stumbled into it quite by accident. Yes, I was promptly propositioned. I immediately went with the "sorry, no German" language excuse, but of course, they came right back with "we speak English, American man!".

Lisa thought this was hilarious.

"Are they good looking hookers?"

"Let's just say that Swiss Misses got some marshmallows in their mugs…"

So we scratched this neighborhood off our list as well. Michael was right: you don't want to live on the Kleinbasel side of the river. This still left us with options. Not knowing the neighborhoods, we had been simply picking listings by the looks and amenities of the apartments themselves. So now, with our little jaunt about town, we could start to narrow things down. With half the city off our list, we could better focus on finding the right place without being overwhelmed by options.

Lisa turned to her coworkers who recommended the Gündeldingen neighborhood, colloquially known as The

Gündeli. It was close to work, close to the SBB (main) train station, the Zoo, and Old Town. They described it as a neighborhood that was becoming hip again, with a large influx of different cultures and young people, and a fantastic restaurant scene. One of our top picks was in this area, so we decided to check it out.

Outside of the Old Town, this was the first neighborhood that felt wholly European to me. It was buzzing. The streets were alive! Shops of every kind lined the block, cafes and bars had tables strewn across the sidewalks, and every building had character. Depending on where in the area we found a place, Lisa could walk to work. This area gave us good vibes. I began to set up apartment viewings for the following week.

Lisa had to start up full time in the office once the new week started, and the weekend was nearly over. Lisa had booked a *Man With A Van* who was available to help us with our move on Sunday. The problem we faced, however, was that a noisy activity, like moving house, was not a Sunday activity. But it was the only day we could make it work. We would have to move quietly. Frankly we were surprised we were able to book anyone on a Sunday, but I suppose, like anywhere, a buck is a buck.

Right before we left Austin, we shipped six boxes of household items we thought we would need in the time between our arrival and all of our belongings coming by boat across the Atlantic (we arrived in early August, but our belongings did not show up until mid-November). So we had eight suitcases, filled to bursting, six cardboard boxes that seemed like they held 20 anvils each, and three large pet carriers filled with five confused, flustered, and oh-so-over-this-shit cats.

"You have many *katzen*"

"Yep, five of them. *Fünf katzen.*"

"My mother in Cyprus has *fünfzehn* (fifteen) *katzen*. She is crazy."

"So you don't like cats?"

"I LOVE KATZEN!!! You have very pretty *katzen*."

Lisa rode in the van with the Man With A Van while I closed up shop at the studio apartment and made my way by tram. En-route, I got a text:

> *Oh, fuck me. We're on the top floor. The fifth floor. There's no elevator.*

Ah, the wonders of the European walk-up.

Both of us have terrible knees. Lisa's heart flutters when she exerts herself too much. I have a bad back, and at the time, almost completely non-working shoulders (which I would get fixed by a surgeon for the Swiss Olympic team, details in a later chapter). Basel was also in the midst of an unusual heat wave. It was, on this day, nearly 100F.

By the time I arrived at the flat, I found the *Man With A Van* sitting on the rear bumper, soaked to the bone as if he had taken a swim in the Rhine. Lisa had asked me to stop at the store and grab some cold beverages on the way, and when I handed this poor swarthy soul an ice cold Coke, he smiled with the most sincere gratitude I could ever remember seeing.

"Oh, danke, danke, danke, danke, danke, mein freund!!! Danke!!!"

Once refreshed, this beast of a man grabbed two small suitcases and tucked them under his arms, grabbed two large ones by the handles, and stormed up the staircase as if charging up San Juan Hill. And true to being Swiss, he did it without making a peep - you couldn't hear a single footfall on the wooden stairs. He made no loud grunts. He simply ghost-thundered up the winding, spiral staircase.

I was not so quiet, lugging the heavy cardboard boxes with all my might, footfalls sounding like a drunken Yeti, a stream of profanity echoing angrily down the stairwell. Alongside the *Man With A Van*, who was working like a coked-up Nepalese Sherpa, we had all of our belongings upstairs in no time. I think Lisa and I separately tipped him handsomely for his efforts and sent him on his way with a fresh zesty drink.

Our new abode was cozy and Nordic, nestled in the attic space of the building. Thick heavy beams stretched in sharp angles from floor to ceiling, creating a head-bumping maze. But it was bright and airy with a proper kitchen and bedroom. Bonus, it had a washer and dryer. We finally had some space to move about, and room for the cats to stretch. Well, we couldn't really stretch-stretch, or we'd bang our heads on the sloping roofline. But it was a good place to call home, if only for three months. It certainly was better than trying to do a hotel stay for that long. For now, we had a place to lay our heads and plan out our future.

We looked at about 10 different apartments before narrowing it down to The One. Some were easy to *eighty-six* from our list like the rambling attic flat in an 800 year-old building where every room was either up or down a flight of 5 steps; the penthouse flat that had three outdoor patios but no living room; the river-side apartment with the wedge-shaped bedroom that was only 5 feet across at its widest point.

At one viewing, after a few minutes of chit chat with the agent, he stopped, looked at my application, back at me, and then tilted his head in confusion.

"It says here you are from Texas. I thought you were British?"

"Why do you think I was British?"

"You are wearing a tie."

He then asked me what I did for a living. I gave him the same response I gave everyone.

"I am a *hausfrau*"

The Swiss thought this was hilarious.

I had been tasked with viewing our list of flats as Lisa was now working in office on the daily. Lisa gave me one more that she found to add to my list. I had seen this listing before and for some reason I just wasn't sure about this apartment. It seemed a bit too perfect, which raised a red flag with me. But I had been striking out with other listings, so I made the call to go see it. I was also a bit leery of it being on such a busy main street. To my surprise, however, the tram stopped just half a block away, making it perfect for Lisa's commute and my ability to get around town. A bakery sat across from the tram stop (you soon realize that there is a bakery on every street, at every tram stop, on every corner), and at the end of the street, just another half block away, was a picturesque dairy farm on a serene and green sloping hill, complete with a historic chapel whose bells chimed the hour. The flat itself was inside a long row of stately 1920s apartment blocks that lined the boulevard.

I fell hard for this apartment. It was the rare gem that was better in person than in the listing. It had immaculate parquet floors, floor to ceiling windows along the entire front of the building, and a wide balcony in the back that ran the entire length of the apartment. The balcony overlooked an incredibly green courtyard, and both bedrooms and the kitchen had French doors that opened out onto the terrace. It had the largest kitchen of any place I had seen thus far, and the bathroom had just been remodeled, complete with the very, very rare double sink. The whole place felt very European to me - so very Parisian in its style. It exuded expat romance. It was cozy and warm and breezy. It was pretty much what I had pictured in my head when I would imagine our new European home.

The Basel Zoo was a five-minute walk away, the train station and a large Coop grocery store were both only ten minutes by foot. Lisa's commute would be less than 15 minutes by tram. If she really wanted to, she could walk to work in less than 25. I later found that I could be in the very center of the Old Town in less than 20 minutes on foot. The location was perfect, the apartment was perfect, and the price was perfect. It was also not available until November 1st, which was when our temporary place was up, so even that part was perfect. We happily snatched it up. We would now be residents on Margarethenstrasse in the fabulous Gündeli neighborhood.

Once we finally moved in, and anxiously awaited our belongings from America, we could explore the ins and outs of our new place in earnest detail. We found that things can be quite different in a Swiss apartment.

We had two ovens. One was a conventional oven. Best part was that it came with a pre-programmed menu to perfectly cook every single possible meal/food on earth with the touch of a button. It was also a steamer with a little pull out drawer to add water. The second oven was not just an oven, but also a microwave. Yeah, you read that right. A microwave, with metal oven racks. American readers know: no metal in the microwave! But this magical microwave could also be used as just a plain old oven! I never stopped marveling at this.

All Swiss toilets have two buttons for flushing (and all Swiss toilets are built into the wall instead of being free-standing). The smaller button is for a quick flush for pee-pee, and the larger button is for a more forceful flush for poo-poo.

Also in the bathroom of Swiss apartments is a compartment in the wall for your water shut off and meters. Cold and hot water are measured separately, and every three months, you will be asked to report the meter readings to IWB (the water department – their headquarters are at a tram stop, which lends the stop its name, and is pronounced *ee-vee-bee*). We were shocked to the core when we got our first real water bill. See, we got our first bill at the end of the year, but had only been living in the apartment for two months, so we thought it was just a quarterly bill. Fast forward to the following December and we get our water bill, and it is for the whole year. I guess we were a bit stupid on our part, not realizing that we hadn't been getting any water bills throughout the year, but we also thought that our quarterly utility bill (electric) included water, since they are administered by the same authority (IWB). So now it's a week after Christmas and we're faced with an 880CHF water bill due in two weeks.

Our flat was just two blocks from the IWB office, so I headed there to speak to someone. Having not realized that the bill was a yearly one, we hadn't budgeted for it, and forking out nearly 900CHF right after the holidays was going to be impossible. True to form, the Swiss were completely sympathetic to our misunderstanding because they trusted that we were telling the truth. The honor system, right? The Swiss are simply incapable of lying, and inherent trust in others, to be up front, true, and honest, is the hallmark of their clockwork society. I was able to negotiate a quarterly payment plan without any fuss, and it was, truly, the easiest time I have ever had with any public utility, anywhere.

We also learned that not only do we pay for the heat and electricity in our apartment, but contribute to the common areas of the building as well. Our bills had our flat totals and the common totals listed, and you paid the sum. The common area portion is not equally split amongst the five apartments, either. No, it is based on each apartment's individual usage. If our flat used 20% more heat than everyone else, then we would pay 20% more of the common area's usage as well. It was an incentive of sorts to keep all usage as low as possible.

We did find a unique way to save a few francs. Lisa came home from work telling me how one of her coworkers was over the moon with excitement because Switzerland had reduced the national interest rate. A strange thing to be celebratory about, no? She then explained to Lisa that when the national rate is lowered, you can petition your landlord to reduce your rent by the same percentage. So I immediately wrote to ours, asking if we qualified for such an adjustment. Sure enough, we were informed that our rent payments would now be reduced by 79 CHF per month. The rates never changed again during our stay, so we kept our reduced amount for over a year. When Covid hit, that small savings was actually pretty damned huge.

When you move into a Swiss apartment, there will be no light fixtures. The Swiss take them with when they move. Every ceiling fixture (with the exception of built-in can lighting and vanity lights in the bathroom) will need to be installed by the new resident. The nice thing about this is that you aren't stuck with someone's questionable taste mistakes. We knew that in many apartments in Germany, you were required to provide your own kitchen (yes, the whole kitchen), and in some parts of the Netherlands, the flooring (yes, the whole floor). Thankfully, in Switzerland, it's just the lights.

Swiss windows open in two different ways. They swing out, like doors, and they also tilt in. You can pull the window towards you, and it will open about six inches at the top, toward the ceiling, pivoting at the bottom of the sill. Because European buildings don't use drywall, but rather, concrete, it is necessary to keep airflow moving to prevent mildew buildup (some leases will have a clause requiring a certain number of hours per day or week with the windows tilted open to prevent mold growth). It's also a nice feature to allow just enough fresh air in without having to open the whole window. Also, there are ZERO screens in Europe. This drove Lisa mad. She asked a co-worker about it.

"Why don't you have screens over here? Don't the bugs get in?"

"But if you have screens, how do the bugs get out?"

Lisa ordered rolls of screens and made me put them up in all the windows. Which was not only to keep the bugs out, but the cats in. Elvis (our one-eyed tiger tabby) loved to explore and had no concept of danger. He'd be leaping James Bond style onto the top of a passing tram if he wasn't corralled properly. Though considering he only had one eye, that would have been incredibly bad-ass.

Swiss fridges and dishwashers always have cabinet-matching facades on them so they blend in. Our dishwasher had a lovely feature - it would project, onto the floor, a readout letting you know where it was in the cycle so you didn't open it prematurely. All of the appliances in our place were Miele brand, and I have to say, unequivocally, that every other brand out there are shite in comparison. When I hit the Lotto big time, I'm making damned sure all my stuff is Miele.

Keys are incredibly expensive in Switzerland, and for good reason. Instead of having jagged edges like American keys, Swiss keys are smooth on all sides, but have an intricate series of divots carved in them (picture the crater-pocked surface of the moon). What makes them especially unique is that you will have only one key that will open both the front common door to the building and your own apartment door (but not your neighbors' apartment door). So if you should lose your key, it can cost anywhere from 800-1000CHF to replace. Weirdly, our Half-Fare train card carries key insurance with it. Should you lose your key, contact SBB and they'll cover the cost of your replacement (one time per calendar year). Strange, but great bonus on the... train pass?

Doors are also designed a bit differently. There will be a beveled edge that will create a full seal around the frame of the door, so you will never have a single gap around your door. No need for weather-stripping for the front door, or lack of privacy with a gap at the bottom of the loo door. It also makes things that much more sound-proof, as quiet is a priority for the Swiss. That, and the concrete walls make for incredibly quiet apartments.

The idea of an open-concept home is not a thing in Switzerland. I quickly became a fan of the separate kitchen. Being a popular protein in neighboring France, I had begun to cook more and more duck. Duck has a LOT of fat, and that fat gives off a LOT of smoke. Being able to close the door to the kitchen, and open the French doors to the patio was a godsend. The house didn't suffer from cooking smells because I could contain them. I could also make as much noise while cooking as I needed without disturbing Lisa working at her desk in the next room. I came to love the idea of the kitchen as its own contained room and now the whole open concept conceit sets my teeth on edge every time I watch House Hunters.

When we were in the temporary apartment, we discovered that European clothes dryers have a feature that American ones do not. Having no idea about this one tiny, important detail, led to a comedy of errors with the rental agency over what I was insisting was a broken clothes dryer.

"The dryer is broken. It turns on, but when I press start, it will go for about 10 seconds and then stop and beep at me. I've cleaned the lint trap, and I can't find anything out of the ordinary"

"We will send someone right away!"

Cue the non-English speaking repairman no less than fifteen minutes later. Using my rudimentary German and Google translate, I get across my problem. He steps over to the machine, looks at it for all of ten seconds, chuckles, and then turns to me with a smile, and puts a hand on my shoulder and pulls me close. Unbeknownst to me, in the front of the dryer, is a drawer. It is full to the brim with water. He pulls it all the way out, takes it to the sink and dumps it out, and replaces it in the machine. He turns the dryer on and it runs perfectly.

"*Verstehen?* (understand?)"

"*Ja. Ich verstehe.*"

Because these dryers are not vented to the outside, they have a drawer that collects the condensation and moisture from the wet clothes as they go through the drying cycle. You have to dump it before every load or else the dryer will not go. The first time I did a load of laundry after moving back to the States, I sat for five minutes trying to find the water drawer on the dryer before the light bulb went off.

We were lucky to find a flat with its own washer dryer. To find a washer is lucky, to find both is extremely rare. Most Swiss apartment buildings have a shared laundry, and use of them is regulated through an insanely strict assigned schedule that can never be deviated from, lest you incur the wrath of your neighbors and, I shit you not, a visit from the *polizei*. Laundry must never be done after 10pm, and never, ever, ever on a Sunday. Even hanging laundry on the line outside is *verboten* on a Sunday. There was simply no way I was going to deal with that *Bünzli* nonsense and if an apartment listing didn't include a washer/dryer, I simply crossed it off the list, no matter how spectacular the rest of the apartment might be. With cats, having access to laundry facilities 24/7 is a must. Again, after returning to the States, I had to remind myself over and over that I could do things on Sunday, like laundry or vacuuming or yard work. Quiet Sundays became so ingrained in our psyche that it took months to break the cycle once we were back.

The Swiss love of silence is a weird one. In many older buildings, you cannot even flush your toilet after 10pm lest you wake or disturb your neighbors. Our building was a "new" building, so it was pretty soundproof. The pipes gave away none of the neighbors' scatological secrets. We could, however, occasionally hear our upstairs neighbor, Christoph, when he brought a lady friend home.

He was a very… enthusiastic fellow.

But it was a rare thing, and he was barely home. What we heard more was the banshee-esque screams of the two satanic children who lived below us. We never actually learned their names. We simply called the youngest boy (maybe 5 years old) "Buckethead" because he was just SO incredibly dumb. The screechy older sister (maybe 8 years old) we called "Singing Shit". She would swing around the laundry line pole in the middle of their yard and scream-sing for hours on end. She loved nothing more than tormenting her brother and making him cry. She was a cruel little shit. Then again, a strong breeze would make that boy cry.

For as much as the Swiss love their quiet, we had to live above a family of thunderous iconoclasts.

These neighbors would become the bane of our existence. It was a complicated relationship. They were our best source of local information, customs, things like that. While local natives, they spoke perfect English and at first, were very helpful and welcoming. As time went on and we settled in, our disdain of their constantly-at-eleven volume cooled our relationship. The mother was around our age, and had no inside voice, just like her children. Dad, whose name I never quite got, as he always mumbled in a disdainful whisper, didn't offer the same openness and welcome that his wife did. He was everything his wife was not: quiet, meek, and shy. He also never, ever, disciplined his rowdy and evil children.

Seriously, those children were evil.

They destroyed things, rambled over fences to climb on the neighbors' prized fig tree, or harassed every animal that came across their path.

They also never shut up. Ever.

They screamed. When they talked, it was a scream. When they played, they screamed. When they ate dinner on the patio, they somehow screamed while they chewed. Bath time screams echoed up through the pipes into our own bathroom. There were weeks on end in the summertime that we could not sit out on our patio because of the non-stop wailing in the yard below us.

In the building next door to us were the most adorable elderly Danish couple. They had lived in their flat, right next door to the Demons-From-Hell Family, for 40+ years. As we were packing up to move back to the US, we noticed that they, too, were packing up house.

"You're moving, too!?"

"I've listened to those horrible children long enough. We're too old for this *scheisse*. We're heading to a nice house with no neighbors in Allschwil (a neighboring burb)"

"I bet I'll still be able to hear them back in America"

"I'm sorry they ruined your stay in Basel. You were very good neighbors and we will be sad to see you go – them, not so much."

Between our downstairs neighbors and the *Swiss Family Robinson* that lived across the courtyard from us who loved to sit all night around a campfire and sing Swiss folk songs until dawn, we began to believe that the Swiss love of silence was nothing more than an urban myth. The only time it is quiet in Switzerland is August, when everyone goes on their month-long holiday to Spain or Turkey or Corsica. I pity the Mediterranean in the summer time.

Of course, when we looked at the apartment, the family wasn't at home, so we had no idea of the cacophony that awaited us. Had we heard those kids that day, we would have never taken the apartment. Which is a shame because everything else about it was absolutely perfect. To be honest, we truly came to hate our downstairs neighbors because they intruded so rudely into our European dream and were so absolutely unapologetic, or self-aware, about it. When the time came to head back to America, just listening to them as we packed eased the sadness over leaving.

Two flights up from us, however, were the loveliest, wonderful young couple who, had Covid not hit, would have become very close friends. We didn't really meet them until right before the lockdown, so we didn't get to know them well enough until a month or so before we had to leave. Claudio and Judith were young, native twenty-somethings who loved to stop and chat for hours in the stairwell about our two country's cultural and political differences. They, too, had no patience for the hellions below, but were not afraid to discipline them themselves for leaving messes in the common areas or running up and down the stairs. I think because they knew how much noise they made, they told us not to worry about making our own. When we left Basel, they gave us a box of Swiss treats, games, and trinkets as a farewell. Upon our return to the States, I sent them a similar box of American goodies, and a hearty thank you for being so lovely. In retrospect, I should have sent them earplugs, too.

When we needed to escape the cacophony, we had many options around us.

The moo cow farm, as I called it, was basically three steps away. It buttressed an enormous, heavily wooded city park which held a myriad of trails through this strange stand of woodland in the middle of the city. Built up against a bluff, the top of the park, and the palisade of the Margarethenkirche (St Margaret church) at the dairy farm, afforded amazing, unobstructed views of the whole city. On clear days, you could see the Vosges mountains of France and the Black Forest of Germany. At the far end of the park was a massive ice skating complex. The center of the park was a large open space where Baselers would sun themselves. In the winter, the slopes of the park became the best place in the city to go sledding.

The moo cows at the dairy farm loved the attention of passersby and would let your pet them as they munched on straw and hay. Lisa tried to pet a cow once. It licked her hand and then greedily tried to swallow her entire arm. She was covered in a thick layer of cow spit from her elbow to her pinky finger. After that, every time we'd pass the cows on walkabout she'd mutter under her breath "fucking cows tried to eat me."

A milk automat was available to buy fresh cow juice. Bring your own container, slip in a couple of francs, and take home farm-fresh milk from the dispenser.

The one downside to living near a dairy farm is "cow stank". In the summer, when the temperatures would rise, so, too, would the heady smell of wet hay and cow farts. For some strange reason, this phenomenon only seemed to occur after sunset. We'd open the windows and take a whiff.

"Cows", we'd declare, if the air was thick with farm ephemera.

I think we experienced it because the farm was at the top of a hill whose slope ended at the main boulevard that went past our house. The canyon-like street funneled the smell from on high down into the depths of the Gündeli. Being only blocks from the Zoo, we thought for sure we'd smell baboons before we smelled cows, but no. On those nights when the smell was nearly visible, we'd have to close up all the windows. It didn't happen often, but when it did, it was never subtle. In all our time there, we never figured out a pattern to discern which nights would yield cow stank. It was completely arbitrary. And it only ever happened at night.

The Zoo was only a five-minute walk away. Heavily wooded, it is an absolutely amazing zoo, and a lovely park to walk through. We bought season passes and spent time there at least 2-3 times a month. It had a fabulous restaurant where we could get schnitzel the size of a blue whale, a bottle of wine, and patisserie-quality desserts for dirt cheap. And the quality of the food was top notch. There is actually a fine dining restaurant at the zoo, with reservations-only tables, white linens, and a sommelier. While in the US, zoo fare is usually a hot dog or a $20 burger that looks like a toddler made it, in Switzerland, zoo fare is top quality, hot, restaurant level food. Swedish meatballs, steaks, schnitzel, *rosti*, and goulash are regularly on offer. Beer, wine, cider, and champagne are available, and desserts like Black Forest Cake, crème brûlée, or kafloutis are the norm.

We ate at the zoo at least once a month.

I also frequented the bakery across the street. It was a tiny, tiny little place. So tiny that no more than two people could be inside at one time. I would always get the *apfelkopfen*, a ginormous apple turnover, for 2.50CHF (cash only!). It was their specialty. This thing took two hands to hold. The pastry was sooo flaky. Almost every Saturday morning, I'd skip across the tram tracks to grab one before they sold out. During the week, if Lisa was having a rough day, I'd grab her favorite *linzer* cookie (again, ginormous!). As time went by, the woman behind the counter would complement my improving German language skills, and give a friendly wave when she saw me pass by (not a Swiss thing to do, btw).

On one occasion, I was ordering at the bakery and did not realize it was three-for-the-price-of-two. I had only asked for two items, so she asked if I wanted two or three, to clarify. I held up three fingers, then quickly caught myself, and changed it to the German three (those who have seen the movie *Inglorious Basterds* know what I'm talking about). The clerk completely busted up laughing, probably because I sputtered out "sorry, German three, German three!". For those who don't get it, Americans put up three fingers to indicate the number three, but the Germans use their thumb, index, and middle finger to signify three. Damned near gave myself away.

I got very fat eating so many pastries, and having them in such close proximity was really bad. But, my gods, they were good. Lisa says I cannot live on pastry alone, but I strongly beg to differ.

When there was maintenance work on the tram tracks, the Italian construction workers would pop over to the bakery and grab demitasse cups of espresso. They'd drink them while running their excavators, and then return the porcelain drinkware at the end of the day. There's nothing like seeing a sweaty contractor set his jackhammer down to take a sip of coffee with his pinky in the air, light up a cigarette, and then return to work. Every construction site I passed was staffed exclusively with Italians (or Italian-speaking Swiss from Ticino). Had I hung around long enough, I could have picked up an encyclopedia of Neapolitan curses and cuss words. I also would have picked up cancer from all the second-hand smoke.

The surrounding neighborhood was lovely as well. The Gündeli was a vibrant neighborhood that was incredibly diverse. It was a newer part of town, having been developed in the Victorian era. It was the only part of town that followed a strict grid pattern, and was a wonderful mix of old row houses, brutalist Cold War era apartment blocks, gleaming new architectural wonders, cafes, bodegas, and leafy parks.

It was also dotted with cigarette machines.

Randomly, in the middle of a residential street, you would find these rusty old cigarette vending machines from the 70s, fully stocked and operational. The first time I passed one, I was gob smacked, especially when someone nudged past me to use it. Weeks later, I discovered another one about six blocks further. When I would take walks around the area, I made it a point to try and find as many as I could. In all, I found four in the Gündeli, but never a one in any other neighborhood in Basel.

Baselers love to smoke. Europeans love to smoke. Even before Covid hit, you'd have to wear a facemask at the tram depot in front of the train station due to the heavy, persistent cloud of French cigarette smoke. I noticed that European cigarettes have a nuttier smell than their American counterparts, but it didn't make them any less unpleasant. I never stopped marveling at the Swiss who value such clean, pristine nature, will climb entire Alps on a weekend jaunt like it's a Sunday stroll through the park, and then light up a fag at the first opportunity. Everyone in Switzerland seems to smoke. Old people, young people, babies, dogs. You cannot get away from it. What sets Swiss smokers apart from everyone else, however, is that you'll be hard pressed, anywhere in the country, to find a stray cigarette butt on the ground. The Swiss do not litter. Period.

Thankfully, no one in our building smoked, but the neighbors next door to us did, and would sit on their back balcony to do so. It would infuriatingly waft into our bedrooms. When they weren't smoking cigarettes, they were lighting up some powerful doobies. This was not so bad a problem because we could sit on the patio and… relax. At no cost. Weed is legal in Basel (weed laws are set by each Canton), so long as you keep it at home and don't use it in public. On the days the neighbors toked up, we took advantage because it helped calm our frayed nerves from the dervishes below us. .

Across the courtyard was a man who made guitars. You'd think the noise from his apartment would be musical, but, oh no. He would sit out on his balcony and sand his guitars. For HOURS.

Scratchscratchscratchscratchscratchscratchscratch

Blow. Wipe, wipe, wipe.

Scratchscratchscratchscratchscratchscratchscratch

The only truly quiet people in the whole of the courtyard were our elderly Danish neighbors next door, and Claudio and Judith two floors up. Otherwise, we apparently lived in the noisiest apartment block in all of Basel.

We found, too, that the noise out front was no better. I knew living on a busy road would be challenging, but I hadn't any experience with trams before. The trams run every eight minutes, one in each direction. So this thunderous clatter would drown out everything every couple of minutes. In the summer, if the windows were open, you would have to watch TV on the highest volume. Or sit with the remote and pause the TV every time a tram would go by.

The cats, however, loved the "green monsters". They'd sit on the back of the sofa and watch them glide past through the large picture windows. Having always lived in quieter suburban areas, they had never had so much activity outside to look at. The constant parade of people, bikes, cars, and trams fascinated them. When we moved back, our house was now on a tiny side street in a quiet suburb where one car might pass by all day long. It took them a long time to give up looking for the green monster.

Having the tram just below, however, was a godsend. We didn't have a car, nor were we planning on getting one. For one, it was cost prohibitive. Buying a car in Switzerland is expensive. Registration, insurance, licensing can all end up costing you twice the amount of the car itself. Beyond that, the thought of driving in Europe scared the hell out of me. I would sit, waiting for a tram, at Aeschenplatz, one of the busiest intersection/plazas in the city, and watch the traffic. Nine roads all converged in the same spot as five different physical tram lines. There were NO traffic signals of any kind. If you didn't know how it all worked, you would simply crash and die. I never stopped being amazed at this area. It was this most fluid, synchronized ballet, with seemingly no conductor.

Lisa had driven a few times (using a rental), heading to Munich for work. She had taken the train before, but decided driving would be faster.

"Aren't you intimidated by this?"

"I want to drive on the *Autobahn*."

She relayed that driving in Basel wasn't as bad as she thought it might be, but did her best to avoid Aeschenplatz, and the other insane intersections that dotted the city.

"How was the *Autobahn*?"

"So. Fucking. Cool"

I was insanely jealous. But I still had zero desire to drive in Europe. I'm an aggressive driver. I'm an impatient driver.

I hate driving, actually.

Everyone is a distracted idiot. The one thing I was looking forward to most, moving to Basel, was not having to drive again. Ever. And the effect on my nerves was immediate. Not driving was the biggest weight taken off my shoulders. I didn't miss it. At all. Not for one single second. Then again, the public transportation in Switzerland is phenomenal. You can literally get to every single solitary city, town, burg, and hamlet by public transport. From one end of the country to the other, you can make the journey entirely by train and/or bus.

In Europe, you can live normally and comfortably without a car. Of all the things I miss about living in Europe, it's the public transportation, bar none.

I loved the tram. It was my lifeline in the city. I had the entire route map memorized in no time. I had favorite seats. I knew how much time I had to switch trams if I was taking multiple lines. I knew whether to sit near the front or the back depending on where I was going and what the tram stop was like at my destination. I also figured out that if I missed a tram, it was sometimes faster to walk. Lisa would laugh at me because of my impatience.

"Why don't you just wait for the next tram? It's only eight more minutes"

"Because I can walk there faster"

"So why do you take the tram at all?"

So I stopped taking the tram for short distance runs. If I was heading into the city center, I'd walk, if the weather permitted. But if I was heading home from the city center, I would always take the tram, because it was all uphill on the way back, and one hill in particular was a beast to walk up. It was always faster to walk to the train station than take the tram. The only times I HAD to take the tram is if I went grocery shopping in either France or Germany. Both were 35 minute commutes, one way, by tram. If I had a small grocery run to make, for just a handful of items, I could walk the ten minutes to the Coop down the street.

I found that I ended up walking far more places than taking transport. I became obsessed with tracking how many miles I walked each month (my best was 78 miles in February, 2020). Basel is an immanently walkable city. And once you knew all the back-alleys and cut-throughs, you could be just about anywhere in town in less than thirty minutes by foot. I preferred to walk anyways. You got to see more that way. With so many tiny obscure details and sights to take in, you got so much more of the town that way. You'd stumble on some excellent graffiti, or a hidden walkway, or notice that a house was dated from the 13th century. Every single time I took a walk, I stumbled on something new, different, or interesting that I never would have noticed had I been on the tram. Basel is a city of hidden gems and treasures. Every single time I *flanneured*, I always, always, discovered something new.

This was another reason why I loved our apartment: it was in walking distance of everything. The tram at our doorstep made longer commutes easy. The proximity to the train station made excursions and exploration days a breeze. We were right in the middle of a vibrant neighborhood, and also right on the edge of quiet nature areas and farmland. Depending on what you were seeking, you could be immersed in either solitude or whirlwind in a matter of minutes. While our new place had its faults (still looking at you, Satan's Spawns), it was perfect in every other way. This was where we were going to make our new home. This is where we were going to put down our expat roots. This is where we were going to immerse ourselves in everything Swiss.

We were, at long last, home.

Chapter Three - Shopping

Becoming familiar with the ins and outs of shopping would be a huge part of daily life in Switzerland. We would have to learn what kind of stores sold what, where were the cheapest goods and services, and how beneficial was it, really, to shop across the border. It's easy to take for granted your knowledge of and accessibility to all sorts of shops where you grew up and are familiar with. We all know the benefits of a Target or Walmart, the differences between a Kohl's and a Bloomingdale's, or whether the item on your grocery list can be found at an Aldi or a Whole Foods. But what happens when none of the stores, or what they sell, is familiar? Where do you start? How do you navigate?

When we moved to Kelowna, in Canada, we faced a similar situation. Target hadn't reached the Canadian market yet (and would eventually fail miserably when they did) and we had a new house to set up. There was a Walmart in town, but it wasn't the all-encompassing monster box that we are used to in the States (besides, I'm not a fan of giving the Walton family any of my money). Where oh where to get our non-grocery household goods?

"Canadian Tire. You need to go to Canadian Tire."

[Look of utter confusion]

"Seriously, go to Canadian Tire."

I thought that maybe, because my neighbor was South African, that we were having a lost in translation moment. But when Lisa came home from work and told me her coworkers were strangely suggesting we go to a tire store, I knew something was there, I just didn't believe it.

So we drove ourselves down to the Canadian Tire store on the main road into town. The parking lot was full to capacity. There was absolutely nothing on the outside that led anyone to believe that this store sold anything but tires. But upon entering we were met with the Canuck version of a Sears. Endless aisles of cookware, clothing, electronics, appliances, and athletic gear. Seasonal items, hardware, and, of course, automotive needs.

Yes, they also sold tires.

Had we not learned of this place from the natives, we would have never, ever set foot inside. The Canadian Tire became one of our most frequented stores, and we never once bought a set of tires there.

Basel had their own strange agglomerations. The two local grocery chains, Coop and Migros, offered their takes on department stores. The Coop City was one option. These stores were, like their namesake, located in busy city centers, and only in busy city centers. They offered everything any American department store might, akin to a Macy's. And like a Macy's, their prices were laughable for what they offered.

Once we had moved into the temporary fifth-floor walk-up, we noticed that, true to the European style, the bed came with no top sheet. "Duvet only" is the Euro way, but being stubborn Americans, we really wanted a top sheet. Actually, we needed a top sheet because Lisa sleeps hot and the duvet was too much for her. Even in the dead of winter, it's usually just a sheet for her. So I headed to the Coop City in Old Town to look for one (at this point not knowing where else to look). I found the linens department and set about buying a cheap one since this would just be temporary until we moved into our own place and got our stuff from the boat.

I searched that tiny little department for at least thirty minutes trying to find one. Sheet "sets" in Switzerland are a fitted bottom sheet and two pillow cases. They don't come with a top sheet. I could find separate single fitted bottom sheets, but no single top sheets. I finally flagged down an associate and asked if they had one. Her face twisted with confused amusement.

"I think we might have... one."

"Just one?"

"Why stock things that are not purchased"

Swiss logic, man.

After searching high and low together for about ten minutes, she excused herself to check the inventory on the computer.

"Yes, we do not have it. We sold it last year."

I thanked her with wild bemusement and decided I would maybe just get a duvet cover and use it as a sheet. So I circled back around and started looking. I made heads turn when I guffawed loudly as I started looking at prices. The cheapest duvet cover I could find was 180CHF. Most ran in the 250-300CHF range. Then I began to make note of the prices of other goods in the area. A standard size bed pillow was 100CHF. A set of two pillow cases was 80CHF. Even perusing the small appliances, the cheapest toaster I could find was 100CHF and the lowest priced iron was 120CHF. I was both shocked and angry. A realization fell over me.

"Oh, god, we're fucked here"

If this was indicative of Swiss prices for standard home goods, we were going to be in quite a pickle.

That evening I reported my story to Lisa who had spent part of her day getting some advice from her new coworkers. She said many had recommended Coop's competitor, Migros, and their home store, called Micasa. Just a couple of tram stops past her office was a large Migros shopping center called M-Parc. Here, there was the largest Migros grocery store in Basel, as well as Migros Electronics, Migros Office, and Migros Micasa (furniture, lighting, decor). So we decided to head over there on Saturday so Lisa could accompany me this time.

Most Swiss businesses close at 6:30pm, including grocery stores, and are closed completely on Sundays. When we arrived at the M-Parc, a line of cars stretched down the boulevard for a mile, waiting to pull into the double-decker parking lot. All of Basel, it seemed, was out doing their shopping on Saturday. It was like going to the Kroger on the day before Thanksgiving. Times a hundred. It was absolute chaos. I would later learn that most Swiss who shop during the week do so as solo shoppers, but the weekend warriors were families with screaming children and clueless husbands.

Some things in life are universal.

Here in the Migros grocery, we found the closest thing to a Super Target, with a large section devoted to clothing, shoes, and kitchen and bath ware. The prices were much better here, but still beyond our comprehension. Migros sell their own brand (everything from food to clothing) while Coop sells brand name items. This allows Migros to set their prices slightly lower, but also means that much of the time, your selections are limited. In the end, based on proximity and variety of goods, I became a Coop man, but still popped off to Migros when I needed the very basic of basics.

Upstairs was the home goods store. Beautiful sofas and dining sets for the price of a Bugatti Veyron. Again, bedding for the same price as a three star Michelin dining experience in Hong Kong. I found the toasters, and the cheapest one here was 70CHF (the most expensive was 260CHF). In this moment, we became a bit panicky. Would we ever find affordable furnishings and appliances for our new home? Were all the warnings about Switzerland being one of the most expensive places on earth not hyperbole but cold hard truth?

A light bulb goes off above my cartoon head.

"Ikea! They have to have an Ikea in Basel, right?"

Indeed, there was an Ikea in Pratteln, one of Basel's industrial burbs. You could hop the commuter train and be there in fifteen minutes. The store was then a short ten-minute walk from the train station. To help people find their way, the city painted the whole route in purple, as it snaked down tiny walkways between industrial buildings and warehouses. Follow the purple squiggles on the pavement to Ikea! Thing is, if you didn't know about the purple pathway, you'd never know it was the way to Ikea, as there are no signs to indicate its purpose. Our downstairs neighbor was the one who told us to look for the purple sidewalk when we got off the train, so we were in the secret know.

We also learned that Americans pronounce Ikea wrong. It is not, in fact, *aye-kee-ah*, but rather *eee-kay-yah*. The layout was completely familiar, and, thankfully, so too were the prices. Here were the discounted items we needed. We found our top sheet for 25CHF and a duvet cover (just in case) for 40CHF. We bought some kitchen utensils and other odds and ends as well, relieved that this option was here and would work for us. We decided to grab dinner at the cafe.

"I'm always hearing about how good the Swedish meatballs are here. We didn't pass a single restaurant in town on our way here, so we should just get a bite here."

My friends, this was no ordinary cafe. You could get meatballs, you could get schnitzel, you could get a sausage plate. You could get Princess torte, Black Forest Cake, rhubarb cheesecake, soft serve ice cream. You could get a beer, wine, cider, champagne. When we asked for meatballs, the dude behind the counter asked how many we'd like.

"What's a normal amount?"

"Between ten and twenty"

"Twenty it is!"

Eating out in Switzerland is expensive. But here, we had a plate of meatballs, mashed potatoes, steamed vegetables, Princess cake, and rhubarb lemonade, and it was cheaper than our first meal at McDonald's. And it was delicious! We would end up making the trip out to Ikea a few more times just for dinner. On our return to Colorado, we hit up the Ikea to once again buy much needed home goods, and decided to stop by the cafe for some tasty meatballs.
I've never been sadder. The only things sadder than me were the limp, bland, grey "meatballs" they plopped on my plate. There were no fancy cakes, no tasty flavored lemonade drinks. There was a pile of marble-sized meh-balls and a plastic cup of overly-sweet Pepsi (your taste buds come to life when you stop ingesting corn syrup in everything). Why is the American version of European things always so disappointing?

We would end up buying our beds from Ikea. Our beds were old and the frames were falling apart, so we sold them before we left (which also saved room in the shipping container), and decided we'd buy new ones once we got to Basel. Based on what we saw at the Micasa, we knew Ikea was going to be our only option. The prices for mattresses were cheap even by American standards! We had the frames and mattresses delivered to the new house, which was a week before our things would arrive, leaving us plenty of space to build the damned things. I did pity, however, the poor delivery guys who had to lug it all up a flight of curved, narrow stairs. But then, apartments being the norm here, I'm sure they're used to it.

We noticed that if you live anywhere above the first floor (the second floor to Americans), deliveries will be made through your windows via a crane/escalator contraption. They'll park underneath your window, load the item on the platform, then send it upwards on a cherry-picker type machine to your open window where a second delivery person will retrieve it and bring it inside. This is true for moving, as well. No way are these guys hauling things up and down five flights of stairs! They do it all through the windows using these machines. The tallest one I saw was six stories. But I believe any building taller than that is required to have a lift. Also, you should be prepared to have coffee/espresso on hand for your delivery people. And if it is a whole house move, breakfast and lunch is expected as well.

Yes, expected.

They will not work until they've had their *z'Nüni*.

Well what about Amazon, you might ask.

Switzerland hasn't exactly embraced the delivery giant. It remains, for the Swiss, primarily a book warehouse. Media is about the only thing you can get delivered via Amazon in Switzerland.

There is German Amazon, but they will not deliver in Switzerland. You have to rent an Amazon drop box in one of the border towns and go retrieve your package there. Commuting a half an hour on the tram to get an Amazon delivery pretty much negates the whole purpose of Amazon to begin with. Plus, depending on the cost of the item, I would have to pay custom taxes on those items as well. And much like their Swiss counterpart, the selection on the German site is incredibly anemic.

We did find a site within Switzerland that specialized in American goods, so we could order packets of Kool-

Aid and jars of Jiff peanut butter and cans of baking powder, but even that was cost prohibitive. The only really great online delivery service we used was *PetPlus*, the Swiss version of Chewy, to order food and litter for the cats. We had to order them proper litter online. The cheap grocery store Fatto brand really pissed them off.

More important than any other shopping was grocery shopping. With a tiny fridge, a freezer the size of a Pop Tart, and no car, I spent at least two to three days a week at the market. Lisa always felt guilty about this change in lifestyle and thought it was a major inconvenience to me. I had always been the one to do the grocery run, so this wasn't a new thing for me. I didn't mind it so much. It got me out of the house, it got my steps in for the day, and it gave me an opportunity to constantly explore and find new culinary things. I developed very specific routines, each customized to the store, or country, I was going to that day.

Just down the street from our flat was a Coop. It took me exactly ten minutes to reach by foot. This is where I would go for a quick grab of items I needed on a more immediate basis. Think milk, creamer, eggs, pastries. Within a month I had the layout down pat. See, I like to write my grocery lists in the order I walk through the store so that I don't forget anything. Lisa says it is the perfect hallmark of my being an old man. She'll add things to my list, and then I will have to rewrite it so that everything is in walking-through-the-store order. This Coop became my local supermarket and I got to know it very well.

But it is not cost effective to grocery shop in Switzerland. The most common thing to do for Baselers is to cross the border and shop in Germany or France. Cross-border shopping became a way of life for me. The country I chose depended on what was on my list. Some things were better bought in France, others in Germany.

So let's talk about shopping in these different countries - what was great, what sucked, and what treasures I found.

Switzerland

If you want to go grocery shopping in Switzerland, you need to go between the hours of 9am and 6:30pm, Monday - Saturday. You will find a mad rush of business-clad Baselers rushing through the aisles the last twenty minutes their local Coop or Migros is open, having dashed off from work at six, hoping to grab a few needed items on their way home. Should they miss their tiny window, the train station is the only other recourse. Every train station in the country has either a Coop or Migros grocery store inside (smaller stations in smaller towns have Coop or Migros Express stores, like a Swiss 7-11) that will stay open until 9pm, and will be open on Sundays. If you run out of milk on a Saturday night, you're making a run to the *bahnhof* on Sunday.

Coop stores sell beer, wine, and liquor. Migros stores do not. In 2022, Migros held an online poll asking whether they should start selling beer and wine, and the country overwhelmingly asked them not to rock the boat and to stay dry. The Swiss are not ones to wantonly abandon tradition for convenience.

It is common for cases of beer to be broken open by shoppers so that they might buy an individual can or bottle, at which point you'll be asked if it is *laufenbier*, or a "walking beer". If you plan to drink it as you head to wherever you are going, then, yes, it is a walking beer, and the cashier will open it for you. There are no open container laws in Europe, and people will be seen in all parts of town, at all hours, enjoying a cold one on the tram, in the park, or just walking down the street. It is not unusual to see someone enjoying a *laufenbier* at 9am, either. I would pass folks sitting at cafe tables at 9am drinking wine with their breakfast croissants. Americans only enjoy a tipple at Sunday brunch, but in Switzerland, every day, and every hour, is a perfectly acceptable time for a drink.

They do this with ice cream as well - you'll find dozens of open boxes of ice cream bars or drumsticks in the cold case. In the Coop by our house, there was a reach-in ice cream freezer at the end of the frozen food section. It had all the individual ice cream treats you'd expect to find, like cones and bars and ice cream sandwiches. Locals, however, knew it was cheaper to grab one out of a box in the regular ice cream section than it was to get a pre-packaged individual item. So it was next to impossible, could I have afforded it, to buy a fully intact box of ice cream sandwiches. The Swiss love tidiness, unless it comes to the ice cream case in the freezer section.

We had just moved to our temporary apartment and I went down to the Migros at the end of the block to stock the kitchen up as best as I could. This was to be my first real grocery run. I got to the check out and the cashier starts to scan my produce. She turns the plastic bag over, and around, sets it aside, grabs the next one, does the same, and sets it aside. She looks at me confused.

"*Wo sind die Preisschilder?*"

This German was beyond me at this point, so I apologized with a meek "*keine Deutsch* (no German)".

Instead of being angry or frustrated, she smiles, turns the light off above her station, grabs the produce I have on the conveyor, and leads me back over to the produce section. Here, with a joyful demeanor, she shows me how there are numbers underneath the description of each item. So the bin of oranges will have a two or three-digit number on the sign that says "oranges". You take your bag of oranges over to the scales, type in the number, and then weigh it. The scale will print out a sticker (*preisschilder*) for you to put on the bag for the cashier to scan.

Unlike the US, the cashiers do not weigh anything at the checkout. Of course, this system relies implicitly on the honor system, which, honestly, just wouldn't fly in America. After showing me how the system works, my friendly cashier watched me weigh and sticker each of my produce items before walking me back to her stand, where she finished checking me out. By this time, a different cashier stand had opened, so there were no angry Swiss shoppers wondering where we had wandered off to.

A week or so later, I was back, and when I made my way to the checkout, she recognized me. I raised my stickered bag of *knoblauch* (garlic) with a smile. She gave me a hearty thumbs-up and a throaty *"ja, ja, richtig!* (correct)".

Well over a year later, after having moved to the other side of town, I had an appointment in the area and needed to grab a few items from the store on the way home, so I popped into this Migros. There was my favorite cashier, who, after so long a time, immediately remembered me. She was thrilled that on this visit I was able to chat with her in my rudimentary German. After telling her that I was now living so far from here, she made me promise to come see her whenever I was in the area. If it wasn't so inconvenient to get to her store from our flat, I would have done all my shopping there just because of how lovely she was.

In fact, I encountered many instances of patient Baselers behind counters who encouraged my German language skills. I had developed a default greeting when dealing with strangers:

"Es tut mir leid, aber mein Deutsch ist sehr schreklisch; sprechen Sie English, bitte?" or "I'm sorry, my German is terrible; do you speak English?".

This usually let them know that I had some German language skills, but that they were rudimentary. My neighbor Judith later remarked that using the word terrible (*schreklisch*) implied a larger vocabulary than I actually had, leaving people convinced I was either being lazy about wanting to speak in German or I was being overly modest. But it usually helped me feel less embarrassed about communicating in English when my German vocabulary failed me.

One day at the post office, I used my standard greeting, and was met with "well, that sounds like very good German to me!". I laughed and said I just didn't know enough to carry on a conversation so well for what I needed.

"Nonsense. We will try together, in German!"

And she made me use all the German I knew, even if it was at a preschool level. When I slipped and used English numbers instead of German, she's slam her hand down on the counter.

"Nein! Auf Deutsch!" and make me repeat myself in German.

When we finished with my transaction, she lowered her shoulders, spread out her arms, and smiled.

"See, you know more than you think! Be confident and you will do well!"

My physical therapist, my doctors, my neighbors (even the crap ones), the pharmacist, were all extremely patient and helpful whenever I tried to use the language.

Nevertheless, there is nothing that induces a feeling of immediate stupidity than standing at the meat counter trying to order a 1lb roast and realizing that everything is metric and you really haven't any idea of how bigger or smaller a pound is to a kilo so you have to mime with your hands to the perplexed butcher how large a piece of meat you want. Thanks, Jimmy Carter, for not trying harder to convert us to the metric system in '78.

You cannot buy any over-the-counter medications in a grocery store. Aspirin, Tylenol, Nyquil, cough syrup, Nexium and the like can only be bought at the apothecary, and are prohibitively expensive. So many expats ask what they should stock up on before moving to Switzerland, and OTC medications are the thing you need to bulk buy. Ibuprofen can be as much as 15CHF for a blister pack of six pills. Most cough syrup is by prescription only.

The best chocolate in Switzerland can be found at your local Coop. All Swiss grocery chains sell their own store brand of chocolate, as well as the bigger name brands. Chocolate in Switzerland is dirt cheap. And all of it is a bajillion times better than anything you have ever had before. The Coop Prix brand of chocolate bars are available in milk, dark, or with cornflakes (called *knusperflake*, they are like a Nestlé Crunch Bar, but instead of puffed rice, they use cornflakes, which hits SO much better). These simple store brand bars are some of the best chocolate bars you can buy. Full size bars cost 40 cents for milk or dark, and 80 cents for a *knusperflake*.

We hoarded the shit out of these things.

Every Swiss grocery will have an entire WALL of chocolate. The importance of chocolate in Swiss daily life cannot be understated. When Covid hit, the three things that stores were consistently sold out of were flour, sugar, and chocolate.

Lindt chocolate, while Swiss, is considered, by the Swiss, as swill. It's their Russell-Stover, if you will. Probably the most famous chocolate brand out of Switzerland (besides Toblerone), Lindt is hated by everyone in Switzerland.

Callier is the premium chocolate bar. This lilac-wrapped piece of heaven-sent manna is made with Alpine milk, which means that you can actually taste the wildflowers and pristine mountain grasses in the milk. It's the most extraordinary sensation, and it leaves you giddy. It's definitely pricier, but worth every single penny (or franc). When we were packing up to head back to the States, I bought an entire case of Callier bars and three canisters of their hot cocoa mix (duuuude!).

Sliced white bread is known as "American Toast". The average Swiss will buy their bread as freshly baked loaves from the store's bakery section. These bakery sections make American ones seem positively anemic. There will be at least thirty different types on offer, and they are baked fresh throughout the day. Unlike France, where the price of a baguette is controlled by the state, bread can actually be a bit more than you might expect to pay (but if you hit the store an hour before they close, you can get that day's loaves for half price). But it is always, always amazing. Many stores (especially in Germany) have bread slicing machines for you to use; in Switzerland, just ask the person behind the bakery counter to slice it for you.

Americans love their flavored coffee creamers. Pumpkin spice, mocha, peppermint mocha, double toffee caramel chocolate mocha, yadda-yadda-yadda. In Europe you have one flavor, which is no flavor. Called *kaffeerahm*, it is simply a sweet cream with no added flavors. Each store sells its own one brand of *kaffeerahm* and that is it. It's also UHT, so while real dairy, it is not refrigerated. Unless you are steaming milk for your espresso, the "adulteration" of coffee is seriously frowned upon, which is why coffee creamers are impossible to find.

Speaking of coffee, the use of ground coffee, or drip coffee makers, is quite rare. Instead, over 90% of the Swiss use Nespresso pods. So, too, then, did we. While Starbucks offers their own version of Nespresso pods in grocery stores, we generally ordered ours online direct from Nespresso for next day delivery. Nespresso pods are much cheaper than buying a pound of ground coffee, and are a third of the price in Switzerland than they are in the States (one of the very few things that is cheaper in Switzerland - in Basel a 10 pack of Starbucks House Blend pods was 4.50CHF, while in the US runs $9.50). There are also brick and mortar Nespresso stores in town where you can buy your pods, but the lines are usually so long they stretch out the door (it's that popular). Nespresso will also collect all of your used pods for recycling. They give you a plastic bag for the pods, and when it is full, you put it out in your post box for the postman to collect and send back to Nespresso for free. And yes, George Clooney's fantastic mug graces the window of every Nespresso shop in town.

Allow me to completely shock you with some prices (figures come from Facebook posts I shared with my folks – and these are 2019 prices. Remember, add 10% to get US dollar amounts):

    A 7oz (equivalent) steak filet = 71CHF(or $78)
    A two-pack of chicken breasts = 39CHF ($43)
    A liter of lactose-free milk = 2CHF ($2.20)
    A pint (yes, a pint) of Ben & Jerry's Cherry Garcia = 12CHF ($13.20)
    A 10-pack of Quölifrösch beer (cans) = 3.50CHF ($3.85)
    A bottle of French cabernet sauvignon = 3CHF ($3.30)
    A 6-pack of Coke (bottles) = 10CHF ($11)
    A 1kg bag of sugar = .50CHF (55¢)
    A kg bag of flour = 1.20CHF ($1.32)
    A bag of Cool American Doritos = 8CHF ($8.80)
    A 1kg bag of macaroni = .30CHF (33¢)
    One Granny Smith apple = 1.25CHF ($1.37)
    One kilo of apricots = 19CHF ($20.90)
    10 rolls of toilet paper = 24CHF ($26.40)
    A six-pack of frosted donuts = 18CHF ($19.80)
    Two pack ears of sweet corn = 4.80CHF ($5.20)

Eggs are not pasteurized, and so, do not need to be refrigerated. As Europe uses the metric system, eggs are sold as five or ten packs. Boiled eggs, however, are available in three or six packs and are dyed various colors (so that you can tell they're boiled), which makes things much easier come Easter time.

Toilet paper is white in Switzerland, but is generally blue in Germany and pink in France.

Quality wise: German TP > Swiss TP > French TP

Price wise, German TP is half what it is in Switzerland (same for paper towel). I bought all my paper products in Germany.

I was corrected on my American pronunciations of Gouda cheese (*gow-duh*, not *goo-dah*), Edam cheese (*eh-dahm*, not *eee-dum*) by the cheese monger at the Coop.

"Have you never been to the Netherlands!?"

Philadelphia cream cheese is strangely popular, and is nearly half the price it is back in the US. There are about fifteen different flavors on offer, as well. Bagels, however, are impossible to find. Instead, the Swiss use it primarily on *smørebrød* (open faced sandwiches).

The quality and freshness of the produce section, from the sweetness of the tomatoes to the deep aromas of the herbs to the crispness of the apples, cannot be overstated. The produce section at the local Kroger here in Colorado is so colorless I sometimes feel like I've gone colorblind. I literally laugh at the "tomatoes" every time for trying so hard to be real tomatoes. For the first time in my life, I felt like I was finally tasting what food is supposed to taste like. There are no flavorless apples like America's misnamed "Red Delicious". Every variety of apple, and in Europe there are hundreds and hundreds, are all, every one, crisp, juicy, and sweet. Oranges from Spain punch a thousand times harder than the ones from Florida or California.

Rhubarb is incredibly popular. Every bakery will have a rhubarb tart on offer. You can bet your life savings on this. When it is in season in the grocery stores, it's thankfully very cheap (around .80CHF a stalk compared to $2.80 a stalk in the US). But you have to get to the store when it opens or it will all be gone by noon. The Swiss LOVE their rhubarb

(Swiss rhubarb soda is to die for). I think Swiss rhubarb is much sweeter than its American counterpart, which tends to run much more sour (which could explain why it never really caught on in the US).

Potatoes come in color-coded bags, so that you get the right kind of potato for whatever it is you are making. Bags are either green, red, or blue. Green bags are for boiled potatoes, or potato salad. Red bags are good for roasted or baked potatoes and French fries. Blue bags are best for mashed or au gratin. Due to their popularity as a Swiss food staple, potatoes are incredibly cheap, and because of this, we had potatoes with just about every meal.

You cannot buy any kind of garbage bags you like. You must purchase a particular kind of garbage bag, issued by the city, called a *Bebi Sag*. If you want your trash picked up, all of it must be in a blue *Bebi Sag*. The *Bebis* in Basel are bright blue, but I preferred the ones I saw in Solothurn – they were white with cartoon faces on them, so that they looked like sad melted snowmen. Bags left on the curb or in the bin in any other color of garbage bag will be left behind. A roll of 24 60L bags is 34CHF, and that is all you pay for trash pick-up - just the cost of the bags. There is no monthly or quarterly sanitation bill like in the US. You simply pay as you need more bags, which are available at every single grocery store in the city. You can also purchase a special sticker for large items to be picked up, called *Sperrgut*. Slap one of these on anything less than 100kg and the trash man will pick it up. You can use two per month, and each sticker costs 10CHF.

All Swiss grocery stores have a plastic bottle recycling center. Every time I would run to the store, I would load up my shopping cart with our empty plastic bottles and drop them off before I started my list. These centers are almost always located just inside the front door, and also have slots for battery recycling. Glass and aluminum must be taken to special depot areas dotted around the city (no more than a kilometer away from any one spot in town). There are massive sealed dumpsters, one each for clear, green, and brown bottles, and one for aluminum cans. Because they are outdoors in busy intersections or near public squares, you are only allowed to do your recycling between 9am-Noon and 2pm-6pm, Monday through Saturday. You cannot disturb the lunch hour with your breaking glass and clanking tin cans, nor can you recycle on Sunday, the quiet day. The Swiss take recycling as seriously as their chocolate, watches, and punctuality. Recycling also reduces the amount of trash at home, so you don't need to buy as many *Bebi Sags*. We kept a plastic bin on the balcony for all of our recycling, and I would take my plastic in every time I went to the store, so it never piled up. Same for glass and cans – kept them in a bin and took it down to the recycling containers once a week.

Shopping in Switzerland is not cheap. In general, a full two bags of groceries would cost upwards of 100CHF. The "discount" options of Aldi and Lidl (both German), or Denner (Swiss) didn't actually save you anything significant, and their selections and quality weren't worth the penny savings. We learned very quickly that we had the option of going across the border to either France or Germany to grocery shop, and that it would save us a significant chunk of change. We had only to follow the import rules for meat (no more than 2kg), alcohol (no more than 3 liters), and cost (anything over 300CHF would be subject to customs import taxes). While there were no border crossing customs buildings to go through, the trams did have stops right at the border so that shoppers could disembark and declare things if needed.

Swiss shoppers could also claim exemption from European VAT - they'd get a slip from the cashier in either Germany or France and present it to the customs office on the border. Once stamped, that VAT amount could be used as a voucher for the next shopping excursion in that country (never redeemed for cash). It acted like a perpetual coupon.

Customs officials would randomly jump on the tram while it was stopped to randomly check receipts of those with shopping bags and loaded carts. I had read about an American woman living in Basel who went to Germany to shop for all the fixings for a full Thanksgiving dinner. She bought the equivalent of a 24lb turkey and had well over 300CHF worth of goods, and did not declare any of it at the border. She faced a fine of 1200CHF for customs violations. I was only ever checked on three occasions, but then, I was always careful to never exceed any of the allowances. I was only ever checked on my way back from Germany, never France. In fact, I don't think I ever saw anyone checked on the tram from France. Guess that's the notorious French laissez faire-ness for you.

———

Germany

When I first started cross-border shopping, I took everyone's advice and went to Germany. The town of Weil am Rhein sits right on the north side of Basel, nestled between the Rhine and the Black Forest. It's not a pretty town. It's more of an office park. A very clean, orderly office park, lacking any hint of character that would let
you know you were in Baden-Württemberg, Germany and not, say, Akron, Ohio. It was strange to me how every ounce of European-ness seemed to evaporate as soon as you crossed over into this part of Germany. It was entirely devoid of character of any kind. It just... was. But it was also home to a variety of German grocery stores as well as a shopping mall and a tiny outlet mall. This was the one town in Germany that the tram went to, and was covered by my tram pass. The shopping center sat directly on the Rhine between two bridges. Take the bridge south and you're back in

Switzerland; take the one west and you're in France.

It took me 40 minutes to get to Weil am Rhein. From home, I would have to go to the main train station and catch the #8 tram. Only every other #8 went to Germany, so if you missed it, you had to wait 14 minutes for the next one. I soon found that if you caught the #8 at the train station, you wouldn't be able to find a seat because it is always the most packed tram, and everyone went to Weil to shop, so I began to walk to the stop before the train station, to beat the crowd and secure a seat (I would do the same on the way back, walking an extra stop away from the shopping center so that I could get on before everyone else at the center stop). With my pull trolley, finding a seat with room for it was paramount. So heading to Germany to shop was never on a whim - it took strategic planning and logistical acumen.

The Marktkauf was a cavernous, two story grocery extravaganza. Located inside the shopping mall, it is probably the largest grocery store I have ever been in. It is also the most popular market in the Basel area and is always, always packed. It is so busy that it has thirty-four checkout stands, and ALL of them are ALWAYS open. You could probably fit two whole Costco box stores inside it. It takes up two floors, and to get upstairs, you have to take the people-mover ramp. Like the long moving walkways in airports, this one is on a steep 30% angle, and not only does it move people up and down, but carts as well. Unlike the cart escalators you find in American multi-story Targets that grab your cart in a vice and pull it upwards while keeping it perfectly level, this angled ramp is also for your cart. So you're on this incredibly steep ramp while holding a shopping cart, with no wedges or stops to hold the cart in place. You simply have to hold on to it for dear life and hope you don't lose your grip, lest it go flying down the embankment, knocking over other shoppers like bowling pins.

Going up is far easier than coming back down. When you do

head back downstairs, you are coming from the canned food, beverage, and home goods section, meaning your cart has become exponentially heavier than it was when you started downstairs. I always started shopping upstairs because I didn't want to have to stand behind a half-full cart on the way up, hoping I didn't lose my grip and have it roll back on top of me, and then have an entirely full cart to hold on the way back down. You have to plant your feet and lean back while holding onto the cart with both hands when you head downstairs. If you have items stacked too high, they'll tumble forward and out because of the angle. I would dread the descent down, not just because it was so dangerous, but because I hated seeing eighty-year-old women holding their fuller-than-mine cart with one hand while looking bored and unconcerned. But I never once saw anyone take a tumble or lose their cart. Still, those ramps scared me.

In the upper deck of the Marktkauf is a wall of gummy candy. Not a section, not an area, an entire wall. How big of a wall? This one was 50 feet long. Yes, 50 feet of nothing but gummy candy. One cannot stress enough just how much the Germans love their gummies. They are, after all, the inventors of the gummy bear (Haribo is one of the largest companies in Germany). And there are at least forty different varieties of gummy bears available. Every animal in your imagination can be eaten as a gummy candy. Mice are the most popular, as well as worms, cats, pigs, rabbits, lions, penguins, sharks, and *Schrumpfs* (the German version of Smurfs). Gummies come in both bags and buckets. Yep, you can take home two and three gallon buckets of gummy mice. Gummies also come in mallow-cream variations, which I loved. The wall is so popular that they have a team of three workers who do nothing but restock the wall throughout the day.

"So, what do you do?"

"I'm a Haribo stocker at the Marktkauf"

"Ah, doing the Lord's work!"

"Blessed be the gummy fruit"

If you want non-gummy candy, you have to go to an entirely different section of the store. In Germany, British chocolate is quite popular (Cadbury, Lion bars, Bounty bars, Picnic, Flakes), but they also have a huge variety of their own chocolate bars: Milka and Ritter. Ritter Sport are square-shaped chocolate bars that come in a huge variety of flavors like Malted Milk Ice Cream, Lemon Meringue, *Knusperflake*, Rum Raisin, and Speculouos Cookie. Kinder Chocolate is also hugely popular, with the original Kinder Eggs being one of the best-selling candies in Europe. Banned for decades in the US because a small plastic toy is hidden inside the chocolate egg, the Europeans give their kids a modicum of common sense not to eat said toy, while in the US, we err on the side of dumbness and ban them. A new version of the egg has been introduced to the American market in recent years, but without the toy center. Maybe if they put a gun inside it, Americans would be okay with it…

The American section is always fun to visit. Here you will find microwave popcorn, Reese's Peanut Butter Cups (if they haven't sold out), jars of off-brand peanut butter, Pop Tarts (at €13 a box), off-brand root beer, Miracle Whip, bottles of Sweet Baby Ray's BBQ Sauce, and, strangely, jars of hot dogs (this is a common misconception that the Europeans have about American hot dogs - in every single American section I visited, be it in Switzerland, Germany, France, and the Netherlands, hot dogs were always jarred).

You can find many oddball beverages in Germany. Lösch-Zwerg, or cola-beer, is a combination of Hefeweizen, cola, coffee, and lemon. Not only insanely tasty, it is refreshing as hell. And, yes, it is both alcoholic and caffeinated. Becks beer comes in lemon-mint and green tea infused varieties (which I did not try, even in the face of my "try all the things" mantra). There is also a European brand of beer called Mixery that infuses beer with either cherry juice or guarana (think Red Bull). Nope, didn't try those, either. As I would linger in the beer aisle, taking it all in, I noticed that these flavored beers were snatched up by the younger set. These seemed to be the German answer to the flavored seltzer drinks that are super popular in the States. I also found that hard liquor was cheapest at the Marktkauf.

If you buy bottled water (which I didn't because Basel tap water is extraordinary), you need to check the label for "*Mit Gas*" or "*Ohne Gas*" - with carbonation, or without. Sparkling water is insanely popular in Europe, and everywhere you go, when you are offered water, you will be asked *"mit gas, oder ohne?"*. Lisa abhors sparkling water.

"I don't drink static".

The produce section in Germany operates just like the Swiss - you must enter the posted number of the item into the scale and print out a sticker. Again, this honor system is incredibly effective. Produce prices in Germany were also much cheaper than in Switzerland, and because the store was so big, it had far more options on offer. I thought the quality of produce was slightly better in Switzerland than in Germany, but both were still heads and tails above America.

Our first Thanksgiving in Basel, we were just moving into our new flat and didn't have enough time to properly plan a traditional feast. The following Thanksgiving, however, Lisa was intent on cooking a big, fat American-style Turkey Day dinner. I love Thanksgiving. I could eat Thanksgiving Day leftovers every day for the rest of my life and be happy. This meant finding a turkey. By this time, I was familiar with cross-border shopping, both to Germany and to France. Getting a Swiss turkey was out of the question. A 6kg turkey (about 12.5lbs) was over 100CHF at the Coop. At this point, I was shopping far more regularly in France than in Germany, but I simply could not find a whole turkey there. Remembering the story about the American woman who was fined for bringing a large turkey over the border without claiming it, I was very leery of getting one in Germany. But this was the only place I was going to find one, and one I could afford. I did, in fact, find an 8kg turkey for only 40€, at the Marktkauf (at this time, the Euro and the dollar were equal value). It exceeded the weight allowance by 7kgs, so how to get it home?

I had noticed that the border checks only occurred on the tram. I had never seen or heard of any pedestrians being stopped as they walked across the border. Again, there is no real gate or building to walk through to cross the border. There is only a small sign. So I decided I would walk from the Marktkauf across the border to the first tram stop inside Switzerland (the border checks were done by the Germans, not the Swiss), and then hop on the tram there. Sure enough, I simply sauntered across the border with my contraband and waited for the next tram to arrive. As soon as I was aboard, I was in a huge panic, as two uniformed men approached me. Luckily, they were just ticket checkers, and after showing them my monthly pass, they moved on. I was free and clear, and now clearly a renegade poultry smuggler. My shame, however, tasted delicious later that week.

Usually the overhead muzak is playing, appropriately enough, '80s German techno pop, alá Kraftwerk and Nena. On American election day, however, it was tuned to the local news station, giving minute by minute updates to the Presidential election between Joe Biden and Donald Trump. I was happily surprised at how much I understood. But my heart swelled three sizes that day when I heard the German political pundits predict (before any of the polls had closed) that Biden would win, and cheers erupted all over the store.

My absolute favorite moment at the Marktkauf was witnessing this conversation in the pasta aisle. A young American twenty-something couple, with the most Deep-South 'Bama accents:

Girl: I can't read any of these labels! I don't know what any of this stuff is!

Dude: [picks up jar of Barilla pasta sauce] It's sauce! It's basil spaghetti sauce. We buy this exact same shit at home!

Girl: German is too hard!

Dude: There's a picture of basil on the front! It's literally the SAME STUFF WE GET AT KROGER!

Girl: I hate it here

———

France

Michael had told us there was no reason to go to St Louis, France.

In fact, for a while, they stopped running the tram across the border after dark because it would get pelted with bottles and paint and eggs (though to be fair, this was during one of the infamous Yellow Vest Strikes). It is true, St Louis is a bit of a shithole, though I never found it to be as bad as all that. I never felt unsafe there, but I also never felt happy there, either. It's a depressing town, and like Weil am Rhein, feels nothing like the country it sits in. Other than the signs being in French, everything about the town felt like a rundown mining town in the Australian Outback. I felt like everyone I passed knew I did not belong there, and made me feel as such.

Everyone always talks about how rude Parisians are, but I had the very opposite experience and found every single Parisian I encountered to be cheerful and helpful. Everyone in St Louis, however, made me feel like I was wandering through a gulag. I honestly never saw a smile when I went to that town. Not once. We would venture up to the picturesque French village of Colmar on weekends and everyone there was simply delightful. It wasn't a French thing, then - it was a St Louis thing. I had spent time touring the old Soviet Union (before it collapsed) and there were many a time that I felt I was back in Moscow or Tashkent or Leningrad whenever I stepped off the tram to do my shopping there.

When you ride the tram over to St Louis, France, the minute you cross the border, the announcements switch from German to French. More importantly, the minute you cross the border into France, not a single solitary person will know how to speak German. You can stand ON the border and if you leaned to the left into Basel, you could speak German to the person standing next to you, and they would not know any French, and likewise you could lean to your right into St Louis and the person standing next to you would not know a single word of German. These two strangers could live on the same street, across from each other on that imaginary line, and neither would know the other person's language. Even within Switzerland, those in French-speaking cities do not know any German and the German-speakers will not know any French. Language barriers here are strange indeed. I was hiking once near the ruins of a castle on the French border. You literally cross the border a few times along the trail. As I passed a couple on my walk, on the Swiss side, we greeted each other with the traditional Swiss greeting of *"Greuzi!"* We passed each other again a short time later, but this time on the French side, so it was now *"Bonjour!"*.

Greeting passers-by etiquette: always in nature, on hikes, in forests, or on alps; never on the sidewalk in a city or town or any urban setting.

There were two main options for groceries in St Louis: Carrefour or Géant Casino (which did not, sadly, offer any gambling). The Carrefour was much too far away to reach. I would have to take the tram to the end of the line at the main train station in St Louis and then take the bus for another 20 minutes to reach it (making it a nearly one-hour trip just to get there). This was the fancy store, the Whole Foods of France, if you will. Instead, I was to make do with the Géant. Imagine if a K-Mart decided to sell food. It was a sad place. It was a run-down place. It was where the French notion of *laissez-faire* nested, took root, and snaked its tendrils across the land. It was the epitome of "meh". But it was cheap, and the quality of goods was actually pretty spectacular. You could find amazing things here, if you could get past the ever-lingering ennui.

They had an entire case dedicated to escargot. In shell, out of shell, in pastry. Lisa and I both love escargot (snails are yummy), so we decided to buy and try all the different kinds for New Year's Eve. We loved escargot so much that we would take the train an hour north to Colmar, France just to sit at a cafe and eat order after order of escargot and drink pink wine until we wanted to explode.

The cheese section is larger than both the produce section and the meat section - combined. Swiss cheese sections are depressingly small affairs. You can get Emmentaler, you can get Gruyeres, or you can get Raclette. That's it. If you want all the cheeses, you go to France. This place had over forty different kinds of brie alone.

The meat section would freak out the average American. Beside the pork loins and beef roasts and chicken thighs were packages of ground horse meat, skinned whole rabbits, tripe, and whole beef hearts. Veal and venison were also regularly stocked. I have to say that the best meat and poultry came from this store. And the prices were literally half to three quarters what I would pay in Switzerland. I could buy a three pack of duck breasts for 9€ (whereas one duck breast in Basel would cost me up to 22CHF). Marrow bones were practically free.

While the horse and rabbit may freak some out, what got to

me were the abominations known as "chicken donuts". Compressed processed chicken meat in the shape of a donut and breaded, like a nugget, sold in a six pack. Yes, they are as vile as you are imagining.

The produce section was enormous (maybe even larger than the Marktkauf), and was the cheapest place for fruits and veggies. France, too, made you print your own labels for your produce, but instead of numbers, you had to search for the pictogram. Divided into *Fruits* and *Legumes*, you had to scroll, alphabetically (in French, of course) to find your item, then print your label. I much preferred the number system. Still, creating your own scanning labels saves an inordinate amount of time at the checkout.

Nothing in this world hits better than a French strawberry. American strawberries are simply thoughts about what a strawberry should taste like. You have not truly experienced food, or life, until you have tasted a French strawberry. It could also be that the French pick their strawberries when they are small and packed full of flavor instead of letting them grow the size of Chryslers where the texture becomes akin to decades old rich Corinthian leather and tastes about the same.

When it comes to in-store bakeries, no country can best the French. I became obsessed with the basketball-sized loaves of sugar brioche. OBSESSED. I could eat that every single day of my life and never tire of it. I bought a loaf every single time I went to the Géant. You could buy a four-pack of rum-baba (an individual sized rum-soaked sponge cake, and I mean SOAKED as in you could not eat one of these and drive) in glass containers for only 4€. Here I discovered the wonders of the *Tarte Tropizienne*: two halves of sugar brioche filled with vanilla and lemon crème patisserie and covered in pearl sugar (this treat was created for Brigitte Bardot while she was in St Tropez filming *And God Created Woman*). The eclairs made Lisa a little bit weepy.

The best chips (crisps to my British friends) can be found in France. And by best, I mean the most creative flavors. It became a habit to take photos of all the weird and wonderful bags of potato chips I found and wondered why Americans were so dull when it came to flavored snacks. If it's not bbq, ranch, or cheese, Americans just aren't interested.

Here are some of the varieties America is missing out on:

>Roast Spare Rib Potato Chips
>Bolognaise Potato Chips
>*Poulet Braise* (Roast Chicken) Potato Chips
>Smoked Bacon and Onion Potato Chips
>Mustard Pickles Potato Chips
>*Confit d'Ognion avec Viniagre Balsamique* (Onion confit with balsamic vinegar)
>Roast Beef with Mustard Pringles
>Peking Duck with Hoisin Sauce Pringles
>Chicken Tikka Masala Pringles
>Flame Grilled Steak Doritos
>American BBQ Doritos
>Paprika Bugles
>Emmentaler and Gruyeres Bugles
>Lay's Wasabi Potato Chips
>Lay's Hot Chicken Wings Potato Chips

I learned my lesson about buying lunchmeat in France. I thought it was quite the steal, getting a package of sliced ham or oven roasted turkey cold cuts for 4€. I snatched up about four or five packs to make sandwiches at home. The first time I opened one, my jaw dropped. Inside were two slices of meat. Just two. Upon closer inspection, in the tiniest of print, it says (in French) that the package contains only two slices. WHO BUYS ONLY TWO SLICES OF TURKEY FOR 4€!?!? The next time I went back, I learned that ALL French deli meat comes in two-slice packs. This was one of the stupidest things I ever encountered in a European grocery store.

Lisa joined me once on a trip to the Géant (I shopped solo 99% of the time). We were standing at the checkout when she noticed all the cigarettes (which feature graphic pictures of diseased lungs, tracheotomy inserts, cancerous tongues, and bodies in coffins).

"I am French. I like to surrender... to cancer!"

Unlike the Marktkauf, the Géant will have two lanes open at the cashier, if you are lucky. Sure, they have 20 lanes, but you'll find just one or two in use. The line will snake all the way to the back of the store. This is true any day at any time. You will wait in line for a longer time than you have spent shopping. This is a Facebook post from one excursion that particularly piqued me:

> *In line at French grocery store, in one of only two registers open. 5 people in front of me. 9:00am hits and the cashier looks at her watch as it beeps an alarm, and she throws down a "register closed" sign. Apparently this means no one in this line is getting checked out before she leaves, so all of us make our way to the ONLY other open register that now has 20 people in line. Three store workers - THREE - are fucking around filling chewing gum endcaps - THREE EMPLOYEES- and not a one opens a register or is asked to open a register. So I now have 25 people in line in front of me, in a line that snakes across the entire front aisle of the store and around the corner and off into oblivion, and in the 30 minutes it took me to get through that line, not a single new register was opened- but a FOURTH EMPLOYEE joined her colleagues in stocking gum and candy bars.*
> *WHAT IN THE NAME OF MARCEL MARCEAU ARE YOU DOING, FRANCE!?*
> *Oh, and because of that, I juuuuust missed the tram, which means a 15-minute wait for the next one.*

Yeah, the trams to France only operate every 15 minutes, so if you miss one, it's a bit of a wait to get the next one. I also had two tram transfers to make when I would go to France, so that made it a bit of an Odyssey, but the money I saved by shopping there made it all worth it. After vacillating back and forth between Germany and France for my cross-border needs, I eventually made France my go-to. If I needed more in the way of canned goods, paper goods, or cleaning supplies, I'd head to Germany. For the most part, though, I spent many a Soviet-style day in St Louis loading up on brioche, strawberries, snails, and ennui.

Of course, all of this changed when Covid hit.

One of the first things that happened was that Germany closed its border with Switzerland (and everyone else around it). There would be no more cross-border shopping. Even those who lived in Germany and worked in Switzerland (and vice versa) were now forced to work from home. For a shorter time, France, too, temporarily closed its border, but for only a few weeks (the German border was closed for months and months). This meant a few changes were on the horizon for me and my trusty shopping trolley.

Immediately, everyone ran to the store when it was announced there was going to be a lockdown. We in Switzerland had known this was coming for some time as we watched the pandemic explode across our neighbor to the south, Italy. In some ways, it helped prevent a super mad rush to the shops all at once. It didn't create a wave of panic buying, but stores did have a run on a few staples.

In Switzerland, it's not called hoarding, but rather

"hamstering".

Baselers were not hamstering toilet paper like in the US (probably because it was too expensive to bulk buy). Strict restrictions were put on items for purchase, and whole sections of stores were taped off. It was a pandemic so you didn't need to be buying socks or oven mitts or Post-It Notes. Bouncers became a standard feature at the front door of every store, counting the number of people they let in so that only a small number were in the same space at the same time. They would spray everyone's hands with sanitizer as they entered, too.

Shoppers were quick to respect personal space. We would stand in a small queue to wait our turn to grab bags of potatoes or crates of eggs. There were no American style boxing matches in store aisles over the last box of Froot Loops (probably because there are no Froot Loops in Swiss grocery stores). Boxes of disposable plastic gloves were available to grab produce out of the bins. As I noted earlier, flour, sugar, and chocolate were consistently out of stock. Pasta and cheese were also incredibly scarce. According to the local paper, demand for sauerkraut and potatoes increased 40% nationwide during the early weeks of lockdown, but retailers were "promised stock from farmers to keep up with demand".

Shoppers were required to make their trips solo ones. Do not shop in pairs, do not shop as a family, all to create as little contact with others as possible. There is always someone who thinks the rules do not apply to them. Again, from a Facebook post:

> *Just watched a store manager refuse a woman with her two children entrance to the grocery store. Though they were speaking in Swiss-German, she was pointing at the woman's kids and shaking her head no as she spoke, while also pointing to the sign at the entrance that has a family pictogram with a slash across it. The woman with the kids was angry but the*

manager stood her ground. I walked past them to go inside, and never did see them in the store, so I'm assuming she left. I know there will be people out there with kids who will rant against this rule, but it's not a new one and has been successfully in place here in Switzerland for at least 8 weeks. The fact that so many kids here have been out in play-groups, at the playground, and are notorious for touching everything in their path, IMHO, this is a perfectly acceptable rule to lower the risk of spreading the disease.

It was actually unusual to see lots of families shopping together during normal times. In my experience, the majority of shoppers in Switzerland and France were solo (or sometimes a pair, but almost NEVER more than two to a group). Germany, well, was different, because the people there loved to shop in large gaggles, like angry geese. But considering it was rare for families to hit the Coop together, it struck me as odd that suddenly it seemed as if everyone wanted to go out together as soon as they were specifically told not to. Humans are weird.

Eventually, France re-opened its border with Switzerland and allowed cross border traffic to resume. This area of France had the lowest infection rate, and the majority of its workforce were employed in Switzerland and Germany. While cross-border shopping was discouraged, it wasn't forbidden. I will admit that while I did end up going back to France to shop, it wasn't until well into the downward spike, and only after I was immunized. And I had to do it to save money. Covid hit everyone hard, which I'll go into in a later chapter. Economics warranted my incursions into the infected armpit of France. Germany would not reopen itself to cross-border traffic for many more months, and by then, I had realized I didn't really miss shopping there. I remained loyal to my shitty French Casino for the remainder of our stay.

To this day, every time I go to the local Kroger here in Denver, I weep a little because I miss the Géant so.

C'est la vie

Chapter Four: Messe-ing Around

Twenty-one years before Columbus sailed the ocean blue and devastated a native population with smallpox and slavery, one hundred and thirty years before Billy Shakespeare wrote a little ditty called Hamlet, and three hundred and five years before some backwater English colonies declared their independence, the City of Basel held its first Autumn Festival.

The annual *Herbstmesse* began in 1471 with a decree of permission from the Holy Roman Empire allowing the city to hold a festival to boost the economy post-plague outbreak. More importantly, the decree allowed the city to hold it in perpetuity. In the Swiss tradition of following things to the letter, the city has held this celebration, every single year since, in literal perpetuity. In 2021, the 550th *Herbstmesse* was held, even in the face of Covid (albeit on a smaller scale, but held nevertheless). It's hard to wrap your head around the fact that this little get-together has been going on twice as long as the United States has existed as a nation. I'm telling you, just when you think you've gotten used to how old things are in Europe, you sit and think about things like this and you can't help but let out a Keanu Reeves-sized "whoa!"

The mere existence of this festival (*Messe*, in German) was a surprise to us, as we knew only of the famous Christmas Market held in the city. I had noticed the enormous, 60-meter-tall Ferris Wheel going up in the Münsterplatz (that's 196 feet for us Americans, or nearly 10 stories tall) and asked our downstairs neighbor about it.

"Oh, just our little fall fair".

Little, we would soon learn, my ass.

Spread out over five of the main squares of Basel, the fair is all about carnival rides, trinkets and food. Lots and lots of glorious, tasty, unusual, wonderful food (found mainly in the Old Town), and lots and lots of glittery and sketchy carnival rides (found mostly in Kleinbasel).

The single greatest bratwurst I have ever eaten, and I say this with conviction and deadly seriousness, was had at the Wurst Chalet (in Old Town's Petersplatz, for those making notes at home). No other bratwurst can ever, and I mean ever, come close to the sweet, fatty perfection of that perfect little sausage. Tears, my friends. 'Twas so good, it brought me to literal tears.

"You're crying! Are you okay, did you hurt yourself?"

"I'm fine - it's this brat. it's just so… amazing!"

"You're crying over bratwurst?"

"I am, and I am not ashamed"

We went back more than once to have one of those brats, and my friends, it made me a bit teary-eyed every single time.

Now, there is one other thing we need to talk about when it comes to Swiss sausages, my dear, backward American friends, and that is how to eat them, properly. This is where, if you are not careful, your 'Murica will show.

The Swiss do NOT eat their brats, or any other sausages, IN a bun.

This is not some alpine Wisconsin cookout. No, the Swiss eat sausages with their hands. Your brat will come half wrapped in wax paper, on a plate, with a piece of rustic bread (NOT a hot dog bun or Kaiser roll or hoagie or any other kind of bread envelope that can hold said sausage) and a dollop of mustard. You dip your brat into the mustard, take a hearty Viking-esque nosh, grab the roll, tear some off with your teeth, and then wash it all down with a tankard of bier. It is a faux pas to expect or ask for your brat to come in a bun.

Sauerkraut is also not as common an accompaniment as you might imagine. Finding kraut as an add-on for your brats is usually reserved for restaurant dishes where you order the sausage plate (that might contain a sample of 3-4 different sausages) and would be served as a side dish along with very common spätzle - and only in sit-down dining establishments, to boot.

Growing up in Chicago, I grew to despise sausage. Specifically Polish sausage (or kielbasa). Because it was so cheap, we had it ALL the time. It would literally make me gag. Just typing the word kielbasa is making my spine shiver. We never had bratwurst, though, because it was both more expensive, and my mother didn't care for it. My first foray into bratwurst consumption came in my twenties when I was able to get out and try all the things! I loved brats. I loved sauerkraut. I loved all the German food. We never ate German food at home because my mother didn't like vinegary/fermented things.

I took German language in high school, and one night, all the language courses got together to cook two dishes from their culture and serve it to the students and their families. Our class made brats with sauerkraut and sauerbraten with German potato salad. Having never even heard of sauerbraten (a beef roast that has been marinated in red wine, vinegar and herbs for three days), I decided to give it a whirl. And I was immediately in love with that dish. It made me realize how much I was missing out on some really great food. So when we arrived in Switzerland, I was itching to try all the local things, especially the sausages. They did not, ever, disappoint (though, to be fair, I steered far clear of any and all kielbasas). In fact, my very first sausage experience was less than two weeks after landing in Basel, at a food cart in the farmer's market in the Market Square. With seven different wieners on offer, I decided to try the Baselwurst - the local dog. It was a beef sausage made with sweet, Christmas-like spices. Completely unusual, it was utterly fantastic. And it was here, at this kiosk, that I learned the Swiss way of eating a sausage. I stood at a tiny, high table, eating my wurst, drinking a bottle of Feldschlösschen bier, under the shadow of the 500-year-old City Hall, and had my first thunderbolt moment of realization that this is my life now, and my gods, is it fantastic!

So at the risk of it becoming weird here, I am unabashedly a wiener man.

One does need a good libation to wash down that tasty link, and European festivals know exactly what you need.

If you're a classic beer and brats kind of guy, then Switzerland has plenty of options. Feldschlösschen, the most popular beer in the country, is brewed just twenty minutes away in the picturesque Rhine River hamlet of Rheinfelden. Crisp and inoffensive, it's the Budweiser of *der Schweiz*. I prefer the heartier Appenzeller bier from the rural southwest of the country (kind of like a Belgian White). Ueli is a local

Basel brew that reminds me, unkindly, of Heineken. Honestly, the best beers in Switzerland are not Swiss. It's just not their forte. Strangely enough, one of the most popular beers in the country is Coors Light, if that tells you anything. Must be the mountains on the can.

On the other hand, what Switzerland does very well, as does the rest of Europe, are hot beverages. Specifically, *glühwein*. *Glühwein* is a sweet, spiced mulled wine (available in red or white) with fruit and brandy, served hot.

My friends, this is the festive winter beverage.

The best part of the weather turning cold means it is finally *glühwein* season. At the *Herbstmesse*, you can indulge in gallons of the stuff. Instead of burning your hands on a flimsy paper cup, you put a small deposit down on a ceramic mug which is refunded to you when you turn your empty glass back in. Or keep it as a souvenir and forfeit the deposit. You can also fill your mug with *glühmost*, or hot spiced apple cider. Like *glühwein*, this hot cup of awesomeness is calvados or rum spiked cider with cinnamon, nutmeg, and anise. A popular addition is a shot of amaretto in your *glühmost*. The Swiss LOVE to put shots of just about any liqueur into any already-alcoholic beverage.

Sadly, there is one other kind of *glüh*-beverage, and it is an abomination before all of man and all the gods in every heaven: *glühbier*.

Yes, it's exactly what you think it might be - hot, spiced beer. I had seen it at one of the kiosks whilst wandering around the *Herbstmesse*, but couldn't muster the courage to try it. A month later, while exploring the Christmas Market in Basel, I decided I had to give it a go - I had made a solemn vow to try all the new things. Not only was I the only person in line to get a glass, I noticed in the following weeks whenever we visited the Market, there was never a single person at that counter buying one.

I quickly learned why.

Imagine you left a can of Pabst Blue Ribbon out in the July sun for a week, then peed in it, left it for another week in the sun, stirred it together with a twenty-year-old stick of cinnamon that was once tied to a candle in the bargain bin of a Bed Bath & Beyond, and then strained it through a used gym sock into a festive little souvenir mug (ironically shaped like a Christmas stocking).

"I warned you."

"But we have to try all the things!"

"I warned you"

"You warned me"

Even Krampus wouldn't make all the bad girls and boys drink *glühbier*. Actually, *glühbier* is a direct violation of the Geneva Convention. In the immortal words of Colonel Kurtz in *Apocalypse Now*: "the horror; the horror!"

Still, as you find yourself snuggled up to a large table with a fire pit in the middle of it, enjoying the glories of bratwurst and *glühwein*, watching the two-story tall pink carousel towering over hundreds of tiny log cabin kiosks selling hats and scarves and candy and toys, all under a canopy of yellow oak trees, you are infinitely happy. You are happy in a way that you cannot remember ever being. You are in the midst of an ancient celebration, amongst all of your new neighbors, in this beautiful city square, and you suddenly feel like you belong here. This festival, this moment, is yours now. This all belongs to you. And your heart soars to Icarian heights.

"We can't just sit here and eat brats all day, sweetie"

"You sure about that?"

We had so many other treats to try, but it was hard to leave this wondrous reverie. My reluctance was immediately replaced with excited indecision. There was SO much still to try, and it seemed that every other stall would make Augustus Gloop piss his pants with glee.

Portuguese egg tarts (if they were this good in Basel, I needed to get myself to Lisbon, like, yesterday).

Intricately pressed anise cookies called *Aniskrabeli* (you can also buy the hand-carved cookie presses used to make them in a myriad of different designs - the most popular are the seal of the City of Basel (the black staff of the Bishop of Basel) and basilisks, the symbol of the city).

Kokosballen were one of my favorites. These are giant chocolate covered marshmallows covered in shaved coconut. Not American-style Kraft marshmallows, but something more like a cross between a marshmallow fluff and meringue. And they come in different flavors like eggnog, Irish crème, whiskey, and amaretto. And they're the size of baseballs.

Magenbrot is a chocolate gingerbread cookie.

Bieberli are the Swiss version of a Fig Newton - a soft ginger cookie with an almond paste filling.

Bars of Alsatian fruited nougat the size of a card table.

Homemade venison sausage.

Emmentaler cheese from Emmental, which is just an hour away. Gruyere cheese from Gruyere which is just an hour away. The epicurean delights were coming at us from every direction. We had to remind ourselves that we could come back to try all the things we missed the first time. If we tried everything on the first day, we'd explode like Monty Python's Monsieur Creosote.

Baseler Läckerli is THE local specialty. If I could eat *läckerli* every day, I would. This magical treat is a chewy, flat, gingerbread biscuit with almonds, lemon, orange, kirsch, and anise. It's a Basel invention, and people flock to the city for it during Christmastime (though it is available year round). There is a shop in town called *Läckerli Haus* that sells nothing but *läckerli*, and when you buy some, you get a freshly baked sample, warm from the oven, and it is a religious experience. If you ask a native what a must-do is in Basel, sampling *läckerli* will be on everyone's list. If I was on death row, I'd request a bucket of *läckerli* to accompany my last meal. Once we returned to the States, Lisa and I were reminiscing about Christmas in Basel and her face lit up.

"I bet I could find a good *läckerli* recipe. I can make that!"

And she did. Apparently, the recipe she found was sourced from Basel's *Läckerli Haus*, and it was perfect. I have never had a memory of a place come to life so viscerally as when I tasted Lisa's homemade version of *läckerli*. I insist she make it all the time. It has become my literal connection to my happiest of memories.

We wandered the 350 different stalls in Petersplatz, but had only seen a tiny portion of the whole fair. In the Cathedral Square were dozens of kiddie carnival rides, including the monstrous Ferris Wheel. What sets these rides apart is the artwork blazoned on the sides of them. These are bad Eastern European knock-offs of American cartoons, like Brad the Builder and Morty Mouse, and my personal favorite, Carrot Bunny (a Dollar Store version of Bugs Bunny). One whirly ride was festooned with an enormous air-brushed Arnold Schwarzenegger-as-Mr. Freeze arm in arm with a lazy-eyed Barbie. It was like Eli Roth had been commissioned to make a children's movie.

The other main square of the Old Town, Barfüsserplatz (no real translation - closest is Barefoot Square, or the Casual Square) had more craft kiosks and a musical stage. The music was a strange mix of Alpine dubstep yodel-pop (which isn't as fun as you might imagine). Across the river, in Kleinbasel, in the Festival Square were the adult thrill rides, including the 15-story-tall drop ride, which is the most popular attraction (after the Ferris Wheel). In this more modern section of the city, it feels less old-school and just a bit seedy, but then, aren't most carnivals? Of course, seedy in Switzerland does not mean unsafe. Rather, it simply means less charming. I always found Kleinbasel to feel just a tad cold. But then, not everything Swiss can be a Hallmark card.

Over the course of two weeks in November, the city celebrated as they have every November for generations upon generations, for hundreds upon hundreds of years. We hoarded so many sweets, drank so many hot beverages, we couldn't possibly imagine indulging any longer.

As the fair played on for the next two weeks, we enjoyed the brilliant colors of a Swiss autumn. Having moved from Austin, Texas, we really missed watching the seasons change. As the sun lowered its declination like a slowly leaking balloon, the light became richer, thicker, more golden and calming. We would walk along the Rhine promenade in the late afternoon, watching the Ferris Wheel turning behind the crimson gables of the Münster, arm in arm under the honey-toned chestnut trees, and watch our new city be gloriously happy all around us. I have never felt coziness so literally in my life as I did during our first autumn in Basel. I've never experienced a community so bound together in festive cheer. It was simply marvelous to experience firsthand. Little did we realize that this was just the tip of the festive iceberg.

Just weeks after the *Herbstmesse* wraps up, Basel's famous Christmas Market begins. Like the American calendar, the last two weeks of November all the way to New Years are just one long lump of days bound together with parties, shopping, eating, and drinking.

One of the things we were looking forward to most when deciding to move to Switzerland were the European Christmas Markets. Growing up, my grandmother dreamed of visiting a Christmas Market in Germany, but never got the chance. We'd watch travelogues on PBS about these magical markets, and as I got older, I'd always watch the Christmas episodes of Rick Steves and relish in the coziness of it all. The closest I had come to experiencing anything like it was a visit to Finland back in 1991. It was only a few weeks after Christmas, and while all the markets had long since closed up shop, the city's Christmas lights remained. The deep blankets of snow illuminated by the warm glow of white twinkle lights was enough for me. I wasn't aware of the word back then, but it had been my first exposure the Nordic notion of *hÿgge,* or warm coziness in the face of darkness and cold. So when I watched these old travel shows about Vienna and Nuremberg and Zurich, I remembered the Finnish winter awesomeness of billowing snow drifts, the smell of spruce trees, and the warmth of holiday lights, and I longed to have all of this magic come together at an actual Christmas market. And oh my stars and garters, it was happening!

The year before we moved, Lisa had been sent to Basel for work, in December, so the Christmas Market was in full swing. Not only did she get to visit a European Christmas

Market before I did, IT SNOWED THE NIGHT SHE WAS THERE. There are no words to describe my level of jealousy.

Of course, it never snowed for any of the Christmas Markets we visited the entire time we lived in Basel. Still, no snow meant no slush to wade through, no slippery cobbles to fall on. I mean, I was planning on seriously partaking in mug after mug of wonderful, delicious, merriment-inducing *glühwein*, and the fewer the obstacles to trip over the better. It was still cold and wintry and it wasn't really about the weather, now, was it? No, this was about cozy wooden chalets, and boughs of pine and holly, and hot adult beverages, and international camaraderie. This was about Christmas lights and festive department store windows. This was about old school, Old World yule time quaintness.

I'm not really a drinker, but seriously, Europeans are masters when it comes to the hot adult beverage. All the partaking's we partook back at the Autumn Fair were going to be on offer once again, and other than the travesty that was *glühbier*, I was in the spirit for spirits. Even Lisa, who shuns vino in general, adores a quaff of warm, spiced, mulled wine. There is something magical in holding a steaming mug of happiness between your wind-chapped hands whilst mingling amongst your fellow wintertime revelers.

There's community in *glühwein*.

Our hellish downstairs neighbors had told us that the Christmas Market was the Fall Fest on steroids. In fact, Basel has one of the largest and most famous Christmas Markets in all of Europe. Unlike the *Herbstmesse*, which is spread out over town, the crux of the market festivities is in the center of Old Town. It circles Barfüsserplatz in the city center and down an alley behind the church-turned-history museum that dominates the square. Here, amongst the cenotaphs for bishops and priests of centuries past, are high wooden tables surrounded by holiday goers noshing bratwursts and clinking frosted mugs of beer. Here are animatronic reindeer singing Christmas carols on the tops of booths selling fried dough and Alsatian nougat. Here, you are immediately enveloped in joyful celebration and wide-eyed American wonder.

A veritable village is constructed of hundreds of small wooden huts, all decorated with pine and mistletoe and glitter and ornaments. Each booth offers intricately carved wooden nativity sets, or blown glass ornaments, or hand-sewn hats and scarves. The longest lines stretch out from the counters selling the nectar of the Christmas gods (aka: *glühwein*). Bags of *läckerli*, cones of roasted chestnuts, batons of peppermint flavored candy floss are all devoured with childlike glee. It is unusual for Europeans to smile at strangers, but here, in this place, everyone greets everyone with happy faces. Every language possible can be heard floating through the chattering crowd. A giant three story high pink fiberglass candle-windmill looms over the scene (called *Erzgebirge Pyramid* in German). Fire pits dot the landscape where families can sit and roast a skewer of sausages or marshmallows and drink schnapps-spiked cocoa on fur-covered log benches.

We wandered up to the second plaza of festivities in the Cathedral Square, the sun dipping lower in the sky so that the whole of the city sparkled under millions of tiny twinkle lights. To reach the square, you have to climb a short, steep, curved alley. This approach is always a favorite of mine because first you are enveloped by this tight medieval street with shops so close on either side that you could stretch out your arms and touch the walls on either side of you at the same time. As you ascend, the 1000-year-old cathedral is revealed, towering above you in all its red granite glory. And there, standing tall and stately underneath the twin spires, is the Basel City Christmas Tree, festively glowing with a thousand points of warm, white light.

On this day, as we entered the Münsterplatz, a small choir

was singing old German hymns, accompanied by a hefty man with a cello and a Santa hat. Where the enormous Ferris Wheel once stood was now the *Märchenwald*, or "Fairytale Forest". Instead of huts full of food and trinkets, this was a small village full of activities for children. There was a small train that circled the whole of the village (on tracks - none of that pseudo-pretend "train" that's actually a car made to look like a train - this was a real tiny train, complete with a railroad crossing for pedestrians with flashing lights). In the village, we watched, with gaping American awe, kids as young as five smith iron, blow glass, carve stumps of wood with chainsaws, and make wooden puzzles using an actual jigsaw. This was no safety-minded Iowa State Fair cushiness with finger-painting and a bucket of Legos. No, this was hard-core European hands-on craftwork complete with open flames and whirring saw blades. Parents would leave their kids to make pint-sized broad swords while they sat around a fire pit downing Jägermeister shots.

While this amazed us to no end, it wasn't a complete surprise to me. I loved to wander the trails in the nearby woods (a most beautiful primeval wood just ten minutes from home). More often than not, I would come across small groups of school kids out on a field trip (Swiss school kids seem to always be out on a field trip), huddled around a campfire. One time, I heard the adult in the group explaining to the small assembly of 3rd graders(!) how to build their fire. I watched in amazement as they constructed their pyres and then expertly lit them on fire. These eight-year-old kids were led into a dark forest so that they could learn to build fires, as a daily school exercise.

In the US, we have to have open concept houses, or ranch-style homes because stairs are just too dangerous for kids to navigate on their own (source: every single solitary episode of *House Hunters* and *House Hunters International*). In Europe, they put them in front of a 1000-degree forge and tell them to smelt silver for bullets to kill Gypsy-cursed werewolves.

On the opposite side of the cathedral square, under my favorite grove of oak trees (I loved, loved, loved that spot), was the food and frivolities village. Giant lighted snowflakes hung from the boughs of the trees overhead, creating a magical scene. It was completely dark now, so all of the light, from the booths and the decorations and giant Christmas tree, and the spotlights on the cathedral made everything feel toasty and cozy. I simply could not recall a time when I was happier. Pure, simple happiness. Glee, really. I was giddy. I was serene and content, and it wasn't just the booze swishing in my belly. It was a bucket list moment, with the love of my life, and it wasn't on a vacation, we lived here, and holy shit, yes, we could come back again and again as many times as we wanted over the course of the next three weeks, and you bet your ass we did, over and over, and it never once got old.

The Basel Christmas Market is spectacular. It doesn't just live up to the hype, it exceeds it in spades.

By the time December had rolled around, we were getting our footing. We were becoming pros at navigating the Swiss rail network, and had been making copious notes on where to go, what to see, what to do. Between the myriad of Facebook groups, Lisa's coworkers, and our neighbors, we had a laundry list of activities. After all, the whole point of living in Europe was to go see it. It's my whole identity: exploring.

I want to see all the things.

There is no corner of the globe I wouldn't kill to see. Living in the virtual center of Europe, I was chuffed to bits being so close to so many things. The problem we faced was narrowing our list down during the busy Christmas Market season. This was no easy task as every large city, and every not-so-large city, hosts a Christmas Market during December. So we polled our local resources for their top recommendations and decided to go with their top destinations: Zurich and Strasbourg.

We figured that we should at least start exploring our new country in earnest first, and we had yet to visit the storied city of Zurich. What better time than during Christmas? So our first post-Basel ambling took us to Switzerland's largest city, for Europe's largest indoor Christmas Market.

Held inside the *Bahnhof* (train station), there are over 100 stalls surrounding a three-story-tall Christmas tree adorned with over 1000 Swarovski crystals. It's a bit cacophonous as the massive hall is jammed with not only holiday shoppers and tourists, but thousands of daily commuters making their way through the terminal. Swiss train stations are notoriously unheated places due to the sheer number of tracks that converge in these places. It's just not possible to separate the platforms from the terminals, so these buildings have hundreds of entrance and egress points at ground level which keeps the indoor temperature the same as the outdoor temperature. So it was quite cold inside the Indoor Christmas Market. We needed something to warm us up.

We had made our circle around the market, offering the usual variety of treats and wares, when we stumbled on this hut with a tall blonde woman leaning over the counter yelling "who's thirsty!?!?" in English.

Me. I was thirsty.

"What do we have?"

"Hütenjack!"

"I'm sorry, what now?"

"Hütenjack!"

"And what is that?"

"You will like it" and she thrust a paper cup of hot, golden liquor into my hand.

No offense to my wife, but this Teutonic maiden could have put anything into my hand and I would have downed it, no questions asked. Couldn't be any worse than *glühbier*. I took a tentative sip and was immediately warmed head to toe with glee.

"Holy shit, Boo, you need to try this!"

But before I could pass the cup to Lisa, my new Swiss girlfriend had already put one in her hands. Lisa took a sip and I watched her eyes light right up.

"In the immortal words of Mrs. Mia Wallace, 'I said goddamn, goddamn, goddamn!'"

Hütenjack is an apple and honey based bourbon liqueur served as a shot inside a mug of mulled cider. This is what the gods drank in the marble halls of Olympus. This is what glorious warriors drank in Valhalla. We had never seen it's like before (and never saw it anywhere else). After making quick work of our samples and ordering two proper walking cups full (*laufenjack?*), we noticed that she was selling bottles of the stuff.

"We're going to explore the Markets in town, but we'll be back to buy bottles on our way home"

"If I see you later, then I will buy you another glass for your journey home!"

True to her word, when we returned to the *bahnhof* at the end of our day, we bee-lined to her kiosk. Remembering us immediately, she put together a small carrying case for our two bottles of elixir, along with a stash of to-go cups, in case we decided to crack a bottle open on the way home. She then gifted us two complimentary beverages, as promised.

After realizing that this was the only place where we could find bottles of *Hütenjack*, Lisa told me, a week or so later, to take the train back down to Zurich and get some more. And after a day trip to the town of Zug, about twenty minutes south of Zurich, I stopped off to grab another bottle, just days before the Market ended. When Covid cancelled the Christmas Markets the following year, we were doubly devastated. Not only would we not be able to experience the magic of the Markets again, we would be denied this ambrosia of the gods. I spent months trying to find it online, but to no avail. Due to the pandemic, their business had shut down. I'm sad about it to this day.

Zurich does not confine its Christmas Markets to the train station. The whole city is a veritable market, with little pockets of festivities dotting the Old Town along the Limmat River. You leave the massive baroque depot and meander down Bahnhofstrasse, Switzerland's answer to the *Champs Elysees*. As you pass boutique after boutique, you will immediately feel poor. Some of these shops make Dior look like a Walmart. The coats and jackets that brush against you as you navigate foot traffic will cost more than your first car. But then you'll pass a small square off the main drag, festooned with holly boughs and plastic snowmen, hosting a small Christmas choir or a bundle of four or five kiosks selling roasted chestnuts and cookie presses. Nearly every department store has an Armani clad *maître-d* standing in the street offering samples of champagne-spiked *panettone* or *glacé* fruit or chocolate bonbons. It is a posher version of poshness. I swear if it had been raining that day, the skies would have poured down bearer bonds and 1000€ notes

We stumbled upon a large open-air series of stalls in the shadow of one of the city's many cathedrals where we enjoyed a non-Christmas-y yet thoroughly tasty gyro (the Mediterranean street food hits SO much harder here. One of my favorite Turkish dishes is *pide*, which is a small eye-shaped pizza made with kabob meat and a fried egg). We washed it down with some brandy-spiked mulled cider. By now, the weather was starting to turn and the wind had whipped up, sending tornadoes of napkins and paper cups scuttling across the cobbled square (to the chagrin of the tidy-minded Swiss). Our faces were red with cold, but our hands were toasty wrapped around our beverage mugs. A hurricane could have magically appeared in Central Europe and it wouldn't have stopped us from enjoying our Market day.

Our last stop was the enormous food market in Sechselautenplatz under the gaze of the Opera House (modeled after the *Palais Garnier* in Paris). Here, a thunderously tall tree towered over the round plaza. This was the place to get your holiday noms on. Sausages, smoked salmon, venison jerky, burgers, gyros, kebabs, turkey legs, you name it. If you could cook it over fire, you were set.

The Swiss love fire. Fire pits, building fires, celebrating fire.

There is a celebration during Lent called *Chienbäse* in the Basel suburb of Liestal. A procession is led through the Old Town of hundreds of torches and burning carts, with massive flames reaching two to three stories high. The fire is carried to a central square where the torches are used to light an enormous wooden cage, creating an apocalyptic bonfire. While we never got to see this festival in person, we did visit Liestal for their Christmas Market and you can see scorch marks in the gables of the buildings all along the main street of the Old Town.

Zurich, too, gets in on the fire craze, every April, right here in this very plaza. In a bizarre take on Groundhog Day, the Swiss will burn a six story tall straw snowman (called a *Böögg*) whose head is loaded with explosives. They will set a large pyre underneath the snowman alight and will watch it burn until the head explodes. How long it takes for the noggin to blast apart will tell you what kind of summer to expect. The longer it takes for the head to pop, the crappier the summer will be.

For now, however, the fires in Sechselautenplatz (Spring Festival Plaza) were keeping people warm and cooking many a tasty treat. Again, fire pits were being used to cook skewers of meat, sticks topped with marshmallows, and to keep extremities warm. A genuine Oompa band played polka-tinged Christmas music. Ice skaters whooshed across the rink at the end of the square (learners get to hold onto fiberglass penguins for support). Our last hot beverage of the day was an apple punch with rum and calvados. With the stinging winter wind, this doubly-strong libation was a perfect way to pickle us for our long walk back to the station.

Along the way we passed the infamous Cabaret Voltaire where the Dada art movement was founded (and the namesake of the '80's New Wave band, Cabaret Voltaire - both quite near and dear to my heart), and what can only be described as the most beautiful *pissoir* in Europe. At the end of a park where the Limmat river meets Lake Zurich stood a small, round Victorian circus of an outhouse where you can take an *al fresco* piss while staring out upon the frosty majesty of the Bernese Alps.

The things that make you say *"ahhhhhhhh"*.

―――

Our other big Christmas Market excursion took us north to the capital of Alsace-Lorraine, the bustling French city of Strasbourg.

I had visited the city on my first trip to the area before we moved and I thought it was cool as hell. A modern metropolis, it is one of four cities where the European Parliament meets, and houses a fantastic modern art museum. But it's what is nestled in the heart of the city that draws people from near and far, and that is the *Petit France.* Situated on an island, surrounded by the Ill river, it is the original medieval city that is a UNESCO world heritage site. Narrow, tilted cobbled alleyways with timber-framed chalets weave you through an endless maze towards the very center of it all, where suddenly, towering 40 stories! above you, is Strasbourg Cathedral. A massive pink granite gothic monstrosity, it was the tallest building in the world for over 200 years. For such a monolith of a building, when you are lost in the labyrinth of the old city, it's surprising how you cannot see it until you are standing directly underneath it.

Strasbourg held a fascination for me as my grandfather's family hailed from the region. Growing up, he told me about his French ancestors who had emigrated from the Alsace-Lorraine to Quebec, Canada. One of them went on to found one of Anchorage's saddest suburbs: Spenard, Alaska. A few years before our move, Lisa and I did the whole *23 and Me* genetic DNA testing, and sure enough, nearly 3/4 of my ancestry originates in a small circle surrounding Strasbourg. Even in high school, on my first day of German class, while calling roll, my teacher, Herr Mensing, stopped at my name and exclaimed "ah, an Alsatian in our midst!" Sure enough,

Spenard is one of the most popular surnames in Strasbourg. So this is why I had made sure to visit on my first trip to the area. The best part was that the city had exceeded expectations and I was excited to take Lisa to see it for the first time. And what better time to see a place for the first time than at Christmas?

To get onto the island and into the Old Town, you had to pass through massive security checkpoints. Just the year before was the tragic terrorist attack on the Christmas Market where eleven people were killed and fifteen seriously injured. It made us a bit apprehensive about going, but then, what were the chances of it happening two years in a row. Plus, we had read about all of the extraordinary measures taken to increase security. There is no way to get to the island without passing over a bridge, and every one of them was fortified by a garrison of *gendarmes* armed to the teeth. This meant that every single person had to go through a checkpoint. They were unavoidable. Our bags were searched and we had to pass through a metal detector to enter. Pairs of armor-clad soldiers patrolled the entire Old Town.

I noticed these patrols, too, when we visited Paris. Around every major landmark were heavily armed soldiers (unlike in the US where it's usually some schlub in an ill-fitting rent-a-cop uniform making $5.75 an hour). While walking in the plaza in front of Notre Dame Cathedral I saw a soldier stop short in front of a large puddle to watch a tiny sparrow taking a bath in the muddy water. If only for a moment, I caught his shoulders relax a millimeter or two and a smile cross his face. I surreptitiously snapped a photo of this moment and it's one of my favorites. Just a year after such a terrible attack on this famous market, however, and there were no smiles on the soldiers' faces. It made us feel both very safe and completely on edge. It was just a constant reminder that we lived in an ever-violent post-9/11 world.

Once across the bridge, however, and all that tension is immediately replaced with a holy jolly smack in the festive face. I've never seen SO much Christmas. Every inch of Strasbourg is bleeding snowflakes and mistletoe. Not content to just decorate their shop windows, the French decorate every single available square inch (centimeter?) of their building facades, turning all these Disney-esque buildings into living gingerbread houses.

C'était comme Noël vomi partout.

It is simply breathtaking.

Spread out across the island are a myriad of small markets nestled in quaint squares and plazas. Strasbourg is the largest city in the area, so the markets are some of the busiest in Central Europe. In fact, our 90-minute train ride from Basel was standing room only. The tight corridors winding through the shops and restaurants become claustrophobic. But whilst crammed shoulder to shoulder with both Marge from Schenectady and Marcel from Bruges, there are hundreds and hundreds of decorations and displays to distract and entertain.

Each main street in the Old Town used to serve a distinct purpose, and mosaics in the cobbles at the end of these streets would let you know which businesses you would find down this particular alleyway. A barrel would signify coopers and wine sellers. A pretzel would let you know this was Baker's Alley. A hammer would signify smiths. In this modern Christmas era, each of these streets were decorated in themes representing their origin stories. Stuffed pigs and papier-mache cows with festive hats sat on balcony railings in the old butchery, and gift-wrapped wheels of brie hung by strings over the boulevard of cheese mongers.

I think the *glühwein* hit a little better in France. You just knew the French would use a higher quality of wine. Here I found that the white *glühwein* was fantastic, while the Swiss did a fair better red. The white also has a punch of cognac, so there's that (laughs in *hon-hon-hon*). And that was absolutely good with me.

We nibbled on heavenly sugar crepes and ate duck fat *frites* (there is no doubt that the French know food). We bought kilos of French nougat candies and Alsatian caramels and pistachio butter cookies.

We experienced the horror of French public toilets. Maybe horror is too kind a word. Even the dingiest toilet in the sketchiest part of a Swiss town is still akin to an antiseptic operating theater compared to what awaits you in the Saw-like dungeon of a French public toilet. Ever see *Trainspotting?* Yeah, it's like that, only French (which, in French, is… *Trainspotting* - go figure).

I find it mind-boggling that the French, who take such meticulous care when preparing food and pastry and art can be so *laissez faire* when it comes to the cleanliness of anything else. There is actually a psychology particular to Japan for tourists who become literally mentally unstable after going to Paris and being shocked at how filthy it is. It's called *Paris Derangement Syndrome*, and in my opinion, is not limited to Paris. France can be a shocking dichotomy of luxe and squalor, and thanks to Hollywood, we only ever see the luxe. This is not a disparagement, but simply, an observation. I still find France intriguing, and I honestly love Paris. But the France of reality is a far cry from the France of television and movies, and many will find the difference jolting. Thankfully, because it is a protected site, the Old Town of Strasbourg is wonderfully preserved.

Just don't pee there.

Lisa was in Munich for a week on business, and it was three weeks until Christmas. We had only been in our new flat for a month, and in order to save space in the cargo container that we used to ship our belongings over, we had sold all of our Christmas decorations. So at this point, our flat was bare, without a festive tchotchke in sight. Christmas was our favorite holiday (well, Lisa's second favorite after Halloween). We decorated inside and out to the hilt. Every year I would put up too many lights and blow a circuit breaker, ala Clark Griswold. We had so many Christmas knick-knacks that we filled ten storage bins when we took it all down. Not knowing how much storage space we would have when we found a place in Basel, we erred on the side of caution and pared everything down to bare essentials. We figured we'd simply get new stuff once we got settled in.

We were not prepared for how expensive Christmas lights and decorations would end up being. Of course, we would have had to buy all new Christmas lights anyway due to the different voltages and outlets. We thought Christmas lights were that much more expensive in Canada compared to the US, but here, a string of lights was nearly four times as much as back home. This put Lisa in a deep funk.

So while she was away, I grabbed my extra-large portable folding shopping cart and headed to the OBI across town (the Euro version of a Home Depot, complete with matching orange color scheme). Here I would buy us a Christmas tree and all the accoutrements. Thankfully, real trees here are incredibly cheap (fake trees are both very hard to find, and are prohibitively expensive). You have your choice of short Noble fir, medium Noble fir, and tall Noble fir.

Oh, you want a Douglas fir, or a Blue Spruce? *NEIN!*

I chose a hearty medium sized… Noble fir, about 5' tall, for just 24CHF. After getting it net-wrapped, I was able to fit it inside my shopping cart, and I wheeled that bad boy to the tram. It's a weird feeling to see that you are not the only person on the tram with a live Christmas tree in a personal shopping cart. When in Switzerland, eh?

After dropping it off at home, propped on the balcony so that the boughs could relax, I headed back to the Obi to get a stand, lights, and decorations. Still new to the city, I couldn't think of another place to go get what I needed (I later learned that there really weren't many other options, and we stuck with Obi for our second Christmas tree. The places my neighbors suggested were in France, and out in the fringes of St Louis, inaccessible without many, many tram and bus transfers). So I travelled back to the other side of town with my trusty shopping trolley and a resigned knowledge that this was not going to be a cheap exercise.

The Swiss seem to have a fondness for pink Christmas decorations. It was nearly impossible to find anything that wasn't part of the *Steel Magnolias* collection. But eventually I found some decent blue and silver baubles and beaded garland (Lisa's preferred color scheme).

What stumped me, however, were lights. They came in plastic buckets and were designed to go on in one single strand (kind of smart, actually). Not being very familiar with metric measurements, I wasn't sure what length to get. Of course, inside this big box store, I could get no internet signal to Google conversions. I had to make my best guess. Too short, and I knew I would have to make a third trip. Too long and Lisa would accuse me of trying to set the tree on fire. Worse still, I was hoping to grab a couple of strands to put around the front windows. Trying to work out the dimensions and find the right strand was beyond this Beautiful Mind. So I figured a medium tree called for a medium bucket, and my large front windows called for the large bucket of lights. My color choices were white, white, or white.

I somehow managed to keep my total under 300CHF for lights, garland, stand, and ornaments. All things considered, I thought I did pretty well. Once home, I turned on some Bing Crosby and put up our little Noble Christmas tree. The sparse boughs lent it that Victorian feel, and to me, made it feel that much more European. It was all I could do not to send Lisa pics, but I desperately wanted to surprise her when she came home

"You carried this upstairs by yourself!? How the hell did you even get it home!?"

The following year when I took her with me to Obi to get our tree, she got it.

"Oh, this is easy!"

"Oh, ye of little faith!"

One of my favorite pictures of Lisa is her getting off the tram with her net-wrapped Christmas tree in the shopping cart, a giant yuletide smile visible behind her facemask.

When we went to the Basel Christmas Market for the second time, now that we had our tree, we decided we should buy a special ornament, and make a tradition of getting one each year. We found two little blown glass blue finches, one for each of us. We had planned on creating a collection of bird ornaments, adding two each year. It broke our hearts when Covid got the Markets cancelled the following year. I suppose, though, that it makes those two little birds that much more special to us.

―――――

I was waiting to get onto the tram one cold December morning, and I see, coming around the corner, a man dressed as a crimson druid followed by six giant Jawas and a donkey. Before I could board the tram that had stopped in front of us, the red-cloaked man put his hand up and bounded up the stairs to the driver's compartment. He handed over a small wicker basket, waved to everyone on the tram, and then climbed down. He gave me a wink and then led his small team down the street towards the next tram stop.

"What did I witness today?" I asked Claudio, my upstairs neighbor, a few days later.

"That was *Sammichlaus!*"

"What about his entourage, and what exactly was he doing?"

And so Claudio told me about Swiss Santa Claus and how Basel celebrates St Nicholas Day.

On December 5th, in the tradition of the venerated saint handing out treats to the less fortunate, *Sammichlau*s and his band of *Schmutzli* (helpers, like elves) will hand out small baskets of fruits, nuts, and *läckerli* to all the bus and tram drivers in town, to celebrate their service to others. St Nicholas rode a donkey from town to town in his day, and so a donkey, laden with these baskets, will follow *Sammichlaus* around as he completes his mission. Unlike the modern Coca-Cola-inspired Santa Claus, the Swiss version dresses as a 4th century monk, albeit in red robes (unlike the brown for the *Schmutzli*). Baselers will bring treats to the *Schmutzli* to hand out, as an alms-giving of sorts, though the majority of the baskets are provided by the Sutter Begg bakery chain in town.

Lisa's office, on St Nicholas Day, would put out large baskets of oranges, walnuts, and *Gratti-maa* (a sweet bread shaped like a woman – almost like a gingerbread woman, but made out of Kings Hawaiian Rolls) as a way of saying thanks to the employees.

When our second December rolled around, I was ready and

waiting with my camera at the tram stop to watch these adorable creatures spread joy throughout the land. You can literally see the joy on the tram drivers' faces. I think it's an incredibly charming tradition and one of those small things that makes Europe feel so much more intimate than America.

I think every single person we know was surprised when we told them that, no, in fact, Basel almost never gets snow. There is this assumption that every part of the country is Alps and snow and ski resorts. Basel sits in a river valley and is protected from most weather. It doesn't get a lot of rain, and is the sunniest city in Switzerland. If it snows more than twice in the winter, it's unusual. Our first winter there, it snowed only once, and only for ten minutes. Our second winter, however, was one of the snowiest on record.

For a city that almost never gets snow, it is incredibly prepared (you wanna take some notes over there, Portland, Oregon?). Spread throughout the city, usually near recycling centers, are large bins full of gritty sand. Is the sidewalk slippery? Here, take this spade and shovel out some grit on the pavement so you can walk safely. Temperature has dropped below freezing? Watch the city blast the tram tracks with flame throwers to keep them ice free. Shoes slippery from the wet snow as you climb on the tram? Well, that's your own problem and I'd probably hold on to something because you are going to slip and fall on the slick linoleum floor. Okay, so the Swiss aren't completely perfect.

When it did snow, the city flocked to the moo cow farm at the end of the street. Usually, the steep hill in front of the farm was used as a grazing field for the cows. Once the snow came, it became the most popular sledding hill in the entire Canton. The owners created a hay bale barrier at the bottom of the hill, to keep little Swiss tykes from flying out into traffic or into the side of a passing tram. There is a walking path that parallels the hill and let me tell you, this hill is steep. If it were stairs, it would be at least five flights. It's on a 30% grade, if not more.

And it is picturesque as all get out.

The old Margarethen church sits at the top of the hill (as part of the dairy farm), with a large stone balustrade that affords sweeping views of the entire city. In the summer months, it doubles as a wedding venue. With this bonanza of snow, the hill was packed with families, sleds, and snowboards. If Norman Rockwell was Swiss, he'd have painted this scene. The best part of it all is that the owners of the farm simply open the gates to the hill when the snow comes and the thought of charging a fee of any kind never enters their mind (unlike America where any chance to make a buck...)

The dairy farm sat on the west side of Margarethen Park, and in the center of the park was the large open community field. This area was surrounded on three sides by a large berm, and this is where tiny toddlers were learning how to sled for the first time. It was a miniature version of the big hill, with young ones sliding down a ten-foot embankment into their parents' arms. At the very east end of the park was the city's immense ice skating venue. Usually home to hockey and curling leagues, during the month of December, it was reserved for family skating time, complete with piped-in Christmas music, fiberglass penguins for learners and little ones, and concession stands selling hot cocoa and cappuccinos.

In the city, the snow, strangely, kept everyone indoors. I was desperate for some pictures of Basel in the snow, so I bundled up and ventured out. I practically had the whole Canton to myself (that, or everyone and their brother was at the sledding hill). It was so quiet. My dad remarked, after seeing my photos, that this is how he pictured Switzerland. I couldn't help but agree. In the summertime, with the iridescent blue waters and emerald green hills, I feel like I'm in a hyper-color fever dream of Europe. In the wintertime, when the sloping chalet roofs are caked with sparking Alpine snow, I feel like I'm in Switzerland.

August 1st is Swiss National Day. Having arrived in the country at the end of August, we had to wait until the following summer to enjoy this Alpine version of the Fourth of July. The Swiss are probably the most patriotic people in Europe, and on any given day, you will come across the iconic red and white Swiss flag in some capacity. The US is the only country I've visited that displays the flag more.

So we were really looking forward to celebrating this patriotic pomp parade with our new neighbors in our new neighborhood in our new nation. I'm not usually someone who celebrates patriotism. I have zero sense of patriotism when it comes to the United States. To be patriotic about a place you were simply born to is odd to me. You should be patriotic about a place that you chose to live instead of one you were born to by chance.

When we lived in Canada, before we became disillusioned and begged to get out, we joined the Canada Day festivities down on the Kelowna lakefront. Everyone was dressed in red and white, had maple leafs painted on their face, wore Canadian flags as capes. Because this was my new home, I was all in on this day. I was sporting the national colors, drinking Labatt's Blue, and eating food cart poutine. When the national anthem was sung by the drunken crowd of Canucks before the fireworks began, I sang along with them.

"How the hell do you know the words to *O, Canada*!?"

"Hockey"

"I forget sometimes you're a boy"

"I am too festive to be insulted by that.
OHHHHHHHHHHH CAAAAAAANADAAAAAAAAA...."

Even after moving back to the States from Canada, we maintained many good friendships we had made up there. Two of our dearest friends ended up moving to Austin where we lived prior to our Swiss adventure. When Canada Day rolled around, we joined them at a Canada-themed bar downtown to celebrate their day with them.

"You just want to go because you know the words to *O, Canada*"

"And poutine. I want poutine"

What I loved most about celebrating Canada Day with Canadians was that I never once heard any jingoistic braggadocio about Canada being the greatest nation on earth, or that Jesus founded Canada after turning water into Moosehead. It was just a fun gathering of people who appreciated where they were from, and keeping it that simple made it a wonderful holiday to celebrate.

So when I knew that we would be able to enjoy the Swiss National Day celebrations in the middle of summer, we were psyched. Every day that brought us closer to August 1st was a day that made us fall harder in love with Switzerland. This was the opposite of our Canadian experience, and as the days passed, I became prouder and prouder of being a resident of Switzerland. I wanted to show my fellow Baselers just how much I appreciated their country. I was going to get myself a Swiss flag t-shirt, maybe some red shorts, a Swiss flag bucket hat (maybe?). I was going to show patriotic pride because I was proud to live here, because I chose to live here, and "here" was a wonderful, exciting, lovely place.

And then Covid hit.

While the lockdown was nearing an end by the time August rolled around, for our first Swiss Day, the city erred, rightly, on the side of caution and cancelled all festivities. There would be no fireworks spectacular-spectacular on the Rhine. There would be no live music in Barfüsserplatz, no carnival rides in Messeplatz. There would be no Alpine Games at St Jakob stadium. Instead, Baselers would have to celebrate with scaled down backyard cookouts. Of course, like the pyromaniacs they are, the Swiss set off their own fireworks after dark. Unlike the US, however, once midnight struck, the explosions completely ceased for night, and quiet time (albeit two hours later than normal) began. The Swiss were very Swiss, even on their night of excusable debauchery.

The following year, the festivities were again cancelled as severe weather ripped through the area, causing massive flooding and wildfires caused by wild lightning storms. Gale force winds tore through Basel on August 1st, causing the fireworks to once again be cancelled. With torrential rains pouring down all week, events in the town center were forgotten as well. The Swiss, being the pyromaniacs they are, did their very Helvetic best to set off their own rooftop fireworks, but the weather beat them down, and the explosions were anemic and sad.

After moving away to Denver, we learned that the festivities were once again cock-blocked by Covid. While the pandemic was well in the rearview mirror by now, the first of the aggressive variants was popping its vicious little head up. By this time, the majority of the populace was fully vaccinated, but boosters were just being introduced. Again, not taking chances, the city cancelled the fireworks show. Even thousands of miles away, we were denied a Swiss National Day.

Though not entirely.

Though past their sell-by date, Lisa and I spent the day gorging on Coop Prix and Callier chocolate bars we brought back with us the year before. I made our favorite weekly schnitzel dinner, and I imbibed an Aperol Spritz or two. Even though we had been absent from the country for over a year, my Swiss patriotism was probably stronger than when we lived there. I may be an American, but in my heart, I am European.

My heart will always belong to Switzerland.

Chapter Five – ERs and Doctors and Surgeons, Oh My!

Let's start right off with some general observations about healthcare in Switzerland, which I will happily elaborate on as we go through this chapter:

1. There is no free universal healthcare here; like the US, the system is insurance based (and that totally sucks)

2. The quality of care is a thousand times better than the US (and it should be for what it costs)

3. Swiss doctors think American doctors are stuck in the Dark Ages (and they aren't wrong)

Getting sick in Switzerland can cost you and arm and a leg, but by the time you leave the hospital, you'll probably be sporting the latest, most top-of-the-line, high tech bionic prosthetics on the planet. We, of course, had our own indelible experiences with the Swiss healthcare system. Some good, some bad. Mostly good. All expensive. Though exorbitantly pricey, I do miss the Swiss system. I miss the five-star quality of care. I have never trusted doctors more than my Swiss ones. I have never had care feel so personal and genuine.

Let's get the ugly side of Swiss healthcare out of the way to start, so that we can focus on the good stuff.

Insurance, insurance, insurance.

You have to have insurance. In fact, it is mandated by law. Within the first two weeks of our arrival, we received an official notice reminding us that we needed to purchase health insurance now. Once you do sign up for a policy, it is retroactively dated to your arrival in the country, so we received a bill for three weeks of coverage that we didn't actually have at the time, but based on the law, technically, we did. These policies do not come cheap. We paid 1600CHF (or around $1760) a month, each, for basic health insurance. We also had a deductible of 2,500CHF (or $2,750) each. Getting the bill from Swica, our insurer, was always a gut punch.

And, no, Lisa's job did not contribute to or offer insurance.

Job-based insurance is not a thing in Switzerland. Vision and dental insurance are not included and can run upwards of 600-800CHF a month. We couldn't afford it. When the time came to for me to get glasses and to get a tooth pulled, we had to pay out of pocket, which, when monthly premiums are factored in, were probably cheaper in the long run anyway.

On a side note, British dentists are egotistical sadists, even if they are slightly cheaper than Swiss dentists. I thought a posh accent might help alleviate my extraordinary fear of dentists, but it only exacerbated it. He was just an expat version of Lawrence Olivier in *Marathon Man*. I kept getting tenser and tenser waiting for him to ask me "is it safe?" Okay, I concede, maybe not all British dentists model themselves on Dr. Scrivello from *Little Shop of Horrors*. But mine did, and he scared the bejesus out of me. After pulling my tooth, I was so traumatized, I didn't go back to get the implant put in (even though Lisa's job offered a significant discount on them). Going to get the implant from a Swiss doctor was out of the question, cost-wise. French and German dentists across the border were a consideration until I asked about them on Facebook and was loudly warned off from them.

On the plus side, when a doctor puts in a request to the insurance company for approval for a medication or a test or a procedure, they universally comply. Unlike American insurance companies, Swiss insurers recognize that doctors went to medical school and know what the fuck they're talking about and don't question their decisions. Swiss doctors still go through the pantomime of pretending to dread waiting to hear the verdict on their submissions for approval, but they are never denied. I mean, when talking to the insurance agent when signing up, I voiced my concern about this being a common practice in the US.

"The doctors know best, so if they say you need something, then you need something"

It certainly took some of the stress out of going to the doctor. If the doc was going to prescribe you something, then you were sure to get it. If you were going to be sent to get an MRI, then you were going to get an MRI, and the insurance company would cover it.

I take a certain medication that, in the US, is used for either asthma or eczema. I take it for my skin, and have for years. In Switzerland, however, the drug had only been approved for use for asthma, and only for three months by the time we moved there. When I discussed this with my new dermatologist, he voiced genuine concern about insurance approving it for non-pulmonary use. But he gathered all of the notes from my US doctors that I had copied for him and sent them in with his request for approval. Incredibly, they said okay. The doc said they usually don't question us, but because it was such an unusual request, he was certain they'd finally come down and say no. As long as I provided proof (through yearly body scans, which themselves were covered by insurance) to show the medication's efficacy, they'd continue to approve it. This kind of trust in doctors by the insurance companies was the one big positive about their system. It meant that I could be sure that I would get the best possible care from my docs because they operated without interference.

When it came time to get a prescription filled, it was time to go to the apothecary. What I love about Europe is that there is a universal sign for the apothecary: a green cross. Go to any city in any country in Europe and you will absolutely see a sign with a green cross. And, no, they are not pharmacies, they are apothecaries.

European apothecaries are far different than American pharmacies. Inside you will find a counter to get your medication refilled and about two or three shelves stocked with holistic and homeopathic remedies, herbs, teas, and tinctures. You will not find aspirin or antacids or feminine hygiene products. There is no candy aisle, no snack food, no beverage case. There are no seasonal items or hosiery or nail clippers. An apothecary is to get your Rx and some ginger tea and that's it.

Should you want any of the other items, you need to go to a Drogerie, which is the European equivalent of a CVS or Walgreens.

You still cannot get over-the-counter medications there, however. Any sort of pain reliever must be dispensed at an Apothecary. You can get Tums but you cannot get Tylenol. You want to have your doctor prescribe aspirin or acetaminophen so that your insurance will cover the cost. These simple pain relievers are incredibly expensive in Switzerland. A six-tab blister pack of ibuprofen can cost

15CHF if you buy directly from the pharmacist without a prescription. Yes, you can buy these meds at the apothecary, but they are kept behind the counter and there are strict limits on how much you can buy. There are no 350 count bulk bottles of Advil. There are tiny boxes with enough to get you through a day or two. We had read that the number one recommended thing to buy in bulk before moving to Switzerland was OTC medications, and it is the sagest advice we received.

Of course, on the flip side, the Swiss have a myriad of non-opioid pain relievers that we just don't have in the US, that are much more effective than aspirin and Advil. They do need to be prescribed by a doctor, but it's a good thing to know that there are options between the usual American extremes of Tylenol and Oxycodone. Swiss doctors will simply not prescribe opioids unless all other recourses have been exhausted. I had surgery on both shoulders and my wife had an entire chunk of bone removed from her arm (what a story) and neither of us ever received a single milligram of opioid pain reliever.

When you fill your prescription at the apothecary, it is a marvel of efficiency. They will take your written prescription (Swiss doctors do not send them in electronically - it's a paper-only system), and as they are inputting all of the information, an unseen person in another room pulls the medication and puts it into a pneumatic tube and sends it up to the counter. The pharmacist will print out an instruction label and slap it on the box (no bottles! All medications are in blister packs). There is no "come back in an hour" bullshit. Your script is immediately ready for you. Once I had a mortified technician tell me that they were out of stock on a particular medication.

"Oh, will it be in by the end of the week?"

She gave me a confused look.

"It will be here by 3pm"

I looked at my watch. It was just past noon.

"Really!?"

"Sorry for the inconvenience"

After a few months, I began to feel like Norm from *Cheers*. The familiar troupe of apothecaries would wave "*Hallo*, Herr Spenard!" when I walked in the door.

They, like other friendly Swiss before them, encouraged my German language skills. I quickly learned how to ask for a medication refill. The whole notion of "refill" is confusing to the Swiss, and is only used in terms of liquids.

I was instructed to tell the clerk that "I need one more of my medications" or *"ich brauche einmal meinen medikament, bitte"*.

They would inquire how Lisa was doing, and always made a point of telling me how lucky I was to have the doctors that I did. At first, they would print the dosage instructions on the box in English for me. After a while, though, they said I was smart enough with my German, now, to stop that coddling nonsense.

The first time I filled a script, I stood and marveled at the whole pneumatic set up and its efficiency. As I was handed my medication, I stood there, waiting. The clerk looked at me a bit confused, and I returned the look.

"Und, wie viele, bitte? (and how much is it?)"

"How much is what?"

"My medication"

"I do not know"

"So how do I pay?"

"Oh, you do not pay here. It will be sent to your insurance"

I never spent a penny (or *koppen*) inside the apothecary. It did, indeed, all get sent to the insurance company, who sent a separate bill for pharmacy co-pays each month. Unlike the US, the copays were, thankfully, cheap (on average 2-3CHF per medication). It took longer to hit the deductible for medications so that they were 100% covered, but the out of pocket was so minimal that it was the one facet of our coverage that I liked. So there were, I was discovering, positives to this system.

Like the apothecary, Swiss doctors' offices operate a little differently than American ones. First of all, while sitting in the waiting room, you must greet everyone who enters with a *"greuzi!"*, no exceptions. It is considered incredibly rude not to. No matter how ill or injured you are, you are expected to greet your fellow patients as they enter.

You will not be waiting long, however. If your appointment is at 10am, you will be seeing the doctor at 10am. You won't be sitting in an exam room wondering when someone is going to be coming in. This is because at 10am (on the dot), your actual doctor (not a nurse) will come and personally escort you to their office (which is an actual office with an exam table tucked in the corner). There will be no redundant repeating of all of your troubles to the receptionist, the intake nurse, and then again to the doctor. You won't have someone taking your vitals, weight, or going over your medications list. You'll sit at the desk with the doctor and tell them directly why you're there. It's that simple. If you need to be examined, they'll just have you strip down right there to your undies and hop on the table. Modesty (and fear of impropriety) does not exist in a Swiss doctor's office. The doctor will not question you, your story, your symptoms, or your pain. If you are at the doctor, you must have a good reason to be there. There isn't this inherent suspicion that American doctors harbor against their patients (especially women and the overweight). Then again, the Swiss are like Vulcans in that it's just not in their nature to lie.

All of your records are available online for the doctor to consult. My records from the rheumatologist, my GP, and my orthopedic surgeon were all in one single file, all from different hospitals and offices, but available for all the doctors to see. A centralized system made care that much better as doctors never had to wait or request records to be sent over to their offices. Sometimes, the accessibility of these records leads to odd circumstances.

While visiting my orthopedic doctor, we were scheduling my second shoulder surgery, when I told him that the dates he was looking at were too close to my wife's own surgery.

"Is everything okay with your wife?"

"Yes. She has a rare condition where her bones can become necrotic and she has to have a section of her ulna removed. In fact, her doctor is here at this clinic."

"Oh! Let's take a look!"

And he pulled up Lisa's x-rays and MRI and explained the whole procedure to me using all of her medical records, right there available to him. I was astonished that he would share any of that information with me, as it's private and confidential.

"But she is your wife, yes?"

"Yes"

"So what is the problem?"

I suppose sometimes the Swiss sense of honesty can be seen a little differently through American eyes.

―――

For years, my shoulders had been getting worse and worse. I had trouble raising either arm above my head. Getting dressed was an Olympian feat. For three years, while living in Austin, I had been getting cortisone shots to help with the pain and mobility. I had been assured that this was the best course of action and that surgery wasn't anything to think or worry about any time soon. So when we arrived in Basel, one of the first doctors I needed to find was an orthopedic shoulder doc. Not knowing where else to turn, I called our insurance agency and asked which doctors in the area took our insurance.

"All doctors take insurance"

"Yes, but which doctors take MY insurance?"

"All doctors"

In any event, they gave me two different clinics to call. One was on the other side of town, but one was just a few blocks away, so I called them first. Yes, of course, we can see you, can you come in tomorrow? This was my first shock, as I fully expected to have to wait months to see a specialist, even more so as a new patient.

When I arrived, I noticed the practice's logo incorporated the Olympic Rings. As I scanned the waiting room, it was adorned with posters of skiers and skaters and snowboarders and gymnasts. Crossklinik was the surgical provider for the majority of all Swiss Olympic teams. At that moment, I knew I wasn't just in good hands, I was in great hands. The more I took in my surroundings, the more I realized that everyone who worked here - the receptionists, the physical therapists, even the doctors, were statuesque models of human perfection. I felt incredibly feeble and unattractive. It was like showing up to a Victoria Secrets runway show in a pair of tighty-whiteys. Nevertheless, I did feel like I was going to get good care here.

I was greeted by a gentleman who introduced himself and led me upstairs to his office. This was my first experience with a doctor personally escorting me to my exam, so for the first five or ten minutes, I assumed he was a nurse. Only when I noticed his degree on the wall with his name did I realize who he was. After explaining my history and him doing a very quick exam, he shook his head and sat down.

"You say your doctor in Texas is an orthopedic?"

"Yes, specifically sports medicine"

"This is a bad doctor"

"Oh! And why is that?"

"You needed surgery on both your shoulders about a year ago. I cannot believe he was only giving you steroid injections, and so many of them! I say again, he is a bad doctor"

With that, he picked up the phone and spoke with someone for a few minutes. Hanging up, he asked me to follow him. We ended up in another office where he greeted another doctor (who reminded me of the great chef and humanitarian Jose Andréas).

"This is Dr. Schwamborn. He is a surgeon. He will explain the procedure to you."

And with that, he left, leaving me with this new doctor, my head spinning from the word "procedure"

"It sounds like you need new shoulders. Let us take a look, *ja*?"

So I let him do an exam, this one far more thorough than the one upstairs. He spent nearly fifteen minutes moving my arms into every possible position. Once he was finished, he nodded to himself.

"Yes, you needed surgery for both of these shoulders yesterday. You say your doctor never mentioned surgery? He just gave you shots?"

"Yup. He said I was 'years off' from surgery"

"Well it's a good thing he's no longer your doctor."

He then explained how, based on his initial exam, that he had a great fear of a thing called "frozen shoulder" setting in, in both arms. He ordered an MRI for both shoulders, and then asked if I wanted a shot to help lessen the pain for a few days.

"I thought you said these shots were useless now"

"*Ja*, for treatment, but we're going to go in and fix them. In the meantime, to give you a little more pain-free mobility, I can give you a mix of cortisone and anesthetic. It will only last a day or two, but if it will help you..."

So I let him give me a booster until I could get into the MRI. As he was prepping, he asked if I had any questions about the shot.

"Oh, no. I've had so many. You spray some numbing freeze and then jam it in, pretty simple"

He stopped what he was doing and whirled around to face me, his eyes wide.

"Freeze spray!? Your doctor uses freeze spray!? How utterly barbaric!"

I told you, Swiss doctors think American doctors are still living in the Dark Ages.

He explained that a surface spray didn't eliminate the pain of an injection into the joint, so what was the point? Instead, he gave me a shot of anesthetic, using a sci-fi gun-like mechanism that was so fast I didn't even realize he had done it already. We waited a minute and then he gave me the steroid injection. I felt nothing. For the very first time, in three years, I didn't feel a thing. He repeated the process on the other arm, and asked what I thought.

"That's extraordinary! I felt nothing"

"And you shouldn't. I cannot believe they put you through that every time"

He was honestly mortified. After getting dressed, he led me across the hall to the scheduling office.

"He will get an MRI next week, and then we will schedule the first surgery in one month. Which is worse, the left or the right?"

"The left"

"He will get the left repaired in one month, and then we will schedule the right for six months later. See you in two weeks to go over the images"

And with that, he was gone. I was pretty dumbfounded at this whirlwind office visit. I came in for pain relief and ended up with two scheduled shoulder repair surgeries. The girl (another statuesque specimen of Swiss athleticism) set me up a time to get the MRI (no need to wait for a referral or a call from the imaging office to get an appointment). I told her I would have to get back to her about scheduling the surgery, as I needed to, I don't know, talk to my wife about it?

Meanwhile she told me how lucky I was that Dr. Schwamborn was doing my operation. Apparently, Olympic and professional athletes from across Europe come to him when they are injured. He had treated many members of, not only the Swiss, but the Dutch, French, and Belgian Olympic teams. He was the best of the best.

My MRI would be taken at the same hospital where the surgery would take place. When I arrived on the day of my appointment, I realized this was no ordinary hospital. This was a boutique orthopedic clinic that only performed bone and joint repairs. The lobby was a scene out of *Westworld*, with gleaming white surfaces, sloping wooden mid-century furniture, and more statuesque blonde Swiss maidens directing incoming and outgoing traffic. Everyone I encountered asked me, before anything, "*Englisch oder Deutsch, bitte?* (English or German?"). Of course, everyone here spoke better than English than I did. Quiet *Blade Runner* style space jazz whispered in the overhead speakers. An espresso and pastry bar were to the left, a small reading library to the right. I was led downstairs to the most pristine white hallway I have ever seen. It was like a Kubrick movie. Every nurse, clerk, and attendant were dressed in equally spotless white. I was led to a locker room and told to change into the provided pajamas. Real, Egyptian cotton two-piece pajamas, with a pair of fuzzy wool socks. - none of this open-back floppy gown shit. Next, I was greeted by the MRI technician who, in turn, introduced me to the anesthesiologist.

"I'm sorry, did you say anesthesiologist? I'm just here for an MRI"

"Oh, this is to make you comfortable. We need to inject you with dye and it will not be pleasant"

"But I've had dye before. Just makes you feel like you have to pee, then it passes"

"Oh, no, no, sir. We will be injecting dye directly into your shoulder. It will hurt very much. We will not let that happen."

"I can't have inhaled anesthetics, I'm allergic!"

"This is local only. No sleepy time for you"

I was put onto a table and the anesthesiologist went to work. At least I assume he did. I never felt anything, and whatever he did, it was magic. Not only did I not feel the local anesthesia, I never had an ounce of pain during the whole procedure. I can only imagine what it would have been like back in the States. I can't picture any imaging center having an anesthesiologist on call.

When we were done, I got dressed (but kept the socks - they were nice). The anesthesiologist was waiting for me.

"We will make you an appointment to speak to the surgical anesthesiologist for your procedure"

Two days later I was back to speak to the anesthesiologist. This was a very important appointment for me because I am very, very allergic to certain kinds of anesthesia. I told her that inhaled anesthetics (gas) induce malignant hypothermia. This is a reaction where your body temperature shoots way, way up and your heart goes into cardiac arrest. I was unaware I had this allergy until I was undergoing a muscle biopsy, and they had used a gas to knock me out. Within minutes, my temperature was 108F and I was dangerously tachycardic. The doctors had to pack my entire body with ice to bring my temperature back down. My heart rate was so erratic I nearly flat-lined twice. So letting the anesthesiologist know this little tidbit was pretty important.

"So we will do two things. We will schedule you as the very first procedure of the day, so there is no chance of any cross-contamination. We will also have the Head of Anesthesiology administer your anesthesia, just to be sure."

We chatted a bit more about my history and it came up that I was originally from Chicago.

"I love Chicago! The International Conference of Anesthesiologists is held there every year. Between you and me, I don't go for the lectures; I go for the pizza"

My file was put inside a brilliant fluorescent pink folder indicating a severe allergy. Back in the States, I had undergone a few other procedures since that episode, and I never noticed anything other than a quick scribble on the line in my chart that asked for allergies. Nothing quite like a brilliant folder to underscore the severity of my allergy.

Everything about this process so far had progressively made me feel less anxious about having surgery. The total commitment to comfort and safety allayed many of my fears. When I returned to see Dr. Schwamborn to go over the images, I learned just how bad things really were. I had massive bone spurs in both shoulders, and the tendons in both shoulders were being torn apart by these shards. Large deposits of calcium were also lodged deep in the joints which prevented any range of movement. The whole shoulder joint would need to be cleaned out, the bones shaved down, and the damaged tendons severed cleanly to avoid ripping further. If they weren't repaired immediately, I risked "frozen shoulder" where my range of motion would be stuck and I would never be able to move my arms upward again. But once repaired, I would finally be able to lift my arms above my head for the first time in three years.

My Swiss doctors were right: things were much worse than my Texas doctor knew, and no amount of steroid shots would fix this. Dr. Schwamborn put me in a bit of a panic when he said waiting a few months was less than ideal and if he could, he would operate on me tomorrow. I discussed everything with Lisa, and we found a time that would allow her to take some time off work while I recovered. We booked the first of my two surgeries, and I anxiously awaited my journey through a Swiss hospital stay.

Having major surgery was the last thing I thought I would be experiencing as a new expat. Plans for outings and explorations would have to wait. Instead of gallivanting across Central Europe, I would be spending four days in hospital and then about three months doing physical therapy. Then I would have about three months before I had to do it all over again. The one thing that helped me consign myself to this fate was the quality of care I had received so far. That, and the knowledge that my surgeon operated on Olympians.

When the day came, I presented myself at the same ultra-modern clinic where I had my MRI. Instead of accompanying me into the prep area (like she would in an American hospital), Lisa was asked to wait upstairs in the well-appointed cafe/lobby.

The Head of Anesthesia did her job incredibly well because

unlike other operations, I have zero recollection about anything between checking in at the front desk and being wheeled upstairs to my room. I'm one of those weirdos that looks forward to that push of anesthesia and the rush of the world going black as you try to count backwards and stay awake. Not this time.

I felt zero pain. There was a IV line in my neck that was feeding anesthetic directly into my shoulder. This was my pain management system instead of pills or opioid IV pushes. It was amazing. There were no loopy side effects, no opioid-related stomach issues. Just localized numbness. It was hard to believe that I had just had my bones scraped.

Lisa was able to visit for a short while, and then it was dinner time.

Now things get interesting.

I have no idea if it was because I was in a specialty hospital or if this was the norm across all Swiss hospitals, but I felt slightly underdressed when my dinner arrived. I felt like I was in the middle of an episode of *Top Chef*.

On proper china, I was served a salmon terrine, horseradish mousse, dill and beet chips, a frisée salad with vinaigrette, a pickled beet, corn, and cabbage slaw, some house made bread, and a poached pear. It was beyond Instagram worthy. It was damned near Michelin star worthy.

Menus were pre-set each day. You either ate what they sent you or you purchased food from the cafeteria on the top floor. If this is what my meals were going to be like, you're damned skippy I was going to eat it all. Some of the other meals I ate over the course of my two stays in this hospital include:

> Roasted pork loin with morel sauce, *spätzle*, navy bean soup, fresh salad, and chestnut rice pudding

> Canapés and a *pomme soufflé* with currants and warm custard sauce (this was extraordinary!)
>
> Cream of chicken soup, nut bread with *Alpenmilch* butter, and *Bircher muesli*
>
> Rack of lamb, roasted potatoes, tomato and pepper salad, *consommé*, Caesar salad, and mango panna cotta
>
> Pork medallions, white asparagus, spinach fettucine, frisée salad, and chocolate fondant with vanilla custard
>
> Tri-tip with mushroom gravy, *spätzle*, carrot-ginger soup, Caesar salad, and citrus *crème brûlée*

The food was insane. I had so much fun posting pictures of my hospital meals to friends back in the States. None of them could believe it. Neither could I. It sure beat Salisbury steak and a cup of Jell-O. Cappuccinos and lattes were readily available upon request as well. Meals came with, and I shit you not, a five-page wine menu. You could have an assortment of complimentary wines or champagne with your meal, or purchase finer vintages if you so desired. Hell, you could have a beer with your hospital lunch if you so wanted.

Most of my nurses spoke English, and of course, all of them were drop-dead gorgeous. I made a comment about it to my dad who said I was being sexist, and had I seen any male nurses and would I make such comments about them like that? That night, I had Denis attending to me, and Denis was the very model of French savoir faire. Yes, pops, even the men were mouthwatering.

I was asked hourly what my pain level was.

"Wie viele schmertz? (how much pain)"

And I would answer with a number from 1-10 (always in German!). Even after taking the anesthetic IV drip out, I never felt anything more than a three. I was given a prescription for ibuprofen when I was discharged and that was all I ended up needing. If this had been done in the States, I probably would have been sent home with Vicodin and Fentanyl and a crippling opioid addiction. Hell, it probably would have been an outpatient surgery.

During my first stay, my roommate never said a single solitary word. He was quiet, I was quiet, it worked out very well. On my second stay, I had a very colorful roommate from Chur, a city in eastern Switzerland. He had travelled the four hours to Basel because of the quality of care at this hospital. He was very curious about life in America and we spent many hours chatting away about the differences between our two countries and cultures. One evening, his father sat and visited with us. Dad spoke no English so his son acted as a translator.

The topic of Donald Trump came up.

"People actually like him?"

"Unfortunately, yes"

"But not you"

"Oh, no, no, no"

"Then we can be friends!"

It took a while to explain to them why Barack Obama couldn't be President again. They suggested, then, that he should come and be President of Switzerland.

"But your President doesn't have any power!"

"Yes, but everyone will love him. Even the carrot-eaters down in Appenzell!"

His father roared with laughter. This was the Swiss way of saying that even the rednecks here would love him. I told you it was a zinger of an insult.

When I was finally discharged and began going to physical therapy, the topic of Donald Trump came up very often. My physical therapist, Christine, was a spry German woman who lived just across the border. She was incredibly blunt and to the point. For example, this is an entry in my notes on Facebook:

> *Today I saw my physical therapist for the first time since Christmas, and the very first thing she says to me is not "hello" or "how was your holiday" - instead she bluntly starts with "well your President is very stupid"*

And then there was this gem:

> *Christine: So, Trump has Covid*
> *Me: Yup*
> *Christine: I hope it kills him*

We had a very good relationship.

My physical therapy was fully covered by insurance, thank goodness, as I had to go twice a week for three months, and then repeat everything all over again once I had the other shoulder done. But the surgeries were a wild success and I had regained all the movement in both my arms. Should I ever require any kind of surgery in the future, I'd do anything in the world to have them in Switzerland instead of the US. The Swiss system spoiled me. I get quite impatient now when I go to see my GP and have to constantly repeat all my woes and ills to four or five people before I even see the doctor. I feel as if my doctors are always questioning my sincerity when I speak to them. I miss the trusting relationship between doctor and patient I experienced in Switzerland.

When I finally got the bill for the first surgery, I was dreading opening that envelope. The total cost, for the surgery and the hospital stay and the doctor's fees was 3411.45CHF. That's it. That was the total for everything. Having met so much of our deductible at that point, our out of pocket was less than 1000CHF.

Lisa, too, had her own experiences with the Swiss healthcare system. As I mentioned earlier, she had her own urgent need for surgery. She was experiencing osteonecrosis in her left arm, meaning the bone wasn't getting proper blood supply and was dying. If left untreated, the bone collapses and the dead tissue can infect the body in disastrous ways. This meant that she would have to have the dead section of her ulna removed. While completely not looking forward to something as major as this kind of surgery, she was reassured that the doctor who would be performing the operation was also part of the Olympic team clinic where I had my shoulders done.

What we didn't count on was a national lockdown due to a global pandemic. Her scheduled date for surgery was two months into the shutdown, and we were afraid she wouldn't be able to get it done. The severity of her condition, though, meant her procedure was still on, as it was considered medically necessary. This meant that I could not be with her in the hospital. I was able to go to the clinic with her on the tram, but had to leave her at the front door. For someone who worked as a surgical nurse for years, Lisa is incredibly anxious when it comes to being the one on the table. It killed me to have to leave her there. I couldn't even wait at the clinic for word on how things went; I had to go home and wait for a call.

She was scheduled first thing in the morning, so I dropped her off at 7am. I was told I should expect an update by phone by noon. As 2pm rolled around and I hadn't heard anything, I tried calling the hospital for an update. I was told she was still in recovery and that someone would call to let me know how things went shortly. As 4pm rolled around, I still hadn't heard anything. I was now in a panic. Another call to the hospital, and again I was told she was in recovery and that someone would call me soon for an update. At 5pm I was still completely in the dark. I hopped on a tram and went directly to the hospital.

"You cannot be here, sir"

"The fuck I can't. My wife had surgery at 8am and I still haven't gotten an answer as to what is going on. Where is she? How is she? What's wrong"

"You cannot be here, sir"

"FIND ME HER DOCTOR, NOW!"

At the time, I was not ashamed to let my American side out in all its loud and demanding ugliness. Lisa had been informed of every step of my surgical journey. They had told her that I was settled in pre-op, that I was being put under, that I was in surgery, that surgery was going well, that I was in recovery, that my surgery had been successful and uneventful, and that I was being wheeled up to my room. Every single step of my procedure had been communicated to her as it was happening.

I had heard nothing.

Zero. *Nada. Nichts.*

I was completely in the dark, and based on my experiences with this clinic so far, this was highly unusual. That alone made me panicky and anxious and angry.

Her doctor was paged and I insisted on standing at the registration desk until she arrived. I was one of those people that scoffed at others who dismissed Covid rules and distancing and mask wearing, so it was with great chagrin that I had to insist on breaking the clinic's rules about visiting. This was my wife, who had just had major surgery, and no one seemed to know anything about how she was, where she was, or if she was even fucking alive. All I wanted was information.

Eventually, her doctor appeared looking greatly confused.

"What is the problem?"

"No one seems to have any idea of what is going on with my wife. Where she is, how she's doing. No one has called me. I know nothing"

"You should have been called hours ago. I told reception to inform you that Lisa was having a bad reaction to the anesthesia and we were having trouble getting her to wake up and stay awake. We are keeping her in post-op overnight to monitor her and we would call you first thing in the morning."

"Um, no one, not a single person, has called me, and when I have called here, no one gave me that information, or any information at all. Three times I've asked for an update and gotten nothing. I'm already stressed about not being able to be here for her, and then I'm left in the dark like this, all while she's having a bad reaction to anesthesia!? I mean, that's bad, isn't it!?"

"I do not know why you were not called. I left explicit instructions for them to let you know what was going on, sir. I am very sorry. The operation went smoothly with no complications, but when we got her into post-op, she would not wake up. This sometimes happens, so we keep her for observation and to slowly bring her around. You should have been told this."

And with that, she gave a furious glare to the receptionist listening behind us. The doctor then went off in rapid, angry German, arms gesticulating wildly. She was pissed that this had happened. I'm sure she was embarrassed, too. She gave me her card and told me she would call me personally first thing in the morning to update me on everything. As I headed to the door, I caught the doctor out of the corner of my eye once again laying into the receptionist with great fury.

As promised, her doctor called me in the morning to let me know that all was well and that Lisa was being taken upstairs to her room. While I could not visit her, I could bring her things that they could take up to her. She was in the hospital for three more days and I was not able to visit her once. Covid was raging across Europe and, at least in this part of the world, precautions were being taken at the most serious level. Sure, I had violated those rules the day before, but in that circumstance, my anger convinced me of my justification.

At the same time Lisa was in hospital, I ran into my Danish neighbor who looked ashen-faced, waiting for the tram.

"Oh my goodness, are you okay!?"

"My husband had a massive stroke and is at University Hospital. They won't let me see him!"

"My wife just had surgery and I can't see her, either. How is he doing?"

"Not good. Not good at all"

He was in terrible, terrible shape. I offered to do her shopping or any other errands for her, but she refused. He ended up being in the hospital for three months. She didn't get to see her husband for three entire months. There is absolutely no way I could have dealt with that. Nope. It would have literally broken my heart. Eventually, he was moved to a live-in rehab facility on the other side of town where she was finally able to be with him for about an hour a day. I brought her some flowers one afternoon to try and cheer her up.

"He will be coming home next week"

"What can I do to help?"

"Make him laugh"

He was a very jovial fellow, and when we did chat, it was always full of laughter. If I saw him on his front stoop, I would always stop and chat him up. He loved hearing about how we were adjusting to life in Switzerland, and I enjoyed hearing about life in Denmark. These wonderful folks felt like adopted grandparents to us. One day, I ran into him taking his short rehab-prescribed walk around the block.

"You're looking better each day!"

"Ja, but my head is killing me"

I panicked. Was he having another stroke!?

"Do you need me to take you to the hospital!?"

"No, no, but you can tell those idiot children below you to

shut their faces up. I cannot heal with all that noise all the time. I cannot relax, I cannot sleep, I cannot sit in my garden. They are terrible, terrible children"

Months later, I learned that, indeed, these kids were preventing him from recuperating fully, and they decided to move. Forty years in the same apartment, and they were going to move across town because Buckethead and Singing Shit couldn't behave. This is how horrible those little brats were (and by default, their parents, too).

Lisa came home after five days in the hospital. I sprung for a taxi to bring her home - I didn't want people banging into her arm on the tram. She had months of physical therapy ahead of her, and had to take a leave from work (she couldn't type, and she was in tech). But Lisa being Lisa, she took off less time than she should have and worked through it anyway. Realistically, she could have taken three months off at 90% pay, but she went stir crazy after a week and a half and ended up back to work, albeit from home. Now that we are back in the States, it's time for the metal rods they inserted in her arm to be removed. She is, and I think, rightfully, apprehensive about an American doctor performing the procedure. She's currently in no rush to get it done.

It's true that our experiences with Swiss surgeons and doctors and physical therapists have made us weary of doctors back in America. The cleanliness of the hospitals, the quality of personal care, the pedigrees of our doctors, the lack of interference by the insurance companies. The cost is exorbitant, but no more so than in the US. But the quality is a thousand times better. Even with the snafus, which were rare, our trust in the Swiss system never faltered. I always felt like they operated on a level that the best American doctors could only aspire to. There was this feeling of living in a sci-fi era of unbelievable medical breakthroughs that I never felt in the US. Machines weren't twenty years old, walls weren't scuffed to shit, staff didn't seem burnt out beyond human recognition. Everything gleamed. Every doctor appeared to be living with knowledge that no other medical professionals had, and it made me put my entire and total trust in them. I had spent time in the UCLA and Stanford medical systems, which are among the very best in the US, and they both pale in every comparison to standard Swiss healthcare.

A few days after my rampage, I received a call from the head of anesthesiology, Lisa's doctor, and the director of hospital operations and management to apologize for the lack of communication. They weren't perfunctory calls, either. There was a genuine horror in their voices that this had happened. In the US, these calls would be to ensure I didn't try and sue them. In Switzerland, it was out of genuine embarrassment and concern about the flow of their operations. Again, it was the Swiss honor system in action. Americans apologize to cover their asses; the Swiss apologize because it is the right thing to do.

When I went in for my second shoulder surgery, the lockdown was over, but precautions were still in place. Lisa, again, was not able to accompany me down to pre-op (which, again, I have no recollection of). This time, her visits were limited to one half hour a day. There were no communication snafus, and hospital management reached out to her to ensure she didn't experience the same fuck-up I did. They remembered, and they acted upon it, as honor, and professionalism, dictates.

This was not Lisa's only experience with Swiss hospitals. Not content with having dead bones in her arm, she decided to go and have a god damned heart attack. Literally.

She had been having flutters in her chest along with sharp

pains. One afternoon she grabbed me and said she thinks she might want to go to the ER. We headed for the University of Basel Hospital, which is the main, and largest facility in the area. They immediately whisked her away and had me sit in the waiting area. This was about six months after lockdown ended, and the hospital was still only letting people inside the building who had appointments or were being seen as a patient in the ER. I was surprised they didn't send me home. My temp and a rapid Covid test was administered to me as I waited (which came back negative). I was the only one in the whole waiting area. You could hear the bustle of a very busy ER behind the double doors, but out in the waiting area, it was calm and totally quiet, which made it all the more nerve-wracking. A nurse came by and told me that because my wife was a heart patient, I was able to stay, as cardiac issues are given top priority. Not being a Covid case also meant that I wasn't a danger to others. I was updated every thirty minutes by a lovely ER nurse who constantly asked if I needed anything to eat or drink.

Eventually, the doctor came out to speak with me. Lisa had experienced a mild heart attack and would be admitted to the hospital immediately. They didn't think she was in any danger at the moment and everything for now was reading normal. There would be a battery of tests over the next few hours, but in the meantime, I should go home. No, I could not go back to see her - no visitors allowed at all in the ER. They hadn't dropped all precautions.

As I left the building, the sidewalk outside was bustling with white-clad nurses, all smoking like chimneys. Doctors, therapists, nurses, aides, all of them were outside in their pristine scrubs fiendishly smoking as fast as they could. There were at least 30 staff members gathered together in a blue cloud of smoke. I told you, the Swiss are strangely devoted to smoking. But outside the ER of a hospital, it was a discomfiting sight, indeed.

Reluctantly, I rode the tram home. En route, I received a call from the hospital letting me know that she was on her way upstairs and gave me her room number so that I could visit her the following day.

At least this facility was communicating properly.

The following day, I was allowed to see her in the afternoon. She was on the top floor in a massive suite, shared with five other elderly women. I think Americans would be shocked to find that most hospital stays are in rooms of this size with this many patients sharing a room. You can pay a higher premium on your insurance to qualify for a double or private room, but the cost is so prohibitive, the majority of the Swiss forgo this option.

All the Swiss *omas* greeted me warmly. Lisa had an amazing wall of glass across from her bed that gave her an unobstructed 180-degree view of the city and the Rhine. It was honestly one of the best views of the city I had encountered so far. All things considered, she was being treated extraordinarily well, and was happy with the level of care she was receiving. Her roommates were kind and friendly, if not fully conversant in English. Again, she was ordered to take time off work, which she initially did, but then predictably got bored and went right back to it.

When it was time to go back to see the cardiologist, Lisa would have to show the bouncers at the main entrance the text message confirming that she had an appointment inside the building. No proof of appointment, no admittance. When I had to see my own docs in the same building, I had to do the same. You then had to get your temp taken, had your hands and exposed arms sprayed down with sanitizer, and were issued a clean mask to wear. All the chairs and benches in the lobby area were taped off or removed completely. You were not to loiter or linger.

When we moved back to the US, Lisa was dreading the task of finding a new cardiologist. After her first visit, she was pretty blunt about it.

"Yeah, he's nice, but I feel like just another number here. My Swiss doctor actually gave a rats' ass about me"

My GP was a hell of a doctor. Dr. Sereghetti was a short, sour-faced Italian woman who brooked no shit. You have an issue, don't pussy-foot around, just tell her what's wrong so she can fix it. And when you did tell her your problem, she took it at complete face value and went to work to fix it. I have an auto-immune disease that causes intermittent anemia. I had begun to feel the symptoms of low blood levels at one point, so I made an appointment to see her.

"And what did your American doctors do at this point?"

"They would infuse me with iron"

"What kind?"

"Venofer"

She looked at me with a very confused and angry face.

"Is it still 1950 in America?"

I laughed. She didn't.

"That's stupid. That's ancient medicine!"

And she went on to explain how one dose of a particular infusion used in Europe did the same job in one session that Venofer would do over the course of three. She was appalled at the level of care I was getting for my anemia, and she wasn't even a hematologist.

"We don't need to bother with a hematologist. I'll fix you. And better than those 'doctors' of yours over in America"

She actually did air quotes for 'doctors'.

True to her word, my iron levels jumped immediately back to normal.

Dr. Sereghetti became my favorite GP of all time. No doctor will ever compare to her.

It had been years since I had so many doctors that I could put my absolute and total trust in. I loved, loved, loved these doctors. I honestly don't know if I will ever find that level of care again. It certainly won't be here in the US. For all the headaches of it being an insurance-based system, it was worth it, simply for the quality of what you were paying for. At least in Switzerland, I got my money's worth, and then some. The Swiss know medicine, and they know it very, very well.

Chapter Six - Scenes of Basel

Basel's most distinguishing feature is the mighty Rhine River. One of Europe's great waterways, it cuts through the middle of the city, and all of Basel seems to congregate along its shores to stroll, drink, and swim.

Yes, swim.

In the US, the last place you want to swim would be an urban river. In Switzerland, the place to swim is in the urban rivers. Not only do swimmers flock to the cold, clear waters of the Rhine, but to the icy, Alp-fed Aare in Bern, too. Instead of being clogged with shopping carts or hypodermic needles, Swiss rivers are clogged with ruddy swimmers and deliciously edible fish. Swiss rivers run blue, and in many places, you can see clear through to the riverbed. Even with barge and pleasure craft traffic, the Rhine is so well regulated that swimming is actually encouraged.

The most popular summer activity in Basel is the Rhine swim. This is such a normal thing to do that nearly every shop in town sells *wickelfisch*: waterproof bags in the shape of a fish that not only hold your dry clothes and possessions, but are used as flotation devices. Baselers will change into their swim gear upriver at the Tinguely Museum, stuffing their street clothes into their *wickelfisch*. They'll float with the current down the river for about two miles, holding on to their *wickelfisch* for buoyancy. Once they've passed under the Mittlerebrücke (middle bridge), they will make their way to the promenade on the Kleinbasel side of the river to exit. Large maps all along the promenade show bathers where to put in and where to get out. A series of buoys marks off the swimming lane on the Kleinbasel side of the river, so that no one is mowed down by a Viking River Cruise. The current is fast, and it is highly recommended that you have a partner with you. Being a social event, you will see large groups of swimmers, one hand on their *wickelfisch*, the other holding an Aperol spritz or a *schwimmbier*, zooming by. Every August, the city holds an Official Rhine-Swim where up to 10,000 swimmers will be in the river at one time (during which time the river is closed to all boat traffic). Google it! The videos are amazing.

The Aare in Bern is the other popular river swim, and is far more picturesque. You start in a wooded canyon and float downriver toward the city, which sits on a bluff above you. The river bends back onto itself and you exit the river at the base of one of the soaring bridges that connects the bluff to the "mainland". The Aare River

Swim is not for amateurs. Not only do you need to exit at the exact right spot, which can be challenging given the speed at which the river flows, but the water is extraordinarily cold. It is recommended that you go with a professional guide for your first swim, and to wear a wetsuit if you are not used to glacier-fed water temps.

We never did get to do a Rhine Swim. I bought us a *wickelfisch*, but our first summer saw record drought, leaving the water level so low that the area reserved for swimming was nothing but exposed rock. The following summer, unprecedented rains caused massive flooding, which again prevented swimming due to strong currents and hidden obstacles. Our only real swimming adventure was when we went to Greece for a week and got to enjoy the warm waters of the Aegean Sea.

There were still ways to enjoy the Rhine. One could walk along the river from one end of town to the other along the tree-lined Promenade on the Kleinbasel side. Not only did it afford excellent views of the Old Town and the towering cathedral, it was always soaked in sunlight. Summer found thousands of Baselers sunbathing on the multiple concrete levels that wound down towards the river's edge.

I loved this walk.

Giant beautiful elm trees lined the promenade, and every six feet a bench could be found to sit and admire the view. Dotted along the promenade were *buvettes*, or beverage kiosks, offering coffee, beer, wine, and cocktails. A few cafe tables would be scattered about, and you could sit all day and enjoy the sun, the river, and a *panaché* (A Basel summertime staple of half beer, half lemon-lime soda). Like the ceramic mugs of *glühwein* at the Christmas Markets, you would leave a deposit when you ordered your beverage and it would be served in a proper glass (instead of a plastic or paper cup). Your deposit was refunded once you returned your empty glass. Of course, you could also, like so many of the younger crowd, bring your own case of beer and sit on the waterside steps and get right proper sloshed. Here in Basel, this was all properly legal. On the weekends, all of Basel was sitting riverside, imbibing and chatting and relaxing. This was Basel's living room.

A row of restaurants lined one section of the walk, with large covered patios overlooking the river. Lisa and I had a favorite where we would always share a *flammkuchen* (Alsatian flatbread pizza made with crème fraiche, prosciutto, and caramelized onions) and drink the local Wilde-Maa (Wild Man) hard cider. In fact, on our very last day in Basel, we stopped here to have our favorite drinks and snacks, indulged in overstuffed apple strudel, and soaked in the epic view one last time.

In the winter, kiosks selling adult coffee beverages, schnapps, and hot cocoa popped up, with small fire pits to gather around. Across the river, Christmas lights from the shopping district sparkled in the dark skies. The Rhine Promenade was the gathering place in the city, no matter the weather, no matter the time of year, and I absolutely loved it.

In the autumn, you could sit in the late afternoon underneath technicolor yellow leaves, and watch the lights of the *Herbstmesse* Ferris wheel click on, towering over the twin steeples of the cathedral. Because the sun was now flying lower and lower in the sky, the sunsets became more and more colorful. To sit on the promenade in October was to experience one of the most amazing light shows of your life.

I could walk this part of the city every single day and never tire of any of it. Everything about this stretch was happy and pretty and calming and exciting. Truly, not a week went by when I did not take a walk along some portion of the Rhine. It was my happy place.

If a quieter river experience was to your liking, you just had to head north to the German border and the Wiese River. Once a canal connected to the Rhine, it now serves as the center of a gorgeous green space, surrounded on both sides by endless forest preserves.

The silence is wonderful. Just you, the babbling of the water, and the breeze-rustled trees.

This was where you came to let your doggos run free, to walk the wooded path along the river, to bike through the primeval forest, and to forage for wild garlic and blackberries. This was where I came when the noise of the city began to wear on me. Lisa and I would bring a picnic and sit in the emerald green grass of the riverbank and drink pink wine and eat grapes and peaches and homemade chocolate chip cookies and feel almost like native locals.

Should you want a more active experience, Swiss woods are home to obstacle and fitness courses called *Vita Parcours*. When the physical fitness craze hit in the '80s (looking at you, Jane Fonda), the Europeans, being far more outdoorsy than Americans, set up simple exercise stations in the woods along popular hiking and biking paths. Usually made out of wood stumps, logs, or beams, these areas were meant for one or two simple callisthenic exercises before moving on to the next one. Courses stretched for a few miles through the woods, and running from one station to the next added to your regimen. I encountered these courses all over Switzerland, France, and Germany, and they are in constant, constant use.

At the entrance to one forest preserve I frequented, there was a small hut where you could hang up your jackets or backpacks on wooden pegs before setting out on your run or walk or *parcours* course. I would marvel at the line of coats and bags hanging unsecured and unattended. In the US, these would be snatched up in a heartbeat. In Switzerland, you could disappear into the woods for the whole day and when you returned, not only would your bag still be hanging there, not a thing inside would have been nicked. Bikes, too, were left at the hut, unlocked without worry.

I loved walking in the woods to forest bathe. It wasn't always the quietest affair, though. Because the Swiss are such outdoorsy people, they don't think of nature as a place for quiet refection or reverence. The forest is just another place to be, and gangs of roving soccer moms would be out power walking and chattering loudly. School children on daily field trips would scream and play like monsters, their screeching scaring off every woodland creature for miles.

The woods can actually be one of the busiest places you can go for a walk. More times than I could count, I would have to make way for a family out walking their goats and ponies on the forest path. Horse riders were a common sight, loping through the forest, leaving an obstacle course of horseshit in their wake (or, as Buckingham Palace calls them, "arisings").

In the woods near the Wiese, I took great delight in sitting on the stone border marker separating Switzerland and Germany, one leg slung over on the Swiss side and the other dangling in Germany. Being from a country where borders are a bit of an ordeal to get over, it never ceased to amaze me that I could just sit ON the border in the middle of the woods. No customs booths, no gates, no fence. Just a small rock with a German flag painted on one side and the Swiss flag on the other.

Quick bit of trivia: In Switzerland, you are never more than 15km away from a lake or river. I never really thought about it, but almost every place I visited in the country was on a river or lake. For being a landlocked country, it has more access to water than most places on earth.

The other water feature of Basel wasn't a river or canal, but was just as big and ever-present. Within the city, you can find over 1000 fountains, and not only are they all unique and beautiful, you can drink from them. I don't mean American style water fountains or bubblers. I'm talking large, public, baroque basins with sculptures and peeing cherubs. The water from the fountains of Basel is some of the cleanest, clearest, crispest, coldest drinking water anywhere in the world.

I hate water. Hate to drink it, hate the taste (or lack of taste) of it. But "trying all the things" meant trying fountain water. All the blogs and all the travelogues insisted that this was the good shit. Baselers don't buy bottled water - they fill up their bottles or thermoses from the fountains. And let me tell you, my friends, there is no better way to quench your thirst than to sip from one of these beautiful bad boys. It's incredible! It's so pure that it's just cold wetness. No mineral taste, no flatness, no blandness. I can't believe I'm trying to describe the taste of water, but I have to try because I have never experienced water so… pure. So perfect. I could not get enough fountain water. Should I ever return to Basel, one of the first things I'm doing is drinking my fill until I have to pee myself. I'm not sure how, but drinking from the fountains of Basel is one of the most fulfilling things you can do. I don't know if they are fountains of youth, but they are most certainly fountains of happiness.

Just a few days after arriving in the city, we were sitting outside at a cafe across from one of these fabulous fountains on a very hot September day. A group of eight teens gathered 'round the fountain, stripped down to swim suits, and sat around the edge of the fountain with their legs dangling in (I suppose it is important to note that you drink from the spigots that feed the fountain, not the body of water in the basin). Our waiter came outside, saw them, and went straight over to them. I thought for sure he was going to admonish them, but instead, he took their order!

A few moments later, a family came and sat down at a table near us with two small children. They stripped the kids down to their underwear and let them join the group in the fountain. The kids climbed right in and started splashing around like it was a kiddie pool. Emerging from the kitchen, the smiling waiter brought the older kids a couple of bottles of wine and a fistful of stemware. A short time later, he was serving them pizzas.

After seeing that the little kids had joined in, he came back with plastic bottles of *Rivella* (Switzerland's national beverage – a tart fruity soda made from milk whey) for them. Out of the corner of my eye, I spied two police officers coming up the street. Instead of admonishing them or asking them to get out, the teens offered them a slice of pizza, which they accepted happily. They hung around and chatted with the group for a good ten minutes before patting the smaller ones on the head and wandering off.

In just thirty minutes, we had observed Basel at its most charming best. I couldn't imagine a more perfect introduction to life here.

Dining out is a much different experience in Switzerland (and Europe as a whole), and I prefer it in every way.

I worked most of my younger years in food service, from waiting tables to bartending to managing family restaurants. Whenever Lisa and would go out to eat, I would be distracted, always analyzing our experience through my "restaurant manager eyes". I knew why our waiter or waitress was behind, or why they dropped the check so quickly, or why tables aren't getting bussed in a timely manner. It can both grate on Lisa's nerves, and entertain her, when I switch into "manager mode". To be honest, it becomes difficult sometimes to truly relax and enjoy my meal out. I look at it all as a business. In Europe, dining out is a part of life; the calculus drops and dining becomes an experience, not a transaction.

Every restaurant will have outdoor seating, and no matter the weather, every one of those seats will be full. In the winter, cafes will leave blankets and throws for people to bundle up in as they eat in the falling snow. There is nothing that will stop a European from sitting outside.

My first experience with this dogged determination to dine al fresco was years earlier when we visited Brighton in the UK. It was early April, and the town was being inundated with fierce storms rolling in off the English Channel. It was around 40F and raining steadily as I stopped into a Costa Coffee for breakfast before I headed out to explore this seaside resort town. Every table inside the café was empty, but every table outside, under the thin and useless awning, was full. As I walked The Lanes of the medieval city, every outdoor table I passed was occupied with Brits and holiday goers enjoying the damp and frigid spring air. I was freezing my baguettes off, and these defiant bastards were lounging outdoors like it was August. I thought them bonkers, all of them.

Until I moved overseas myself.

In quick time, I, too, wanted only to sit outside. Even on the coldest of days, I eschewed the stuffiness of dining rooms. Lisa wasn't quite so enamored of dining outdoors at all costs, which is weird because she is almost always hot and I am always cold. But like Brighton, all of the coffee shops in Basel had packed outdoor tables and empty indoor ones. Some places offered heaters on their patios, but many did not, and Baselers didn't seem to care. Even when they did, they were turned on with great reluctance.

In the warmer months, it became an Olympic sport trying to secure an outdoor table. You didn't wait for someone to seat you. No, you pounced on one as soon as a group stood to leave. Outdoor seating is first come, first served. We learned this quickly, and after a while, could spot American tourists a mile away as they stood confused and angry waiting for a hostess to come and lead them to a table. While you seat yourself, it is still good manners to make eye contact with a waiter in the area, raise your eyebrow and gesture to the open table, as if to confirm it was now yours to enjoy. They will give you a perfunctory nod and go about their business. This serves a greater purpose as well – it lets them know they now have new customers.

Once your waiter arrives, you will be handed menus and asked if you would like water. This is where your American will show if you just say "yes, please".

This will be a grave mistake.

Water is never free in a European restaurant. Never, ever, ever free.

Should you decide you do want water, you will then be asked if you want *"mit gas, oder ohne gas?"*. Your confused look will prompt the waiter to ask you, in English now, "sparkling or still?". Whichever your choice, you will be served an entire liter bottle of water, and once it is gone, you will have to order, and pay for, another.

Free refills are nonexistent in Europe. For anything. You want your coffee topped off? You'll be brought a fresh cup and charged full price for it. Soft drinks are usually served as a bottle with a glass on the side. There are no fountain drinks here, and you certainly aren't drinking your fill for free. Sizes, too, are miniscule compared to the paint buckets you get in the US. What the Europeans consider standard, Americans would consider children's sized. 5-7oz glasses are the norm, not 18-24oz Big Gulps. Starbucks is about the only place in Europe you're finding a 20oz (Venti) beverage.

Lemonade in Europe is not American-style lemonade, like Country Time or Minute Maid. If you order lemonade in Europe, you will get sparkling lemon flavored soda, and it is superior to American lemonade in every way. Mix some of that with some *Limoncello* and you're going to have a good day, indeed.

You will need to ask for ice for your beverage as well. Your drink will be served cold (or cold-adjacent), but it will not, ever, have ice, unless specifically requested. This request will immediately peg you as an American, and your waiter or waitress will bring you more ice than exists in all of Alaska. Lisa needs ice for everything, and it annoys her to think that the wait staff will immediately think less of her for doing so.

Within a week of moving to Basel, she made me go find ice cube trays for the freezer, which was no easy task in the slightest.

Remember, before your waiter leaves to get your 12CHF bottle of Perrier, ask for an English-language menu if you need one. American tourists are wont to forget that they are in a foreign country and assume the menu will be in English. Actually, the Brits are even more arrogant than Americans in assuming that English is the language de rigueur. There is nothing more entertaining than reading Trip Advisor reviews by Brits of restaurants in Spain complaining that everyone spoke Spanish around them and nothing was written in English. To strengthen our language skills, Lisa and I always used the regular German-language (or French-language) menu. Should we have translated incorrectly, well, we were going to be trying a surprise supper and learn from our mistakes.

Once you start perusing the menu, you will notice the prices. Your waiter might be nearby and offer to pick your jaw up off the floor for you. No, you are not hallucinating. That 5oz filet does, in fact, cost 72CHF. That filet of red snapper is actually 65CHF. Yes, your garden salad is 29CHF. Beyond belief, that side of frites is 25CHF. Yes, you just paid 15CHF for a Coke (with no ice).

Switzerland is one of the most expensive places on earth to dine out. These are normal prices, and you will realize that eating out is a very special treat, indeed. At least the wine is cheap, which is why you drink to numb the pocketbook pain.

Other than delivering your food, you will not see your waiter again. He will not hover; she will not ask you how everything is. The manager will not stop by your table to see how satisfied you are with everything. You are now left alone, to enjoy your meal and your company, in peace. The concept of "churn and burn" is non-existent here (in the US, it refers to turning tables over quickly in order to serve as many people as possible in a given evening, which is why you always feel so rushed when you go out on a Friday night). Your waiter or waitress isn't dependent on earning as many tips as possible; they are paid a living wage. They will earn the same paycheck by the end of the week if they serve five people or fifty.

When you are finished with your meal, you will raise your finger towards the nearest wait staff. You will not snap your fingers, and you will not wave your arm like a rabid man-child. You certainly will not call out *"garçon!"* A polite, subtle signal to let them know you have finished. You do the same should you want to order fresh drinks, or need anything else during your meal. It can be a bit unnerving the first time you realize you actually have to flag someone down. In the US, this is only done if you feel you have been unjustly ignored. In Europe, it simply means you are in need of attention.

You order dessert, if you are feeling wealthy. If you order coffee, you will need to be specific. There isn't a Bunn machine in the back with a carafe of black coffee and an orange carafe with decaf. If you just order coffee, you'll be brought an espresso. When you order an after-dinner coffee, you'll order a latte, or a cappuccino, or an Americano (this will be the Euro version of a black coffee). You will once again be left alone until you are ready to leave.

This is where dining out in Europe is so lovely. No one is trying to rush you to leave. You can sit and enjoy the next two hours at that table and never order another thing, and no one will bat an eye. This is your space to sit, enjoy conversation, even read a book or the newspaper. You take all the time you want and let your food digest. After all, you've spent a small fortune, so why not get your money's worth? Your server is not dependent on turning the table over, so they could care less how long you sit there.

The concept of a doggie-bag does not exist here. You will

not be asked "did you want to take the rest home?" or "can I box that up for you?". Then again, your food portions were not designed to feed an entire Boy Scout troupe.

For one last time, you will summon your waiter ever so apologetically. They will present you with the bill, and then stand there. You will immediately pull out your credit card and hand it over. Instead of disappearing with your card, your European waiter will have a portable credit card machine with them, and will run your card right there in front of you. Europeans panic when dining out in the US when their server absconds with their debit card to the dark recesses of the kitchen, out of sight, and unmonitored. It vexes the European mind.

Do not be like the arsehole we witnessed when living in Canada. Out to dinner one night, we watched as an irate American was told that, no, they could not accept American dollars as payment as they were not in America. Even had we been anywhere near the border, the utter gall. Don't be that guy. Switzerland is not in the EU, so put your Euros away, please.

You will not have to leave a tip. The gratuity is included, and, again, your server is not subsisting on tips. It is customary to round up to the nearest 5CHF if you should want to leave something. Anything above that can be read as insulting. Anything above that will confirm, above all doubt, that you are, indeed, a Yank. Still, when out at a coffee shop or at a riverside buvette, a franc or two is appreciated.

You'll pat your belly happily and remind yourself to do this again next year after you've saved up enough money to dine out once more.

Basel has two phenomenal art museums with the Kunstmuseum and the Fondation Beyeler. Both are absolutely extraordinary and house some incredibly famous works of art. The best art, however, is to be found on the sides of buildings, down alleys, on transformer stations and mailboxes and in shop windows.

The street art scene in Basel exceeds anything that can be found in a frame gallery. Even random acts of graffiti are photo-worthy. While the streets and sidewalks are immaculate, flat surfaces are not immune from spray paint, and scribbling can be found everywhere throughout Switzerland. What sets Basel apart is that the city embraces public displays of expression. Enormous, street-long murals can be found down the back streets of Old Town. One in particular celebrates all of popular music's geniuses, from Jimi Hendrix to Bob Dylan to The Beatles. Another 100-yard-long mural depicting scientists and medical achievements is both educational and insanely colorful. Down the block from our flat, the electrical transformer box for the tram tracks was fully painted to look like a giant grinning Cheshire Cat.

In every corner of the city you will find brilliant spray-painted Picassos, underlined with the caveat "Not A Picasso". Throughout my wanderings of the city, I encountered no less than 30 "Not A Picasso" Picassos. I even found two in Zurich. It seems as if Switzerland has its own Neutral Banksy.

On days when I was a bit bored, I would pick a random neighborhood to walk through and I would try to find as many hidden pieces of street art as I could. Murals, wall tags, stickers on light poles, pen-knife carvings in park benches. No matter where I ended up wandering, I would end my walk with a full camera roll and a lifted spirit. The causal viewer saw defacement. The discerning viewer saw life.

On a garden wall, tucked away in a well-to-do neighborhood, was a full-scale reproduction of Picasso's *Guernica*. It was strange to see something so incredibly beautiful bedecking a retaining wall in a parking lot. It was so tucked away in such a non-descript area that when I wanted to take Lisa to see it, I couldn't find it. I searched for over a year and never came across it again.

One of my favorite things was the life-size fiberglass Spiderman crawling up the side of a random house on a random side street in the suburb of Binningen.

There are many underground pedestrian passageways in the city. In most US cities, I wouldn't venture through one of these on the brightest, sunniest of days, in a hazmat suit and armed with an assault rifle. In Basel, however, these passages are painted with brilliant technicolor murals and are so clean that you could probably eat off the sidewalk. There are no puddles of piss, no broken bottles, no meth addicts or werewolves or Dementors. They are as pristine as the day they were built. Instead of terrifying tunnels of doom, they are almost like underground art galleries. Many installations are done by local school children. The best one, by far, was painted by a middle school that featured Lisa Simpson dressed up as Hermione Granger.

One of the three main bridges across the river is a double-decker affair, with auto traffic above, and foot traffic below. The whole length of the pedestrian portion of the bridge is one giant sea-themed mural depicting mermaids and narwhals and water skiers and sailing ships. It stretches continuously for almost 300 yards across the river. Insouciant Baselers have added witty and vulgar balloon captions to many of the figures, adding fun to what was already fun. While Switzerland is known for being a rather buttoned-up society, Basel is much cheekier than the rest of the country.

Even advertisement billboards can be a bit raunchy.

One in particular was an underwear ad with a rather… bulgy gentleman in a pair of skivvies with the caption "Not For Pussies". A clothing store had posters up in the window showing a woman giving the middle finger with the caption "Give Me A Smile" and the hashtag *#fuckexpectations*. There's even a statue hidden in a courtyard depicting a man trying to look up a maiden's skirt. It's all a bit ribald, but you can also tell it's all in good fun. European conservatism doesn't necessarily translate into prudishness.

On the more vulgar side of things, though, are the political statements found around town.

The most popular tag is *Fuck Erdogan*.

Ethnic Kurds have a large presence throughout Switzerland as refugees, and they hold anti-Turkish rallies on a regular basis, shutting down many main avenues in the center of town. When not protesting, they are tagging the large Turkish neighborhoods with this popular slur. All sorts of enclave-based insults and epithets can be found the further into Kleinbasel you go. It never spills over into actual violence, but the tensions are there, and the graffiti is a constant reminder that so many grievances are brewing just under the surface.

That's not to say that there aren't bigoted messages to be found on the other, posher side of the river. Instead of ethnicity-based messaging, the target of wall-screeds in the older parts of Basel are expats. I had a particular neighborhood not too far from our flat where I loved to take my daily walks. One afternoon, I rounded a corner and found "Expats Fuck Off!!!" scrawled on the side of an apothecary, in five-foot-high red letters. It made my heart sink.

These were the thoughts I wrote down when I returned home:

While I love Switzerland, I must admit, sometimes it can be an unwelcoming, cold, racist, and misogynistic place. So many, myself included, have this picture of an Alpine paradise of friendly hikers in dirndls and an enlightened European attitude about everything. Switzerland, however, like any other place on earth, is plagued with prejudice.

I saw graffiti while out on walkabout today, in a neighborhood I like to frequent. As a white male, I know I am at the pinnacle of the privilege pyramid, so until today, I have been pretty insulated from taking any kind of disparaging remarks or slogans or slurs to heart (I'm not a targeted group, regardless of what Trump supporters want you to think). I've never felt the sting. And while this may not be as

intrusive, vulgar, or evil as anything thrown at (to be embarrassingly general) women, gays, people of color, Muslims, immigrants, or Native Americans, it was the first time something like this hit me on a level I have never experienced before. This is my home, and while I constantly feel like an outsider, I've never felt like the people here want me to leave. Though, to be fair, I have always known that the Swiss do not like outsiders. The Swiss are an insular people who do everything they can to make sure that those who are not TRULY Swiss know that they will never, ever, be Swiss.

Even if you are born here, one of your parents must be Swiss born for you to have Swiss citizenship. Even then, if both your parents were not born here, you are forever tagged as a foreigner. You can never truly be "Swiss". Only after three generations of both parents being born in Switzerland can one be considered fully Swiss. And even then, many rural areas will still think of you as an outsider.

Yesterday, Switzerland held one the quarterly national referendum votes, and the country voted to ban face coverings (i.e., hijabs and burqas) in all public places (allowed only at home and in a place of worship). The referendum was put forth by a coalition of far-right political parties, and while the federal government opposed the law, because it was a binding national referendum, the people's vote trumps all - and the Swiss, with a history of anti-Muslim sentiment, passed it. To emphasize the anti-Islamist attitude here, minarets are forbidden - no mosque can have them, save for four that were grandfathered in when the law was passed (again, by national referendum) in 2009 by 60%.

Last week on my way home from grocery shopping in France, I noticed a car pulled over by the French gendarme. The whole family was standing next to their car as it was ransacked by the border guards. This was obviously a Muslim family, as the women were wearing niqabs and the men had dark skin. Another guard stood by, waving all the other cars with white drivers through without so much as a second glance. It was all I could do not to disembark and ask why these poor folks were singled out. I feared I would only make things worse for them if I did.

Which brings me back to the graffiti. While I have always known that I would never be fully welcomed here, I never felt threatened. When I saw this today, I felt, for the very first time, targeted. That selfish anger, however, was swept away when I realized that this was one tag, on one wall, and that I was in no real danger.

The rather noticeable police patrol presence on my walk today, however, made me take note that there are groups of people here that actually do face danger on a day-to-day basis: Muslims. The ban on face coverings was voted on yesterday, and today, throughout this neighborhood I frequent, this neighborhood of Middle Eastern, Eastern European, and Turkish immigrants, there was a heightened police presence that made me guiltily aware that some are more unwelcome than others.

Every country has an ugly side - today was the day I really saw Switzerland's.

You can't let the ugliness get to you. Feeling down, I found myself walking past the Basel Synagogue, and on the side of an apartment block, opposite the temple, I noticed a series of spray painted Arabic words. I used Google Lens translate app and instead of finding anti-Semitic slurs, I found a message of brotherhood and peace for Basel's Jews. I realized in that moment that for all the hate in the world, there is hope, too.

In the US, graffiti is rebellious defacement or gang-territory markers or pointless mayhem. In Europe, it is an expression of politics, religion, hate, hope, and art. I loved all of it because it was the voice of the city, readily available to all, to be heard in whatever voice you chose to give it.

Basel not only has street-sweepers, but sidewalk-sweepers as well. The sidewalks here are not cement like in the States, but are paved with asphalt, just like the roads. They are wide enough to allow a miniature sweeper to scoot down it, or for smaller alleyways, the city employs people with giant vacuums strapped on their backs - like reverse leaf-blowers. In the large city parks, they have vacuums attached to the riding mowers to suck up all the leaves so people can enjoy the green open spaces throughout autumn-time.

Street sweepers (the human kind) also use enormous brooms made out of willow switches to sweep large debris into the street for the machines to pick up. Unlike the US, which runs a street sweeper maybe once a month down a major thoroughfare, in Basel every single street, alley, byway and highway is cleaned weekly. The busiest streets are swept twice a week. Both the streets and the sidewalks here are so immaculate that you would swear the tarmac had just been newly put down days before.

Speaking of the streets, I have never encountered a place where every single solitary road I have seen or been on is in perfect, and I mean perfect, condition. I didn't see a pothole. Ever. Not once. All across the country, every road is a hemorrhoid sufferer's dream. A baby's bottom is not as smooth as a Swiss roadway. They're Santana-level Smooth. It's kind of mind-blowing.

For as clean and orderly as Basel is, there are still those that sully the scene. There are the gangs of young punks who sit on the riverside and blast horrendous Finnish death metal on boom boxes and get sloshed on cheap booze. There are the assholes who blow smoke in your face as you pass them on the sidewalk. There are the groups of tourists who insist on having an argument about which way to go at the very bottom of the escalator in the train station, blocking everyone from moving. Tourists, man.

Homelessness is not a problem in Basel. Many equate the ever-present group of aggressive beggars and panhandlers at the train station as homeless. On the contrary, the Swiss government is extremely proactive when it comes to helping those in need, with a myriad of services and shelters available. Walk the streets after dark and you will not find a single body sleeping in a doorway or dark alley. There are places for the displaced to go when they need a bed to sleep in, a place to eat, or a doctor to see (meanwhile, during the pandemic in Nevada, the city spray painted social distancing boxes in a concrete parking lot for the homeless to sleep on) . So when you find a large group of unsavory characters outside the bahnhof, do not mistake them for the displaced or down-on-their-luck.

Bad public behavior was a rare sight. One evening, I watched some pseudo punk-rock douchebag with a potbelly sticking out of a crop-top lounging across two seats on the tram. This was during rush hour and he was drinking a beer and listening to thrash metal so loud you could hear it through his earphones from six seats away. I watched a few people glare at him because they wanted a seat, but he wasn't budging. Until this old woman, who was probably 100 and looked like she drove tanks during WWII, shoved his legs over and sat down with some sort of German epithet spitting out of her mouth so hard you could see it smack his face like a brick. The woman sitting next to me literally guffawed out loud. It is always the Swiss women who will call out those being shitty.

Fear Swiss women. They brook no shit.

How fearless are they? One afternoon, three women, clearly over the age of eighty, zoomed past me on the sidewalk today on RAZOR SCOOTERS. Not electric scooters - just plain, foot-powered scooters. And they were FLYING. They had to be cruising at 30mph. Pensioners on scooters are everywhere, and it's an odd thing to behold. If I had to bet on a Basler grandma versus a Basler schoolkid in a scooter race, I would put my francs on the Oma in a heartbeat. They will mow your ass down if you get in their way.

These women plainly have places to be.

Ping Pong is strangely popular in Basel.

Many small side streets, in order to keep traffic moving slowly, are built in a dogleg pattern. In these small curbside oases, you'll find gathering areas with benches and planters and... ping pong tables. Built out of concrete with metal nets, they are permanent fixtures. We had just such a side street near our flat, complete with *tisch-tennis* table. Posting a picture of this cozy little avenue, my Dad was confounded. The pattern of traffic, parked cars, and these gathering areas just didn't register with him.

"How the hell do you even drive down a street like that!?"

"Slowly. Very slowly."

Baselers used these tables, too. They were in constant use. It wasn't just kids who played at them, either. You'd find small gatherings of teens, twenty-somethings, even seniors, all having a go. Public playgrounds had ping pong tables, too. Sometimes you'd find families using them as an *al fresco* dining table. Even the Swiss version of Muscle Beach on the Rhine had four ping pong tables among the pull up bars and weight lifting benches.

The age of things never stops confounding.

While being aware that there are thousands more years of

history here than we have in the US, there are literal reminders everywhere letting you know just how ancient everything around you is. Houses have the year they were erected painted over the door, along with the name of the family that built it. Some will note the dates of when the house changed hands, passing from one family to another.

One magnificent old house on the prettiest street in Old Town was built in 1350. Above the door, in gothic calligraphy, are notations about the house's history. In 1456, it changed hands for the first time, passing to the Habstat family. In 1512, to the Froidenbergs, in 1743 to the Fridbergs, and finally in 1807 to the Frieden family. Almost every house in the Old Town will have notations like this, and even after walking these same streets a hundred times or more, I never stopped marveling at how old this city was. I think the oldest house I found dated from 1231.

The cathedral was celebrating its 1000th anniversary when we lived there. The *Herbstmesse* (Autumn Fair) was in its 550th year. I had explored Roman ruins from the 1st century BC. I climbed the ramparts of castles built in the 1300-1400s. The tram would pass by the Spalentor; built in 1356, one of two City Gates still standing sentinel at the northern edge of the Old Town.

Street signs, too, will have bits of trivia posted below the street name. Easy to spot in royal blue with brilliant white lettering, you will find that Rheingasse was first mentioned in record by name in 1336. Nadelbergstrasse was first noted as a street in 1241. Peterkircheplatz, according to the sign, dates all the way back to 1035. Other streets will give a small biography of the person they are named after. General-Guisan-Strasse was named after the head of the Swiss military during WWII. Erasmusstrasse was so named for the famous theologian who is buried in Basel's cathedral, and Edisonstrasse is apparently named after some obscure American inventor.

I always loved that Swiss street names are generally a mouthful. Lisa and I would always imagine my Dad trying to pronounce the longer street names in our neighborhood, like Gündeldingerstrasse, or Nachtigallenweg, or Münchensteinerstrasse. Even our own street of Margarethenstrasse confounded my Dad. Once, he was preparing to send us a package and kept messaging me to confirm that he was spelling the street name right.

"This is all one word?"

"Yep"

"Do I put 'street' at the end of it?"

"No, the *strasse* part means street"

"So you just live on one long run-on sentence?"

"Pretty much"

"Good lord"

Should you fancy having a barbecue, you have a plenty of options. Remember, the Swiss are a nation of pyromaniacs, so grilling out is not just a leisure activity, it's a compulsion. I'm surprised the Swiss national anthem isn't *Firestarter* by Prodigy.

Lots of people love to bbq whilst they camp. Should you go out into the woods, you will find pre-cut firewood for all your flame-filled needs. No need to go foraging for kindling; the local government has already got you covered. Small covered huts are next to all the grilling and fire pit areas and house enough corded wood to last a lifetime.

If a wood fire isn't your bag and you'd prefer to use charcoal, have at it! Just make sure to scoop out your pit and dispose of the ashes in the provided, labelled Ash Bins. These bins are located in every forest preserve and public park. Burn things all you like so long as you clean up afterwards.

Maybe the woods or the riverside park are too dull for a weenie roast. Maybe you need something a little more… dramatic.

Grab your hiking boots and get your butt up to any one of the hundreds of castle ruins that dot the surrounding landscape and set up your rotisserie over one of the government provided bbq pits located inside the ancient ruins of a once might stone fortress. Yes, you can climb up to the hillside parapets of a 12th century Hapsburg fortress, and after exploring what's left of the stone ramparts, grill yourself a cheese. Castle ruins are one of the most popular places in Switzerland to have a picnic and cookout. I suppose after exerting yourself climbing all the way up there (and it's easy to forget that castles are always on the highest point around), a nice glass of Gewürztraminer and a kalbswurst hits the spot nicely.

I loved exploring castles. There are so many within 15 minutes of Basel, and all of them are free. It's the getting there that's the challenge. It's always a steep climb up through the forest to reach these places. But once there, you are afforded spectacular 360 degree views of the valley below. Some are larger than others, some better preserved, but all allow you to explore the standing structures. You can ascend to the top of the lookout towers or bastions and pretend you're preparing for battle. I almost always had these places to myself, which is incredibly peaceful. The views are always top notch. My Dad marveled at my pictures.

"I don't understand how they let you climb on these things. They could collapse at any moment!"

"Well, they've stood this long, right?"

My particular favorite was on the French-Swiss border where I could take in the whole of the Vosges Mountains of France and the distant skyline of Basel. I could take the tram and get off on the Swiss side of the hill that the ruins stood atop, explore the castle, and then hike down the other side and catch the same tram on the French side of the border for the ride home.

If I visited this castle and stayed on the Swiss side for a hike, I would find myself, a kilometer down the road, at the Closter Mariastein, a monastery founded in the 1400s. To get there, just follow the never-ending row of stone crosses and Virgin Marys that line the pilgrimage road to the sanctuary. A large (and obscenely gorgeous) baroque cathedral sits atop a grotto deep in the earth below. Legend has it that a local boy fell in a crevasse and was "saved" by the Virgin Mary. It has been a holy pilgrimage site since the 1600s when the basilica was built and sits in the most serene, green valley you have ever seen. To be sure, it lives up to those pictures of Switzerland in your head.

After you complete your genuflections and almsgiving, listen to the robed monks perform vespers, and explore the underground grotto, you can fire up one of the many provided bbqs in the abbey's flower garden and enjoy a juicy bratwurst.

Spring is probably when Basel is at its finest.

The town suddenly becomes awash in a hundred shades of purple and yellow as trillions of crocuses bloom in every square inch of soil across the Canton. The green of the grass is replaced with a mosaic of color and it is an absolute wonder to behold. The closest I've seen to anything this jaw dropping, in terms of flower blooms, is blue bonnet season in Texas Hill Country. The public parks will rope off all of the grassy areas to protect these sprawling carpets of flowers. Sometimes I would be late to my physical therapy appointments because I would stop to admire the crocus bloom in the sprawling Schutzenmatt Park across the street from the office. It's a display that is so mesmerizing that it's impossible to pull yourself away.

The best place to see flowers in Basel, however, is at Merian Gärten, the sprawling botanical gardens on the far eastern edge of town. Not only will the bucolic glens take on a calico pattern of millions of tiny flowers, the whole of the area will buzz with the giddy happiness of joyful bees. In every park, every slice of green space, every tree-lined median in Basel, you will find a bee house. Almost every large city park as an apiary as well. The Swiss love of nature and all its splendor means that the Swiss also love their bees. In many rural areas, you can buy homemade jars of honey from honor boxes at the end of driveways. The familiar hum seems to be ever-present - comforting, but never threatening or ominous (I'm looking at you, Nick Cage). It's the soundtrack to the painting.

Spring is also the best time to walk through the Gärten's dense rhododendron garden and inhale, heavily, its calming honey perfume. While many botanical gardens will have different biospheres to walk through, this is more akin to the English style of flower garden after flower garden, interrupted by rolling green fields and arbors of yew trees. A lovely Victorian tea house sits at the center where elegant cygnets swim in a nearby pond. It's one of the most idyllic spots in all of Basel.

Once you've filled your nostrils with nature's perfume, you can saunter over to the neighboring Grün 80 park where you can feed ducks, play miniature golf (on one of the hardest courses I've ever played), and then sit on a large shaded café terrace and drink champagne. You can soak your feet in a tiny mineral spring, and bask in the shade of a life-sized brontosaurus statue. You can ride a carousel or take a dive from the ten-meter Olympic diving platform. Perhaps a game of tennis on one of the thirty courts, or a game of beach volley ball in one of the ten sand pits. Honestly, mini golf, cheesecake, and a cocktail was why Lisa and I would hop over there at least once a month. Why wouldn't you? What better way to spend the day?

The one thing you must be on the lookout for, however, while ambling through Basel's parks, are storks. Not because they might sling a swaddled baby at you, but because they are a protected, endangered bird that is enormous and will kill you if you get too close. Their beaks are like long swords, and they're almost 5 feet tall. They were reintroduced to the area almost thirty years ago after nearly going extinct, and are now happily thriving. The Basel Zoo has hundreds of extremely tall poles spread out all across the park, and atop each is a stork's nest. These are almost as wide as the birds are tall. Storks will stand atop their nests, kick their heads all the way back, and clack their enormous beaks in a strange castanet-like clatter. You will hear this cacophony in almost every corner of Basel. It's actually a lovely thing. They're beautiful birds, and in the spring, they clatter the happiest. The clack of the storks, the carpet of crocus, the smell of flowers everywhere, I'm telling you Cole Porter got it wrong: I don't love Paris in the springtime; I love Basel in the springtime.

———

The Swiss are a very hands-on people. Not only do kids get to smelt iron in the Christmas village, at school they get to tend to farm animals. Almost every youth center and elementary school will have an extensive farmyard with pigs, chickens, goats, and rabbits. Some have donkeys, others alpacas. Even the most urban and urbane child will learn how to care for and tend to these important aspects of Swiss life. They gain an appreciation for animals and their importance to everyday life. It teaches them responsibility and treats these kids as burgeoning adults, and not addled toddlers.

Swiss kids are also treated as adults when it comes to public transport. Schools in Switzerland do not have lunchrooms or cafeterias. Kids either go home to eat lunch or run to the grocery store to grab lunch. It is completely normal to see a gaggle of second graders riding the tram to the local Coop and buying a grab-n-go sandwich out of the cold case (kids under 14 can ride public transport for free). And unlike American kids, these youngsters will actually buy a sandwich or fruit or yogurt and not spend all their lunch cash on junk food, energy drinks, or candy. To be fair, it's not out of the ordinary to see a congress of high schoolers slamming a few beers on their lunch hour before heading back to class. True to form, I have watched French high schoolers buying single-serve cans of wine during their mid-day break. But for the most part, Swiss schoolchildren are pretty well behaved when out in public. Probably because they are taught and given responsibility and autonomy at a young age. Like I mentioned before, kids as young as five are being taught how to build fires in the woods and are blowing glass at the Christmas Market, so what's it to them to ride the tram around town?

I think, growing up as a latch-key kid in the '80s, I relate to these kids, and their under-estimated ability to take care of themselves. Kids in Europe are treated like short adults. I don't have kids, am not particularly fond of kids, cannot relate to kids, and am almost never around kids, but I respected these kids for being so confidently self-sufficient. They acted like adults in public, and that made them eminently more tolerable than American children (except for the Lovecraftian demon children who lived below us. How they didn't get hit by a tram on a daily basis is beyond me).

Speaking of trams.

There is a strict Swiss right-of-way hierarchy. It is as follows: Tram > pedestrian > bicycle > car.

Strangely, I found, in Amsterdam, that the hierarchy is: bicycle > tram > car > tulip cart > dogs with sunglasses > earthworms > pedestrians.

In Switzerland, you can step out into traffic in any crosswalk and never get hit. Cars will literally stop on a dime if you are waiting at the crosswalk. Of course, the natives don't really wait – they just plow into traffic knowing without a doubt that cars will stop. It took me a while to get used to this, especially in the busy intersections where there are no traffic signals. I would dawdle at the crosswalk waiting to join a local so I didn't feel like a prat making cars stop for me. Within a year, I was marching across every street with wild abandon.

Should you be at a crosswalk with a signal, however, you absolutely cannot cross until the little man turns green. To cross at a signaled crosswalk on a red little man will earn you the unending disdain of every local around you. They will remember you, for years and years. Every time they come to that same crossing, they will remember the reckless, irresponsible, stupid foreigner that crossed on a red. They will talk about your evil deed at their next Apero (cocktail hour). This will be the fuel that feeds the Swiss fire of xenophobia.

If you step out in front of a tram, well, *hasta la vista*.

My mom asked me once if I had been to a Swiss cemetery yet. She was curious to know if they were any different. Actually, there was a small cemetery at the edge of our neighborhood that we would wander through on walks in the area. Instead of being a place you only frequented if you knew someone and were visiting their grave, in Switzerland, they are considered public parks. Walking paths, benches, flower gardens are all woven into the grounds and you are encouraged to stop and sit and admire the beauty of the place.

Swiss cemeteries are gorgeous parks, and American graveyards pale in comparison. Instead of being large grassy lawns, the Swiss create intricate arbors of pine trees and cedars and flowering fruit trees. Fountains dot the landscape, and each marker sits within a small individual garden. These can be framed by hedges or rose bushes or rock gardens or even moats. Gravestones are intricately carved statues and cenotaphs. Many use stained glass windows in the shape of favorite objects or hobbies – sailing ships and sunflowers and cats and dogs casting a kaleidoscope of color on the ground. There are no simple slabs of granite tucked into the grass.

And every site is tended to meticulously. Tucked away in unobtrusive areas are maintenance kiosks for visitors to pot flowers and fill watering cans. Hedge trimmers, brooms, rakes, and buckets of gravel and stone are available to tidy up your loved one's area. You will find no fake flowers or plants here, either. The Swiss make regular trips to ensure everything is pristine at all times. They really are some of the most pleasant, picturesque, happy places you can visit.

Across the river is the largest cemetery in all of Switzerland. Friedhof am Hörnli is almost 150 acres with over 40,000 graves. Here, the monuments take on an even more ornate quality, with some markers soaring over 30' tall. You could visit every grave in the park and never encounter two stones that looked alike.

The park is home to a herd of white-tailed deer, and seeing them bounce through rows of tulips and buttercups makes the whole scene something out of a fairytale. I'm a cremate-me-and-spread-my-ashes kind of guy, but if I had to be put in the ground, I'd be quite content to linger here.

How long I'd stay there is another story. You don't own your plot; you rent it. Your plot lease can last anywhere from 5-25 years. Most cemeteries will not renew leases. Space is an issue in Europe where people have been dying for, oh, quite a few years now. So you lease a plot, spend a decade or so underground, then you are dug up, cremated, and your space goes to the next generation of the dead. Many families keep rotating out members so that they don't have to keep swapping out headstones – they just add a first name, or economically, just keep a surname on the stone. Others, though, will simply be content to have a nice place for grandpa for the next twenty years and then give it up for another family in need of space.

Even in death, Europeans are efficient.

Not every moment was spent running around town or the countryside. Many nights were spent relaxing in front of the boob-tube. Our cable package was an enormous conglomeration of hundreds of channels from across Switzerland and Europe.

French TV calls *Spaceballs: La folle histoire de l'espace*, or "the crazy history of space".

I once watched *Inglorious Basterds* on Swiss TV. All of the German speaking parts were left as-is, complete with English subtitles at the bottom of the screen. The English language parts, however, were over-dubbed in German, with no subtitles (because, why?), meaning the whole movie was now in German. This became especially hilarious during Brad Pitt's "I want one hunnert Nazi scalps!" speech.

Weirder still was *Star Wars: The Force Awakens* over-dubbed in German. The frothing pseudo-fascist speech by Brenden Gleeson's First Order character came off a little more than Hitler-ish, making this a very uncomfortable watch.

For the most part, we watched British television because those were the English language channels available to us. We also had access to German, French, and Italian channels, Portuguese, Russian, Albanian, Greek, Turkish, and even Polish stations.

There is an Italian version of *The Great British Bake Off*. Let's just say the British have a monopoly on calm, friendly, and genteel competition shows.

I learned, watching *Portugal's Got Talent*, that Portugal does not, in fact, have any talent (at least that I saw).

I found that I liked the sound of certain languages more than others. I'm sure to be excoriated for these opinions, but being exposed to so many for so long, you quickly develop favorites and annoyances. Then again, when you really think about it, English is a pretty ugly language, so who am I to judge?

Turkish is a lovely language. Florid and melodious, you cannot escape it if you are a man in Switzerland. I'm sure that statement sounds a bit odd. Let me explain:

All barbers in Switzerland, and almost all of Europe, are Turkish.

It is the strangest stereotype I've encountered, but also one I found to be hilariously true. In all my wanderings around the city, and in all my wanderings in so many other Swiss cities, I never once encountered a men's barber shop that wasn't run or staffed by Turkish men. Insanely polished and handsome Turkish men. Slick, suave, and slavishly dressed Turkish men.

I found this to be a good thing because they are excellent barbers. The best of the best. Their work is efficient and impeccable. They are the friendliest people you will encounter in Switzerland, too. The only caveat about going to the barbershop in Europe is the music. Every Turkish barber will have Ibiza foam party dubstep blaring at high volume. It is inescapable. After a while, you take it in as part of the experience, but for the first few visits, it's weirdly jarring. Still, I miss my Turkish barbers. Even with language barriers, their skills are so on point, you don't have to say a word and they'll just instinctively know what you want. Turkish barbers are one of Switzerland's greatest assets.

French is always beautiful. Always.

I was surprised by how pleasant and melodic Greek was. I don't know what I was expecting, but I wasn't expecting something so soothing.

For as disjointed as Hungarian is, it is a surprisingly jocular language. Everyone I heard speak it sounded upbeat and positive. Then again, it could have something to do with every Hungarian person I interacted with was upbeat and positive.

Portuguese has always sounded like drunken anthropomorphic bees who have learned how to speak - it's all *zhzhzhzhzhzhzhzhzh* every other syllable. It always sounds fuzzy to me. I told my Brazilian friend this and she thought it was quite funny. Lisa, who used to travel to Sao Paolo for work, thought I was insane.

"I think it's an incredibly sexy language!"

Italian to me just sounds like a boggle of vowels. It's also one of Switzerland's official languages, but unless you are in the Canton of Ticino, you'll be hard pressed to find anyone in French or German Switzerland who knows a lick of it.

Russian is mysterious. I took a couple of years of Russian language in college, and travelled to Russia twice. Maybe it's the ever-prevalent notion of spies and the Cold War and Cossacks and Rasputin, but Russian has always sounded slightly menacing and sinister, but in a fun and intriguing way.

Russians can be incredibly jovial, but only if they know you. When dealing with strangers, a concrete wall goes up and their faces become implacable. Years ago, Lisa and I had been in Moscow for over a week when we decided to visit the Pushkin Museum. Being surrounded by all that magnificent art lifted my spirits and made me happy. Turning a corner, I entered a room bedecked with a dozen Chagall pieces, and I beamed. My smiling gaze met the small eyes of a docent hunched in a corner. I made my smile warmer and willed my happiness at her and was met with a stare of such cold contempt and utter disdain that I could literally see my good mood leave my body and climb out the window. She watched me with dagger-like suspicion the whole time I was in that gallery.

Still, I have a fondness for the Russian language and enjoy spy dramas where I can flex my understanding of it.

As for German, well, now it just sounds as familiar to me as English. You got so used to it that when you did hear someone speaking English around Basel, it sounded strangely foreign. When we moved back to the US, we were watching a German language spy series on Netflix. Lisa got up to grab a snack from the kitchen, so she couldn't read the subtitles.

"You'll miss something. I'll pause it"

"Actually, I understand everything they're saying!"

We may not have been able to speak it fluently, but we were surprised how much we picked up over the course of two years. Reading was easiest (you can take your time to break down the inevitable compound words). But we could generally get the gist of spoken German, enough to have a good idea of what was being said. The inane number of grammatical rules made speaking German intimidating. I knew the vocab, but had trouble with the tenses and genders and it always gave me pause.

That words have genders in German made zero sense to my Dad. Literally made no sense whatsoever.

"What do you mean a chair is masculine? What does that mean?"

"It means that a table is considered to be a male object. A door is female. A car is neuter, or non-gendered"

"Now you're just making shit up"

"No, every word is either male, female, or neuter. Every single object in the world has a gender in German"

"Okay, but why?"

"Damned if I know"

So what does German sound like to me? It isn't the angry stereotype we see in movies (except for that Star Wars overdub - wow, that was Nazi-rific). It sounds like dyslexic English. It is neither pleasant or unpleasant. To my ear, now, it just sounds practical.

On the other hand, Swiss German is completely inaccessible to outsiders. Every Canton has its own regional dialect, making it impossible to learn as a blanket national language. Someone speaking Basler Swiss would be unintelligible to someone in Zurich who speaks Zuricher Swiss. The Swiss version of German is strange to listen to (and impossible to learn as an outsider). When our upstairs neighbor Judith asked if we had picked up any Swiss-German, I just laughed. The only thing I really picked up were two colloquialisms: to answer in the positive with a "Ja-jo!" and to randomly throw the word *genau* into every sentence.

The word *genau* is the Swiss-German equivalent of "exactly" or "right" or "dude" or "fuck yeah". Lisa and I would laugh when we heard it because it sounds like gnu, and it made us think of the '70s kids show *The Great Space Coaster* and Gary Gnu ("no news is good ga-news with Gary Gnu!"), and this is a thing that is impossible to explain to a Swiss person, that we associate the word *genau* with an anthropomorphic wildebeest puppet.

Swiss-German sounds like a Swede trying to speak German. When I gave this opinion to Claudio over drinks one evening, his face dropped, then burst into uproarious laughter.

"I will never not hear that, now, *danke*"

The winter after moving back to the States, I watched the burning of the *Böögg* with my Mom online. It was, of course, broadcast by Swiss television, so it was all in Zuricher Swiss. She validated mine and Lisa's opinion about how Swiss German sounded to outsiders.

"These people sound like the Swedish Chef got into the Schnapps"

The one linguistic stereotype that was quickly quashed, having watched so much British television, is that everyone in the UK has a posh accent, like the ones we hear in Hollywood movies. There are more British accents out there than nations the Empire colonized. The majority of Brits do not, in fact, speak with anything remotely posh or polished. Instead, Britain is a cacophony of blue-collar accents, some so thick as to be unintelligible to the average American ear. Someone from Kansas would not understand a single word out of a Geordie's mouth. A Californian wouldn't recognize a thing spoken by a bloke from Essex.

I did love that adverts on British TV used all of these diverse accents. In America, we look to the standard generic flat articulation that could be from anywhere. It's a bit boring, *innit?*

I also love that British TV (and European TV in general) isn't prudish in the slightest. Swearing is never bleeped, and is considered just normal conversation. Talk shows in particular are quite free of vocabulary censorship. In Britain, you can hear Gordon Ramsay in his true form. Nudity, too, is not something that is shied away from. Nude scenes in movies are not blurred or cut out. In fact, there is a television program that airs on regular British television that would make the average American's head explode:

Naked Attraction

This is an honest-to-God real dating program, in Prime Time, that features completely nude contestants being rated on their bodies. Segments are dedicated to examining and critiquing boobs, dongs, butts, and va-jay-jays, all in full technicolor close up. Not a single areola, butt pimple or pubic hair is blurred.

Our TV faced the giant picture windows. Across the street from us were apartments, and we could only imagine what those poor people thought, looking across the way, to see a giant flaccid dong on our massive TV set.

Go ahead, take a moment and scoot on over to YouTube and take a peek. You won't be disappointed.

On the other hand, you can watch *Family Accordion Night* on Swiss TV, if that's more your cup of tea.

Chapter Seven - Exploring Switzerland

If I could grow a proper mustache, had perfect physical but questionable mental health, and lived in the 1800s, I'd have been one of those bonkers Victorian explorers who couldn't sit still for two minutes and needed to see every inch of the globe. But I don't have a blood-thirst for hunting animals to near extinction or a tendency toward colonial evangelism, and I don't look particularly good in hats, so perhaps I am more suited to this day and age. In any event, I am an explorer at heart, and once we were settled into our new city, I could not wait to get out and see every inch of it.

My curiosity is always getting the better of me. I'm the one who is always wondering what is around the next corner. If I read about an unfamiliar place, I'm immediately searching Google Images to see what this place looks like. My fear is that if I don't keep going down a particular road or up to the top of a hill or around the next bend, I'm going to miss something cool or amazing. And when I do take a place in, I do so through the eye of a photographer. I'm always trying to find the perfect shot to encapsulate the moment or the sense of place. Every single time I am on walkabout, I'm seeing things through the lens of my camera.

Lisa sometimes loses patience with me because I will stand and wait for as long as it takes for people to move out of my way so I can capture an image sans people. Many of my friends are amazed at how many pictures I have of city centers and busy tourist areas with zero people in them.

"Just take the damned picture!"

"They'll move in a second and then I can get it"

"You know you can Photoshop people out, right?

"No, that's cheating"

My mother is also someone who would love to go out and see the world and all its magic and wonder. Her health prevents it, so she tells me that she lives her adventures vicariously through my pictures and stories. It's a family thing, I suppose. Growing up, I was always traveling. My parents divorced when I was around five years old, and as a single mother, my mom had to work a variety of jobs to support us. This meant that I spent a lot of time with my grandmother, two great aunts, and great uncle, and these wonderful Hoosiers loved to travel. I feel like I grew up in the back seat of a brown Buick Electra, tumbling down the highways of 1970s America, stopping at every Stuckey's and Howard Johnson's along the way. By the time I was nine years old, I had already been to the Grand Canyon, Tijuana, The Great Smokey Mountains, Disney World, and Catalina Island. I had visited almost thirty states before my tenth birthday. My aunt Franny and my uncle Earl were both teachers, and they introduced me to geography and map reading so that I could follow along when we made our way across the country. This love of junior orienteering led to learning about the rest of the globe, which in turn made me insanely curious about what other things are out there to see.

When my mom remarried, my new dad fit in perfectly because he, too, loved to travel. Long two-week road trips out west in our VW Bus were heaven. These trips made such an indelible mark on me that when Lisa and I moved to Denver, I took her on a mini vacation retracing parts of a family vacation to the Black Hills of South Dakota and Mt Rushmore. As we grew, the trips became less frequent, but the need to go see new places never left me. When I was at university, I was offered the opportunity to visit the USSR in 1990 and had to ask my folks for the money to go. My dad, for all his love of travel, did not understand why I wanted to go someplace so dismal and forbidden. But that was the very reason I wanted to go. I needed to see this Evil Empire for myself, and if I suddenly had the opportunity, I was going to take it.

"But don't you want to go someplace fun?"

"Oh, this *will* be fun!"

And it was one of the greatest experiences of my life. This was the trip that showed me that there are beautiful things to be found in the most depressing of places. This was the trip that showed me how people live completely different lives than we did in America. I had only just experienced the tip of the iceberg and there was SO much more of the world to see and explore and experience and enjoy. So when Lisa was presented with the opportunity to move us to Europe, I nearly jumped out of my own skin at the chance. This wasn't going to be just a few days or a week in a faraway place; this was going to be life in a faraway place. There was going to be SO much to see!

Hot diggity dog!

Augusta Raurica

My very first day trip out of Basel was just a fifteen-minute train ride east of town. In the tiny little Rhine-side town of Kaiser-Augst are the ruins of the Roman settlement, Augusta Raurica. Founded in 44BC, it is the oldest known settlement on the Rhine and served as an outpost for the Roman Empire to keep an eye on those kooky Germanic tribes across the river. Now, it is an open-air museum where you can visit the baths, a wealthy merchant's home, and the nearly perfectly preserved amphitheater. Spread out across a 10 square mile area, you can walk through fields where dozens of ancient temples once stood. It's weird to be on a gravel footpath, walking through some farmer's rapeseed fields that just happen to have marble ruins of a temple shrine to Venus smack dab in the middle of it. One field had a small temple to Juno where cows loitered like drunken plebeians on the crumbling steps.

Even walking through the town of Augst from the train platform to the museum, you'll pass a large four-foot-tall section of Roman City Wall running directly through the playground of the local school. When Lisa and I were visiting the Museum of London, there is a large section of their own Roman Wall in a courtyard, but it is well protected from curious hands and inaccessible to the general public. In Augst, however, the wall is used as a gathering spot for sticky fingered middle schoolers.

Archaeologists estimate over 20,000 people lived in the city. Quite surprisingly, in 2022, a second amphitheater was discovered in the area, leading scholars to believe the town was much a larger than previously believed. The area is now being re-examined and is expected to reveal a whole new trove of treasures and buildings.

I was already wowed by the cathedral in Basel being a thousand years old, but there is a lack of comprehension in visiting something that is over two thousand years old. Not knowing if I'd ever get the opportunity to visit Rome or Athens, I was amazed to learn that these ancient Roman ruins were just a hop, skip, and jump from downtown Basel. To actually sit in the amphitheater, to touch it, to feel it, was such a geek-out moment. You can't believe these places are still standing, let alone still being used. Yes, the town still uses the amphitheater to put on plays and concerts to this day.

I would have never thought of Roman ruins when I thought of Switzerland. But then, the country's official name is Latin (Confederatio Helvetica). I guess it seemed appropriate, then, that my first excursion in Switzerland was into its very foundation.

Veni, vidi, i obstupui

Lucerne and Mt Pilatus

Alright, we've come all this way, we had better damned well climb an Alp, right?

"Right-o, boy-o"

Lisa had asked her coworkers for advice on what would be a best first trip to the mountains, and they came back with what would be an absolutely perfect recommendation: The

Golden Circle.

Golden Circle of what, you ask?

A circle of *awesomeness*, I tell ya!

A gondola ride to the top of 7000-foot-tall Mt Pilatus on the outskirts of Lucerne, an alpine mountain coaster, a cog wheel train ride down the other side of the mountain to Lake Lucerne, and an hours-long boat cruise back to Lucerne. This was going to be epic.

We hopped a 90-minute train ride down to Lucerne (or Luzern in Swiss-German) at the crack of dawn. Oh, Lucerne. Lovely, lovely, lovely Lucerne. Gods, I love that city. After two years of exploring the country, I can confidently say that Lucerne is the prettiest city in Switzerland, and might be one of the most beautiful cities in all of Europe. It sits on the opalescent Reuss River where it empties into glistening Lake Lucerne. The skyline is defined by the onion domes of the 17th century Church of the Jesuits and the winding 15th century covered bridge that connects the two halves of Old Town. Across the lake are the soaring, snow-capped Bernese Alps. The water of the lake is crystalline blue, and the surrounding hills are all beckoning you to twirl, arms wide, and sing about how they are alive with the sound of music. This is epitome of Swiss-ness. This is the ultimate in picturesque Swiss cities. Lucerne feels immediately welcoming and happy. It feels small and quaint. Even on the cloudiest of days, Lucerne is sunny and warm.

Lucerne is also home to a coffee shop and bakery called Äss Bar.

The train station in Lucerne is located directly on the water, right next to the gleaming black-glass concert hall. You step out into the sunlight and glimpse the medieval old town across the water to your left, and Mt Rigi to your right. It's an amazing way to start any adventure in this town. It sets you in a brilliantly positive mood.

We took a short bus ride across town to the gondola depot where we would soar to the top of Mt Pilatus. We clambered aboard the first of two gondolas we would take on our way to the summit. This was a small four-seater that would take us, slowly, half way up the mountain. Our excitement was a bit tamped down as we had to share our ride with two chatty Cathys who talked nonstop, in outside voices, the entire thirty-minute trip.

The Swiss seem immune to calculated dirty looks.

The views were distractingly awesome. Up and over the pastures of the foothills and happy grazing moo cows. you were suddenly gliding over a dense spruce forest. The windows of the gondola were open and the smell was pure and intoxicating and divine. We were deposited at the gondola-haus at the middle point of the mountain, called the Fräkmüntegg.

This stop is an alpine wonderland. A massive chalet serving sausages and Raclette, cold beer and bottles of wine, sits on a cliff edge overlooking the panorama below. Considering this was June, fondue was not on the menu.

Fondue is strictly a wintertime treat, and you'll stand out as an American the minute you order it wearing shorts. If you do get the chance to try fondue while in Switzerland, there are rules. If you're the first one to lose anything off your skewer into the cheese, then you must pay for the meal. Not only that, if you're the first to lose anything off the skewer into the cheese, you must eat the crusty residue at the bottom of the pot. If you lose anything off your skewer into the chocolate, then you aren't in Switzerland because Swiss fondue is strictly the cheese variety and dessert fondue is an American invention

So you sit there on the sweeping patio, enjoying fondue only in the snowy months, and you look down on Lake Lucerne and the endless expanse of the azure, snow-capped Alps, and you cannot help but be awed.

The view is simply spectacular!

The food is fantastic (and for Switzerland, cheap!). We stopped here and ate a hearty serving of rosti (fried hash potatoes topped with a sunny-side-up egg) and swigged a bottle of cider. While you sit there, basking in the immensity of the view, you can watch kids of all ages tackle the alpine obstacle course set up along the edge of the cliff. A rope course winds its way through the nearby pine forest. Rope ladders stretch up to zip lines. Giant log balance beams wind their way through monkey bars and wobbly suspension bridges. The adventure park is massive, and it was packed with kids as young as three and four years old, geared up in hard hats, gloves, and harnesses.

"This would never, ever fly in America"

"Americans on *House Hunters International* freak out about stairs, for Pete's sake"

Down a short walking path was the alpine coaster. The longest one in Switzerland, 8CHF lets you pilot a single-rider sled down the tubular track overlooking the distant lake. The course wound through pastures of grazing heifers, doubled back on itself creating loops and tunnels, and ended at a small chalet where your sled would be hooked to a cable and you would ride it, backwards (facing the lake) back up to the starting point, taking in the epic vista as your heart pounded with adrenaline in your happy chest. This thing was fast. You had only a stick in front of you to control your speed - push forward to go fast, pull back to activate the brakes.

We loved the coaster (and the whole Golden Circle) so much that a year later, we went back and did it all again. This time, however, Lisa went full *Speed Racer*. I had gone before her and was waiting for her at the bottom trying to get a quick video of her sliding down the mountain. She should have been right behind me.

After two minutes, I was in a panic.

Then she appeared, looking very unhappy. She had wiped out taking a turn far too fast and landed in a cow field with her sled on top of her. He leg was already turning purple.

"What happened!?"

"I went too slow the last time. I wanted to see what this puppy could do. I pulled a Richard Hammond"

It was time to catch the next gondola and head to the very top. To get there, you climb aboard the Dragon Gondola - a huge 40-person, standing room only car that goes so fast, and at such a steep angle, that it actually freaked me out a little.

I'm not one who scares on things like gondolas or cable cars or flying things. When I was eight, I my aunts and uncle had taken me to visit the Royal Gorge in Colorado. My Uncle Earl and Aunt Beulah (the more adventurous pair in the group) and I decided to take the gondola ride across the chasm. Literally half way across, it stopped. The power had cut out and we were left swinging in the stiff breeze almost 1000 feet in the air. This was the '70's, so safety precautions were non-existent. A tiny chain was looped across the completely open doorway on either side of the gondola. From waist level up, there was no glass in the windows; it was all open-air. The slightest stumble and it was a tumble to certain death. We swung in the wind for over forty-five minutes before we were able to move again. My aunt got the vapors, but I was completely nonplussed.

Because the first gondola up Pilatus was slow, gentle, relaxing, I wasn't expecting the second one to be a rocket ship. It takes half an hour to get to the midway point from the bottom. It takes 8 minutes to get from the midway point to the summit in the Dragon. When it takes off, it's like being in a race car peeling out at the start line. You're thrown back and the torque leaves the gondola angled back in a tilt so that the view out the front window isn't of the mountain face in front of you, but the blur of the forest below, whizzing by at breakneck speed.

You are moving so fast that when you approach the summit, you're convinced that you are going to slam into the granite face of the mountain. Instead, you suddenly slow and are pulled into this hulking concrete bunker built into the side of the rock and exit out into what can only be described as an airport terminal. A gleaming concourse of posh Swiss shops leads you out to the observation deck. Here you can buy yourself a Rolex, a Volkswagen-sized Toblerone, and a 100-blade Swiss Army Knife.

Yes, I always do my shopping on top of an Alp. The convenience is… [chef's kiss].

Outside is a sprawling patio area with deck chairs and ice cream vendors. Across the lanai is the 19th century Pilatus Kulm Hotel. Some mustachioed Victorians hauled their tweed asses to the top of this peak, looked around and thought "zis is a perfect place for an inn!"

They weren't wrong.

All around you is an unending ocean of mountains. It is about 30 degrees cooler up here, but the sun also shines harder and burns the skin a bit (so many Swiss were getting their tan on in the canvas deck chairs). The lake looks like a puddle below. It is one of the most breathtaking views I've ever encountered. The mountains just go on and on and on. It's a thing that can never be accurately described - it must be seen to be believed. Even then, I did not believe all of this nature was possible.

"Are those people!?"

Lisa was pointing down below us on the mountainside. Sure enough, there were small groups of hikers making their way up to the deck. Only then did I notice the trails that wound down the side of the mountain and out of sight. Climbing to the top of Pilatus is, apparently, a popular activity, and most Swiss consider it to just be a "day hike". On our second trip up Pilatus, we watched a family with three kids, all under 10 years old, sauntering up the trail like it was nothing. The kids were in sandals.

To get back down the mountain, we climbed aboard the world's steepest cog wheel train. Built on a 40% grade, it takes 40 minutes to reach the bottom at the edge of the lake. The train itself is built like a staircase so that all the seats are level, so it's almost like sitting on an escalator as you go down. The hiking trails to the top wind past the train, and we lost count of the number of hikers we passed along the way. Cows graze on the steep hillside, too. I don't know how they don't just tumble down the side of the mountain. It's too idyllic for words.

Once you're down to the lakeside, you'll board a double-decker lake steamer for a 90-minute cruise back to Lucerne. Grab a seat on the open bow and enjoy 180 degree views of an alpine lake surrounded by soaring mountains, rolling green hills, and countless picturesque chalets. I got incredibly sunburnt on our first trip, and I didn't care in the slightest. The lake is so calm, the breeze so sweet. Order a cocktail from the bar below deck and enjoy the most calming boat cruise of your life. I truly cannot recount a time when I was more relaxed and Zen than I was on that first Lake Lucerne boat cruise.

Your view of Lucerne as you approach the dock is Instagram heaven. Every second on the water is a photographer's wet dream. It will never truly register with you that such a place actually exists, and that you are there, in the middle of it, and your jaw hurts from smiling so much. This will be one of the best days you have spent in your adopted country, and you will fall even deeper in love with Switzerland because of it.

The boat conveniently docks directly in front of the train station. The sun is now getting low in the sky. You have spent the entire day frolicking on a mountain and zooming across the water, and while the beautiful city winks at you and beckons, you'll just have to come back another day to enjoy her. Any excuse to come back. Lucerne still whispers in my ear late at night, asking when I'm coming back to see her.

Soon, my darling. Soon.

—

Fribourg

"So what are your plans today?"

"I'm going to go hike a gorge"

"Okay. Don't die"

I had seen someone post about the Gorge Gótteron in French-speaking Fribourg, Switzerland, and I was immediately determined to go check it out. I love gorges. They're nature with a presence. Fribourg was a city that I was curious to check out anyway. I had passed it a few times by train. You could see the spires of the city towering like sentinels on a large granite butte with a massive suspension bridge stretching out across the gorge below. This area of Switzerland was a maze of stone outcroppings, deep forested valleys, and hundreds of caves and caverns. The train ride felt like I was winding through the Appalachians.

Indeed, the train station sits atop a bluff overlooking the Sarine River, about 200 feet below. The city center is built around the winding main boulevard that snakes its way down the side of the bluff to the riverside. The cobbled street is steep, and on this damp May morning, slickery as hell. The whole of the city was built using limestone quarried from the surrounding cliffs. It gave the town a strangely British feel, like I was in the Cotswolds, but all the signs were in French and there wasn't a pub in sight. Unlike Lucerne, Fribourg exuded no warmth. Maybe it was the preponderance of cold stone, but I felt like an interloper.

Though the longer we lived in Switzerland, I noticed that it was always in French-speaking Switzerland that I felt uncomfortable. I felt like an intruder, as if everyone knew I didn't belong there. I never felt this way when I was traveling through German-speaking Switzerland. The French-speaking towns just always felt a bit too aloof to me. That's not to say that I didn't enjoy exploring them, but I also never felt bad about leaving to head back home.

I figured out how you could tell if you were in French Switzerland or German Switzerland without looking at a single sign.

Window shutters.

The shutters gave it away. German shutters are solid wood and are always left open. French shutters are slatted and are actually used as shutters, so half of them will be open and half will be closed. But they will always be slatted. I told Lisa my theory, and after we spent the day in Lausanne in French-speaking Switzerland, she realized my complete and utter genius.

But for now, snaking through this French-Swiss burg, I could feel myself tucking my head down as I made my way to the river and trailhead to the gorge.

The gorge was why I was here, and the sooner I was out of town, the happier I'd be (it is a city that looks better from a distance). Strangely enough, the gorge began right at the edge of the Old Town on the other side of the river. I crossed a 16th century covered bridge, passed through one of the old medieval city gates and followed the posted sign for the gorge down a dusty path along a babbling tributary of the Sarine. Within minutes, all evidence of civilization disappeared and I was in a lush, damp valley where the river narrowed to a small brook. The further I walked, the narrower the walls of the valley become. The air became saturated with moisture and though I was warm, I could see my breath on the air. The rocks became slippery and the vegetation became dense. The canyon walls grew taller and taller and soon I had trouble seeing the sky. It was dark and primeval. All that could be heard was the running stream of water and the rat-tat-tat of woodpeckers. For those who have been to the Dells in Wisconsin, imagine that, but on steroids. Water-carved limestone formations created a dizzying maze through the moss and ferns. It was the most calming forest I have ever visited.

The gorge extended for four miles away from town where it abruptly and unexpectedly just… ends. You step out of the forest onto a small dirt road and stretched out before you are rolling farm pastures. Route markers told me to take a right and my path took me into the most bucolic farm scene I could have ever imagined.

A centuries-old barn sat in the middle of a swaying field of golden rapeseed. In the not-so-far distance were the towering and jagged French Alps. A small plaque nailed to a wooden fence along a hedge row welcomed me to the edge of the Gruyeres region, home of the namesake cheese. Silver-hued cows lounged in fields along the path. Here, too, it was deadly quiet, with the only sound being the wind rustling the field crops. It was breathtaking. I couldn't have imagined a place existed in real life. It was a scene directly out of an Andrew Wyeth painting.

Soon I approached the edge of town. This leafy area of Fribourg, it seemed, was where the *hoi-polloi* lived. Mansions and ornate chalets sat back from the oak-lined boulevard. Couples on horseback, bedecked in formal English riding kits, passed me by. I found myself at an ornate Italianate chapel on the very edge of a cliff overlooking the city. The view was spectacular. The entirety of Fribourg was stretched out in front of me.

It was then that I realized I was on the wrong side of the river, and that the large bridges across were both a mile in either direction. Below me, at water level was a small pedestrian bridge. I would have to go down, down, down, cross the river there, and then make my way back up the cliff side to the train station above.

By now, the early afternoon sun had come out in full force, and I was sweating, to borrow a phrase, like a whore in church. Once across the bridge, I looked for the easiest way back up. To my surprise, I spied a funicular across the street and made my way over, only to find an out of order sign hanging on the ticket machine. I would have to walk. A woman watching my exasperation from across the street pointed to a staircase, and then pointed up. I followed her finger, and my heart dropped. It was the steepest set of stairs that looked like they went on all the way up to the clouds. I nodded a thank you and set off on my climb.

I counted on the way up. I counted every one of those god damned stairs and there were 99 steps in total. I had already hiked well over ten miles, and now I found myself wheezing up 99 god damned steps to get to my train. Halfway up, I was passed by an impatient woman who had to have easily been 120 years old, with one leg and twenty shopping bags in hand. I hated this city now. Hated, hated, hated it.

Of course I reached the top two minutes after my train left.

Merde

The Rhine Falls

"I need to be near water. Take me to see some water"

Lisa is a water baby. If she could live in a bathtub she would. If she didn't hate Tom Hanks with the heat of a thousand yellow suns, Splash would surely be her favorite movie. He ideal vacation is the beach. She thinks mountains are just ugly rocks and doesn't see the allure. She says the only way a landscape can be pretty is if it has water. If we took walks in town, it had to be along a river, be it the Rhine, the Birs, or the Wiese.

"We can go see the largest waterfalls in Europe, if you want"

"Book it, Dan-o!"

And so we put on our best non-slip sneakers and trained it an hour east, along the Rhine, to the city of Schaffhausen to see the Rhine Falls.

This is the Niagara Falls of Europe, but without all the Canadians and honeymooners and meth heads. Cruise ships and river barges count Basel as their last true port of call because there is simply no way around these massive waterfalls. At one point, two 19th century Italian businessmen proposed buying the falls from the government and then blowing them up so that ships could pass through (and they could charge a toll). The government gave these gentlemen a hearty "*Nein, danke*" and so the falls remain today.

Like Niagara, you can take a small boat out to the falls, experience the walls of mist, and climb up a platform on a tiny rock in the middle of the river to view the falls from above and between. We took the cascading staircase down the side of the riverbank towards the rushing edge of the falls to get soaked there instead. A wire mesh platform stretched out over the roaring rapids lets you feel as if you are floating above them as the water rages underneath your feet. The sound is absolutely deafening.

I SAID THE SOUND IS ABSOLUTELY DEAFENING!

At the top of the falls is a small castle (because, of course there is) where you can grab a coffee and pastry and learn about those crazy Italian entrepreneurs and their hair-brained scheme in detail. From here, one can head into the city of Schaffhausen with its perfectly preserved medieval castle, but we decided, instead, to hop back on the train and scoot another fifteen minutes down the Rhine to what is considered to be one of Switzerland's most beautiful villages, Stein am Rhein.

Located in Switzerland's northern nubbin' (that little bit that pokes up into Germany - go look at a map and you'll see what I'm talking about), this postcard-perfect hamlet sits on the Rhine, nestled amongst vineyards and orchards and quaint forests of maple and elm. On this side of the Rhine Falls, the river is glacial, and it nearly glows phosphorescent blue. The sky here is clear and cobalt, and the sun is Hollywood gold. Every inch of this area feels like it was designed by Walt Disney.

The town itself is one long main cobbled street lined with

ornately decorated 16th century timber-framed buildings. Every eave, every facade, every wooden window shutter is painted with scenes depicting boar hunts or religious pilgrims or fair maidens with baskets of flowers and bashful kneeling suitors. Large fountains with overflowing baskets of geraniums dot the Old Town, and the streets are clogged with cafe chairs and tables, all busy with fat British tourists eating gelato and sugar crêpes.

And us. Our fat asses ate sugar crêpes. Sugar crêpes are delicious!

Even the manhole covers are fancifully decorated with reliefs of St George slaying the dragon. Every inch of every surface has some artistic detail that just makes this tiny hamlet sing. It truly is one of the most picture-perfect places I've ever laid eyes on.

To complete her water themed day out, Lisa walked down to the river's edge and joined a small gaggle of youngsters wading in the shallows. She stood knee-deep in the crystal clear water and smiled.

"Can I swim home?"

Bern

I have a huge crush on travel host Samantha Brown. Years ago, I watched as she visited Bern. At that time, I had zero interest in ever visiting Switzerland and had never given the country a second thought. But then I saw my girlfriend visit the Zytglogge (clock tower) and float down the Aare River (in a fetching little one-piece swimsuit - *rawr*) and drink espresso on the esplanade behind the Parliament building. This must be a great place to visit if my little vixen explorer did a show there. This made me rethink the places in Europe on my list to visit should I ever get my butt over there.

When I joined Lisa on that visit to Switzerland months before our move, I chose Bern as the first place to visit.

I was so enamored of Samantha's wry little smile, that I didn't even think about the fact that she was there in the sunny, sunny summertime, and I was now standing on the same esplanade behind the Parliament building, but I was freezing my tuckuss off under a soul-sucking slate-grey winter sky. Everything was grey. The buildings were grey, the streets were grey, even the people were grey. I felt like I was in the movie Pleasantville. I couldn't find any of the colorful charm that Samantha basked in on her tour through town. It wasn't for lack of trying. I visited the famous Zytglogge and I walked down to the banks of the Aare. I also, quite stupidly, went across the river to visit the famous bear pit, where the living symbols of the city and Canton were kept for visitors to see. It was February. And what do bears do in February? Yeah, they hibernate.

After spending a couple of hours walking the streets of the Old Town, everything started looking the same to me. Without color, with a howling winter wind, and a creeping sense of jet lag, I gave up far earlier than I expected and retreated to Basel and the warm comfort of our hotel.

Once we moved to Switzerland, I decided I was going to visit Bern, Samantha style. I would find a cloudless, warm summer day and visit this UNESCO World Heritage Site properly. I could take my time and not worry about frostbite. I was also now fairly fluent enough to feel more comfortable navigating the city, the restaurants and shops. And those stupid bears would be awake this time.

The nice thing about Bern is that the whole of the Old Town

sits atop a rocky peninsula, surrounded on three sides by the Aare River. There are basically three main streets that run the length of the town, making it impossible to get lost. It is an eminently walkable city. The main drag, Kramgasse, is lined on both sides with limestone buildings that sport the longest covered shopping arcade in the world. You can walk the entire length of the avenue without ever being exposed to the elements. Swiss and Bernese flags fly from every building, creating a colorful display of patriotism from the bahnhof to the bear pit. Flower boxes in windows overflow with crimson geraniums and fountains with decorative pillars add charm and provide many, many photo ops. Other than buses, the street here is car-free - just don't get run over by the big blue tram.

The Zytglogge is a magnificent astronomical clock built in 1218 and dominates the side of the old city gate. It's the most photographed spot in town. Thing is, you have to be very careful of the angle to you take your photo. Stupidly, just feet away, also on the side of the medieval city gate, is a massive McDonald's logo.

Yes, housed inside an ancient 13th century tower is a god damned McDonald's.

While I appreciate the Swiss notion of constantly repurposing and reusing old things and spaces, this gross commercialism bleeding into an iconic piece of history is vulgar and egregious. Then again, the house where Einstein lived, and where he wrote his Theory of Relativity, is sandwiched between a liquor store and, ironically, a bagel shop.

The following winter, Lisa and I made our way back to Bern to visit the city's museums. Her first impression was the same as my own wintertime one.

"Well this place is depressing as shit"

I did, however, find a pair of hand-made woolen slippers at

the Christmas Market in the Bundesplatz. I call them my "swippers" (We would jokingly put an "sw" in front of anything to make it Swiss – slippers becomes swippers, though confusingly, this could also connote Swiss strippers).

The Bundesplatz (People's Plaza) is dominated by the Victorian Parliament building. Interestingly, Bern is not the capitol of Switzerland, even though the Parliament and Supreme Court are located here. It is simply the agreed upon meeting place of all the Cantons, and to make it easier, they built a Parliament and a Court building to do business in. Switzerland actually has no official capitol because designating one would give one Canton an advantage over the others, upsetting the balance of power in a country where all Cantons are viewed as equals (unless you're talking about Inner and Outer Appenzell, which are considered, derogatorily, the Mississippi and Alabama of Switzerland).

As grey as the city is in winter, we did find comfort at both the Kunstmuseum (art museum) and the Paul Klee Center. The latter is a fantastic museum dedicated to the expressionist/cubist/surrealist/Bauhaus painter. The building is a gorgeous Renzo Piano space that looks like a gently rolling stainless steel wave. I think this space, like the Van Gogh Museum in Amsterdam, is one of the best artist-centric museums in the world. We don't usually think of Switzerland as producing great artists - Italy, France, the Netherlands all come to mind first. In addition to Klee, the Swiss have given us some greats: Jean Tinguely (who has a fabulous namesake fountain and museum in Basel), Alberto Giacometti, Sophie Taeuber-Arp, and H R Giger (of Alien xenomorph fame, who has his own namesake museum in his home town of Gruyeres), to name a few. If you're an art lover, the Paul Klee Center is an absolute must see.

Many guide books recommend crossing the river and hiking up to the Rose Garden that overlooks the city. I smartly waited until my summer sojourn to do so. From this elevated vantage point, you can see the entire Old Town, all while enjoying a glass of sparkling pink wine at the Orangery. The rose part of the rose garden is small, but the park itself is immense, snaking along the top of a cliff with perfect views of the whole of Bern. On such a day of sunshine and fully blooming flowers, I took some of my best photographs yet. There was one more vista, though, that I was itching to take my camera to.

On my winter trip to the city, the cathedral, with its towering spire, was closed for renovations. I was told that the best place to get aerial pictures of the entire city was at the top of the church. Now that I was here on a clear sunny day, and the church was re-opened to worshipers and tourists, I was hoping to get some fantastic photographs of the rooftops below.

"You cannot go to the top of the Münster alone. You might throw yourself off the building"

I had received this same unnerving response when I wanted to climb the bell tower of the Basel Münster on my first trip to the city. I heard it again in Fribourg.

What is it with the Swiss and suicide by bell tower!?

Interlaken

"I need to be near water. Take me to some water"

"How about a boat ride?"

"How about hell yes!"

The summer was one of the hottest on record, and walks along the Rhine just wasn't cooling us off the way we needed. After some consultation with the internet, we found just the remedy.

The town of Thun (pronounced toon) sits at the northern edge of the likewise-named Lake Thun. From this little medieval village, one can board a boat for a leisurely two-hour cruise, running the length of the lake down to the city of Interlaken, gateway to the Alps. Along the way, there would be stops to visit the myriad of tiny castles and boutique chateaus that dotted the lakeshore. A first-class ticket bought us seats on the open-air upper deck with unobstructed views and access to a fully stocked cocktail bar. Sunshine, lake breezes, castles, Aperol Spritzes, Alps, and your fully contented sweetheart. What more could a person want?

I had visited Thun the year before. I was told that the view from the top of Thun Castle, on a high bluff, was to die for: all of the Old Town, the river, the lake, and the Alps (specifically the Big Three - The Eiger, The Mönch, and The Jungfrau, among the tallest mountains in Europe). Weather is weird in such a mountainous country. There wasn't a cloud in the sky when I departed Basel, but upon exiting a long train tunnel through a mountain, it was pouring rain. Through another tunnel and it was once again sunny. By the time I reached Thun, it was partly cloudy, but nothing terrible. I lazily skulked about the small but cozy Old Town, explored the covered bridges that spanned the mouth of the Aare River, and enjoyed an al fresco lunch. By the time I started my climb to the top of the castle, the sun had disappeared completely behind a carpet of low clouds. The lake could not even be seen at this point, and its shore was only a kilometer away. I was a fool for not having done the castle first! A fool, I tell you! So I never did see a single mountain across the lake.

I decided to take a walk along the lakeshore anyway. The breeze had picked up, the temperature had started to drop, and the first inklings of autumn hung in the air. Even if I couldn't see the Alps, the lake itself (at least, what I could see of it), was lovely. Mist clung to the hills along the lake's edge. The first hints of leaves changing color could be seen on the rows of oak trees that lined the promenade that snaked along the curve of the lake. It was atmospheric and haunting and wonderfully calming. I grabbed a seat on a bench and stretched out for a spell. I could sit here for hours, I thought.

"I don't care if we are in Switzerland and I should be drinking schnapps and shit - I want a margarita SO bad!"

And like that, my reverie was broken as two twenty-something speed-walkers tumbled by in all their Lululemon American glory.

Today, however, there was no chance of this glorious view being once again hidden from me. The sun was shining so brightly that all the colors popped that much harder. Even my sunglasses needed sunglasses.

The boat dock was right beside the train station, and soon we were off. Like a Hollywood movie, the lake was slow to reveal itself, hidden behind a bend in the river, thick forests on either side. We had to go slow in this narrow passage of river. It was hilariously suspenseful waiting to clear the river and see what I had missed the year before. Suddenly, the foliage cleared and out before me was a scene so unreal that I would swear I was in The Matrix. The lake is such a deep shade of blue that it looks artificial. Sloping Kelly green hills peel away from the lake, dotted with dozens of the most wonderfully cliché Swiss chalets. And in the distance, at the far end of the lake, peeking over the grassy hills, are the snowy peaks of the Swiss Alps. I don't know if I have ever been so shocked by something. Shocked because it was literally too perfect to be real. As we steamed out into the lake, we could see the first of many castles approaching on our port side. A small stone fortress stood on a tiny peninsula, its technicolor red and white Swiss Cross flag fluttering tall in the lake breeze. We considered disembarking to explore this little port of call, but decided we just wanted to be on the water.

Half way through our journey, the Eiger, Mönch, and Jungfrau growing ever taller and taller in our view, we docked at the village of Spiez. On the edge of a tiny little harbor was a fairytale castle, with soaring ramparts and stone walls dripping ivy and wisteria. Nestled in the center of the town, amongst the wood-shingled rooftops, was a gleaming white church, and atop its steeple was a shiny golden cross reflecting sunlight in every direction. Behind this scene were hillside vineyards and orchards and pastures full of cows wearing sweetly clanging bells. Spiez was a living, breathing stereotype of everything Swiss. It was so breathtaking from the boat that we thought we might spoil the magic if we got off to explore. We didn't want to break the spell. We just sat with our jaws open, pinching each other because neither of us could believe we lived here.

As we neared the end of the lake, we prepared to make our first and only stop. I had read about a series of cliff-side caves and waterfalls high above the lake and was curious to see it. Lisa agreed that the cool dampness of a cavern would be a fun way to cool off on such a blistering summer day. We jumped off at the tiny dock with just two other people. A small wooden sign pointed up the hill. This dirt path was the only way to go as we were surrounded by thick forest. As we began to climb, the path got steeper and steeper and steeper. The grade became more and more vertical, to a point where I seriously thought we might need ropes and crampons to continue on. Our knees began to scream and we were now both drenched in sweat. Lisa was NOT happy.

"Screw [gasp] these [gasp] caves"

"Yeah, you're right. Screw these caves"

And we mostly tumbled ass-over-teakettle back down to the

dock and waited for the next boat to arrive so we could continue our journey.

Once back on board and thoroughly re-hydrated, we approached the town of Interlaken. Located on a narrow stretch of land, the town served as a bridge between Lake Thun and Lake Brienz, and also as the official Gateway to the Alps. The town was nestled in a tiny green valley between the Jura mountains to the north and the Swiss Alps to the south. The two lakes lay on either side. Cutting through the town from one lake to the other was a canal, and we snaked down this narrow waterway to the quay by the western train depot.

From here, we disembarked and walked the main drag through this Victorian resort town. A storm of skydivers rained down upon us, landing in the large field across from the Hotel Interlaken. Shops sold two things - hiking gear and skiing gear. Just before reaching the train depot of Interlaken *Ost* (East), we veered off the main drag to catch a gondola. We were heading straight up the sheer Jura mountain wall behind us.

Harder Kulm is a mountaintop vantage point 650 feet above the town of Interlaken. A large restaurant sits perched on the mountain's edge where you are afforded the most perfect and stomach-churning view of the city, both lakes, and the Three Sister mountains of Eiger, Mönch, and Jungfrau. If you are brave enough, a small walkway extends out over the edge so that you can feel as if you are floating over the valley. I don't know if there is a better total view in all of Switzerland. We had experienced a lot of amazing vantage points, but none encompassed so much wonder at once. The giant mountains are so close you feel as if you can reach out and touch them across the valley. The lakes, from up on high, are bluer than any blue you have seen, or will ever see again. This is a scene that would make Bob Ross break down in happy little tears.

We sat there, drinking house-made apple *schorle* and just marveled at it all, for hours. We were transfixed. We couldn't leave. I've never felt so glued to a spot.

Eventually, we made our way to the gondola and the station below to catch our train back home.

Neither of us is religious, but that day, we saw the divine, and it blew our god damned minds

---

Lauterbrunnen

We knew we were heading back to the States in August. I had time to make one last day trip. I had to decide what the last place in Switzerland I was going to see. Choosing Lauterbrunnen was no contest. I never read it, and am not a big fan, but this was the place that JRR Tolkien based the elvish land of Rivendell on. This was also a favorite spot of the divine travel minx Samantha Brown. She biked the valley and bought cheese from a vending machine and I was going to find that vending machine come hell or high water. For Samantha.

This is the picture you most often see of Switzerland. The small village with its quaint church steeple in the foreground, the soaring granite cliffs behind, and a stunning waterfall tumbling down the mountainside, seemingly right into the center of town. Yes, this is the famous waterfall village in the alpine valley, and I was going to hike the entire length of that valley, and dance in the mist of waterfalls and find the magical cheese vending machine and take about a bajillion pictures. I was going to soak up the most Swiss of Swiss places before we had to reluctantly leave.

To get to Lauterbrunnen, I had to take a three-hour train journey to Interlaken where I changed trains for a picturesque chug into the foothills of the Alps. I was heading directly for the Jungfrau, one of the tallest mountains in Europe. My destination was a teensy tiny little hamlet at the head of a deep gorge valley that led all the way to the foot of this magnificent alp. Disembarking from my train in the town of Lauterbrunnen, it was a little bit crazy to be so close to these magnificent mountains. They towered so closely overhead that it felt like you were standing in the apse of a great cathedral.

The town itself is tiny. One small little street with about four or five souvenir shops, housed in dark brown shingled chalets with cascading flower boxes and bright green shutters. I had no interest in these cutesy little shops. I was interested in what towered over them: Staubbach Falls. One of the tallest waterfalls in Europe at 980 feet, they're the main attraction here. On days when the breeze blows just right, the whole of the town is misted from the tumult. They're that close to town. The village is built directly buttressing the sheer cliff wall. The scale of everything feels distorted because all of these massive walls of granite are so close to you that it can actually induce a strange sense of vertigo. Imagine going into your backyard and your fence is now made up of an unending wall of Sears Towers (I'm from Chicago and I will never, ever, call it the Willis Tower, sorry). That scale and that intimate forced perspective creates an overwhelming sense of majesty.

I walked to the end of the street to get closer to the falls and discovered that you can hike up behind them. You bet your ass I was going up there! Climbing a waterfall is one of the coolest things you can do on a hike. This wouldn't be my first rodeo.

When I turned 25, my good friend Chris took me on a birthday hike in Turkey Run State Park in southern Indiana.

It had been rainy for quite some time, so we knew it would be muddy, but were well prepared. We set off and decided that we were going to tackle the toughest trail in the park. Little did we know that we should have done the loop in a clockwise route instead of going counter-clockwise. One direction meant descending a waterfall. The other meant climbing it.

We ended up climbing it.

Better still, it's not technically a waterfall, but there had been so much rain, that this rocky cliff became a raging one. This meant free climbing up the slippery rocks as icy cold rain water pummeled us in the face. It took us the better part of two hours to make it up the 100' rock face. By the time we reached the top, we were both completely caked in mud and soaked to the bone, and had another five miles of hiking ahead of us. But we were completely happy and pumped. We had accomplished something rather dangerous and unexpected, and it was incredibly thrilling. After that experience, I purposefully sought out trails that included waterfalls to navigate, or hike near, or peer over. So when the idea of hiking up behind the tallest waterfall in Europe was an option, you're damned skippy I was going up there.

It's a steep climb for about 100 feet, then you enter a long tunnel carved into the mountainside where you meet a long series of soaking wet metal stairs. Up and up you climb until you are on a skinny precipice. On your left is a sweeping view of the village and the Alps across the valley. To your right are the thundering falls dumping hundreds of gallons of water a second just a few feet away. You still have more steps to climb to reach the back of the falls where you can cool off in the cold, snowmelt water. Standing now about 450 feet higher than you started, you can see from one end of the valley to the other. On all sides are sheer rock cliffs zooming a thousand feet or more into the air. Peeking out behind are leviathans of snow frosted Alps. Standing sentinel at the end of the valley is the queen of the Alps, the

Jungfrau (or Young Lady). It looks like a painting. It doesn't look real. Places like this just cannot be real.

Back at the bottom, I stop to use the public loo before I set off on my walk across the valley floor (spotless, of course). I notice that all the signs in this area, for the loo, for the tourist office, the directional signs, are all in English and Chinese. It is such a tourist hot-spot that I realize that almost nothing is in German. Looking around, I am surrounded by Chinese tour groups. Most come just to look at the falls and will then take the cable car up to the top of the mountain to the towns of Gimmelwald and Grindelwald. I usually appreciate a good mountaintop vista, but being on the valley floor afforded such a unique perspective that I had no desire to go up.

This mean that my hike should be free of tourists and groups and loud chatter. Just moving a few yards past the falls and I was basically alone. A perfectly flat, perfectly paved path led away from town, through the valley, and off towards the Jungfrau. I thought the views from town were amazing, but the further I travelled, the more epic everything became. The cliffs grew higher, and the valley grew narrower. For most of the walk, the valley was never more than 300 yards across. This created an incredible sense of scale and awe. The rolling green fields are all active farms, and, as always, sleepy cows grazed in the warm sunshine. Every quarter mile or so, I would pass a farm house. These were the exact buildings everyone pictures when thinking of Switzerland. Three story chalets, with stone bases, dark shingled wood, flower boxes full of geraniums and edelweiss, green shutters with hearts carved in the middle, and a sharply peaked roof. Every house had a garden of flowers out front that would make Martha Stewart need a towel. Massive granite cliffs with tumbling waterfalls provided an unparalleled backdrop. This was, after all, the "Valley of 79 Waterfalls". It seemed that the whole of the valley was weeping from on high there was so much cascading water.

At one farm, along the walk, was an honor box. I love Swiss honor boxes. You will encounter them all over the country, and they can only work in a society where honor is ingrained into the psyche.

If Klingons yodeled, they'd be Swiss.

Here was an actual refrigerated case, built into a wooden shelter. On offer were glass bottles of milk and wedges of homemade cheese. I took a block of Emmentaler and left my 10CHF in the cash box (which is not locked in case you need to make yourself change). When I got home and tried my purchase, I was floored. You could actually taste the wildflowers in the milk used to make this cheese. It was one of the most unreal and epic culinary experiences I've had to date. I'm not a big cheese person, but this stuff was Biblical.

As I was packing my purchase away in my pack, a woman sauntered up from the trail behind me. She looked the whole case over and then looked at me quite confused.

"Where do you put the money in?"

"Oh, no, you use the cash box, there"

"It's not locked!"

"No, of course not"

"Wow. This shit would never fly in Jersey. How do they know I'm even paying for this stuff?"

"Honor system"

"Holy shit"

We chatted for a bit about these Swiss honor box wonders. I had bought honey from one in Flüh, and strawberry jam from another in Bettingen. I told her there were even ones that sold booze.

"Oh, get the fuck outta here!"

When we were in the small town of Frick, Lisa and I walked the Cherry Blossom Trail (*Chriesiweg*) through the Jura foothills to take in the spring cherry blossoms. Here, too, were honor boxes, sitting under the orchard trees, offering bottles of cherry liqueur and cherry wine. Large dispensing jugs allowed you free samples of each before you bought a bottle.

"You're telling me they had booze just sitting out in a field for people to take, and nobody stole anything?"

"That's how it works here"

"I live in the wrong place"

She selected a few cheeses and put her money in the box, smiling from ear to ear.

I continued on my walk in a fabulous mood. It was forecasted to be 60F and partly cloudy on this day, but instead, there wasn't a cloud in the sky and the temperature hovered near 75F. For long periods, I had the footpath to myself, and could linger and take pictures, and breathe in the sweet Alpine air. Soon the road turned and crossed a small rushing stream. It was milky blue. Pure glacial runoff. Even the footbridge was festooned with overflowing flower boxes. From here, I would meander over to the other side of the valley to visit Trummelbach Falls

These waterfalls are inside the mountain.

This is one of the very few places in Switzerland were you will have to pay to see some nature, but at 12CHF, it was totally worth it. First, you enter a funicular which takes you half way up, inside the mountain. Now, you will climb a series of stairwells and carved passageways 460 feet to the top of the falls. You'll watch the falls come flying over the top of the mountain into a large cavern. From there, it will carve its way down through a series of dells, like a maze of limestone Swiss cheese. The temperature inside the mountain, from all the water and moisture and spray is just above freezing. Every surface is slick and you have to hold on to the railings or you'll be screaming down the world's toughest Slip 'n Slide. The roar of the water is absolutely deafening inside the echo-y caverns. As you descend deeper and deeper towards the valley floor, sunlight from above is replaced by artificial spotlights. The lower you go, the colder it gets. Soon, the falls exit the mountain and once again pour along the outer walls of the canyon. You are back in the warm sunlight and standing on a promontory overlooking the whole of the valley below. The slopes of the canyon are covered with herbaceous pines and the scent is overpowering. A gentle sloped path leads you back down to ground level through a picturesque forest of firs. In no time, your wet clothes are dry again and you're ready to continue your journey.

Back on my valley path, I came across a small wooden hut with a few red benches and a small fountain (where I refilled my water bottle). Here was the famous vending machine.

Which was empty.

I was too late. The early *oiseaux* got my *fromage*. Still, I let my fingers linger over the buttons that Samantha had once caressed, and comforted myself with the knowledge that I had at least hit the honor box in time to get some treats. Damned tourists ruined my pilgrimage. I failed you, Samantha, my love.

The rest of my walk was quiet, through the working farm fields of rapeseed, wheat, and cows. I passed many more picture-perfect chalets, all framed by waterfalls and limestone cliffs. I sat for a spell underneath the large Dragon-style gondola whisking people up to the mountaintop village of Mürren, where travelers would catch their scenic train rides to the top of the Jungfrau (and Europe's highest train depot).

I was nearing the end of the valley, as it was narrowing and narrowing and I was completely in shadows now from the surrounding Alps. I had been on my journey for hours, and so I stopped at small eddy in the creek and took a quick splashy-splash in the icy water.

I had reached the super tiny village of Stechleburg, which consisted of a Bed and Breakfast, a post office, and three houses. A banner of Swiss and Bernese flags fluttered above the roadway and not a soul could be seen or heard. This is where I would catch the Post Bus back to Lauterbrunnen (it was true – you could get to any city, village, town, or hamlet, no matter how small, by public transport!). The air conditioning felt wonderful as I (the bus was empty except for me) slowly lumbered back to where I started. By the time I got on the train back to Interlaken, I was beat. But it was a happy tired, a fulfilling tired. I had completed the best walk of my life. I have seen many fantastic things in my life, been to many of the world's wonders, but I'm not sure anything, ever, will top the Lauterbrunnen Valley. Go Google it, and marvel, and then put it at the top of your bucket list. If you ever make it to Switzerland, you find a way, come hell or high water, to get your ass to Lauterbrunnen.

Sprinkle my ashes here, please.

I realize that it sounds like everywhere you go in Switzerland is epic and amazing. And you would be right. Even the ugly parts (and every country on earth has ugly parts) are honestly not that ugly. Sure, Olten, the transportation hub of Switzerland, is the butt of thousands of jokes amongst the Swiss, but it's not really that bad. It has a castle and an Old Town and is surrounded by the bucolic Jura mountains. Every town in Switzerland has a castle and an Old Town, and if you can at least spend ten minutes admiring those things, you'll realize that even the drabbest of cities (looking at you Biel/Bienne) have hidden charms.

Even the ordinary suburbs of Basel were full of wonderful things. Ten minutes south, in the village of

Arlesheim, are the Hermitage Gardens. Hundreds of acres of pristine woodland, hiking trails, and, yes, castles, is the most relaxing place to find nature and solitude. I loved to go there in the autumn when the leaves were at their peak. There is nothing like the turret of a 15th century castle poking its head above a sea of red, yellow, and orange trees rolling on forever around you.

Head to Rheinfelden, twenty minutes down the Rhine, and sit in the 15th century baroque Italianate church of St Martin and listen to the soft, piped in chamber music. Better yet, do it at Christmas and listen to choirs singing yuletide hymns.

Stop in Lenzburg in the Jura Mountains and visit a sprawling 13th century castle and fortress with 360 degree views of the pristine Aargau Valley. Take a train to St Ursanne in French-speaking Switzerland and visit the tiny walled city that sparked the Victorian "Grand Tour". That cliché in costume dramas where some old rich person claims the young couple must take a Grand Tour of Europe? It all started in pretty little St Ursanne.

While you may never be more than fifteen minutes from water in Switzerland, you are also never more than fifteen minutes from stunning nature, breathtaking cathedrals, wonderfully preserved castles, or charming city squares.

Sometimes, the further you get away from the touristy areas, the more amazing your finds. I never once spent a day out, on either a neighborhood walkabout or a day trip in some far flung corner of the country, without finding something amazing.

It is impossible not to be constantly wowed.

239

Chapter Eight - Exploring Other Places, Too

The idea was, once we were settled into our new Central European home, the whole of the continent would be at our beck and call. I'd ping Lisa at work and tell her, sorry I won't be home for dinner, I'm skulking about Belgium. Of course, the reality is, things are further away than you think, and while train travel is the best travel, it's not the cheapest. Oh, and then a pesky little thing called the Global Covid Pandemic kind of put the kibosh on all of our travel plans. One of the things we were looking forward to most was visiting friends in Edinburgh and Brighton up in the UK, but the plague of our century prevented it.

Lisa's job was originally slated to be nearly 40% travel, with opportunities to visit other offices and clients in places like Munich, Leipzig, Lisbon, and Copenhagen. I was champing at the bit to tag along. Once she was settled into her new position, and we had our lives pretty well set up, I'd book a ticket on the next train or plane with her, and wander and wonder while she was in the office. I'd accompany her to Milan, check Italy off my travel list, and zip thirty minutes north to sip Nespresso with George and Amal Clooney at their Lake Como villa. You know, stuff like that there.

It never happened.

We waited too long, and the global shutdown kept her not only confined to Basel, but to working from home. My only Clooney contact was limited to his wryly squinting eyes on the large posters hanging in the Nespresso shops of Basel. If Lisa couldn't even go across town to the office, I had little hope of hopping the ICE Express to Gräfelfing, Germany any time soon. But we did get out of Dodge as often as we could, when we could afford it, and when time permitted, and obviously when the world wasn't masked and shuttered. To be sure, most of my journeys outside of Switzerland proper kept me in the French and German vicinities, and that was perfectly fine. There were plenty of things to check out in our immediate surroundings, and it was always fun to experience the differences between neighboring countries and cultures. We were fortunate to get out and see some burgs in farther European climes as well, just not as many as we had hoped. Above all other things, though, and making me happiest, was getting to cross off one of my ultimate travel bucket-list items.

We had been in Basel for a month or so when it dawned on me that I could walk to both France and Germany from my house. Pretty cool, right? I sat down with Google Maps and decided to see which was quicker to get to, and exactly how far was I from each border, and could I, indeed, walk there. After plotting the closest border crossing, I figured out that Germany was 5.7km from home, and France was 4.6km. Some maths later and I had 3.5 miles and 2.8 miles to traverse to reach my destinations. That was nothing! That's just an afternoon stroll. I had this in the bag. This was going to be so cool.

"I'm off for a walk"

"What are you checking out today?"

"France"

"You going shopping?"

"Nope. Just for a walk"

"To France?"

"Yep"

"Um… why?"

"Because. I. Can."

I set off towards the French border first because it was the shorter of the two walks. Less than three miles wasn't much, especially since it was all urban walking. I wasn't going to be scaling hill and dale to reach my destination. I just thought of it as an opportunity to explore the outer reaches of town that I wouldn't ordinarily be in.

I'm always down for urban walkabouts. From our leafy little quarter of the Gundeldingen I headed toward the chic Schutzenmatt neighborhood on the other side of the Zoo. One of Basel's largest parks was here, all hidden under a sprawling canopy of chestnut trees. In the fall, the park is swarmed with nut collectors, snapping up buckets and buckets of chestnuts. It becomes impossible to walk the park paths because of the sheer number of nuts on the ground. It becomes a slapstick adventure, like trying to run across a marble-strewn floor. These chestnuts, though, aren't the kind for human consumption, but are prized as animal feed.

The Swiss are notorious urban foragers and scavengers. You will find hundreds of Baselers out in the city parks and local forests picking wild garlic, blackberries off bushes, and fruit hanging juuuust over the fence of the tree's owner. Yes, if you walk down a neighborhood street and a house has an apple tree in its yard, you can pick any fruit that hangs on the public walkway side of the fence. I used this loophole to occasionally bring bouquets of flowers home to Lisa.

As I moved on past the park, the rows of apartments went from tony brownstones to concrete bunkers. The further from the center of town I got, the more I understood why I didn't frequent this part of Basel. Feeling very Soviet, this part of the city was mostly 1970s personality-free apartment blocks. Nothing here gave any character indication of my still being in Switzerland. I was taken aback at just how generic the whole area was. Soon, housing gave way to industrial warehouses and office parks. The area began to look a lot like suburban Indianapolis, with apologies to both Basel and Indianapolis.

I came upon an enormous walled cemetery that seemed to stretch forever in both directions. Walking along the stone wall for a few blocks I found the street that held the border crossing. Turning the corner, I stopped up short.

The only thing that has disappointed me more was Tom Brady un-retiring from the NFL.

There before me was a tiny little service road leading to a concrete mill and factory in a large dirt field. A bent metal pole held a small *Landesgrenze* sign (country border) with decals of a Swiss and French flag. Beyond the mill was open miles of nothingness. The city of Basel abruptly ended at the border. Even the paved road ended at the signpost, and a gravel trail began on the French side. On the Swiss side of the street was industry, housing, roads, and life. On the French side was a concrete mill and fallow farm fields. There was no customs kiosk, no road barrier, no "*Bienvenue à France*" sign, no indication that anyone in the entire world cared that these two nations met at this spot.

It was one of the most underwhelming experiences of my entire life, and I watched Geraldo open Al Capone's vault on live television. Here I had proudly walked from my new Swiss home to the nation of France and I was met with… dust and ennui.

Bien merde.

I snapped a few pics. No one would believe that a border crossing could be so dreary. True to form, my Facebook post that afternoon elicited exactly what I thought it might. My mother wrote "wow, that sucks" and my sister said it was "super depressing". Another friend posted "see, this is why you should never go to France".

Point taken.

But I did it. I achieved my goal. I had walked to France. From my house.

Backtracking, I hopped the closest tram and made my way back to town. I was starting to wonder if it was worth going to the German border. I mean, I had already taken the tram over to Weil am Rhein to shop, but my walk to the German border would take me to another unfamiliar part of town, and I wasn't sure I was ready to be disappointed a second time. But I had to walk to Germany from my house because I could. This time, though, not only would I bring snacks and water and Haribo, I'd pack some tempered expectations

It was a few weeks later while on casual walkabout near the Rhine that I realized I was already halfway to my intended jaunt-to-Germany end point. It was a muggy late summer day and I wasn't really prepared for a longer journey, but figured, what the hell, let's do this. Unfortunately, I did not have my pack of treats and water and Haribo and tempered expectations with me. This would be a wholly unexpected and unsupported journey. I would be taking my chances. I would become an urban Bear Grylls.

To quote Farmer Ted from the 1984 John Hughes teen comedy classic, Sixteen Candles: "I'm a gambling man by nature…"

My intended crossing point was at the far eastern edge of Basel on the other side of the river. Here, the sprawl of Basel gave way to the edges of the Black Forest. Just across the border was a German yacht club, and that was where I set my sights. A yacht club had to yield a far better experience than a cement factory. I just had to get myself there.

I followed the Rhine past where it meets the Birs River. A gorgeous park surrounds this juncture and a small sandy beach is one of the most popular places for Baselers to cool off during the warmer months. I had never ventured past the Birs, so this was new territory for me. The park was lovely, complete with the requisite small animal farm at the local daycare center. Of course I had to stop and give noggin' rubs to a friendly donkey and chat a bit with the goats. The park and the river began a sweeping bend here, and as I continued on, I was surprised to find myself at a massive dam and locks spread out across the river. You cannot see these massive structures from the city, so I didn't even realize they were there. Unsure of which way to go from here, I spied a pair of joggers who crossed a short footbridge onto an island where the locks were and followed them. Fully loaded barges queued to make their way down-river towards Strasbourg, then Cologne, on to Rotterdam, and finally the North Sea. Another footbridge put me on a pedestrian and cycle path atop the hydroelectric dam. A mid-century masterpiece, it's a striking example of form-meets-function architecture.

It even had a fish ladder for all the… fish.

On the north side of the river now, I had only to walk along the water's edge until I reached my destination less than a kilometer away. But the footpath suddenly ended at a stairwell heading up to the busy road above. Climbing up, I was face to face with a four lane highway that was under construction, in both directions, as far as the eye could see. The sidewalks heading to the east, and to my destination, were blocked off.

Scheisse!

At that moment, like a cliché, the skies opened up and it began to rain. I was thisclose to my destination, but I couldn't find a good way around the construction closures that would get me to the border without making a massive detour. My shoulders sank and I could feel my lip curl in frustration.

I decided I would have to try another spot on another day.

Not only did it take me almost an hour to find my way to the nearest bus stop, it took me longer to get home on a series of busses and trams, because of all the detours, than it did to walk there.

Sadly, I never did get the chance to walk from our flat to the German border. I crossed the border many, many times, but never after leaving home on foot. It was a goal I failed to achieve, and my shame hangs heavy around my neck. I feel as if I should wear a crimson letter L around my neck, but I'm afraid Boomers might think my name is Laverne.

It occurred to me, though, that I could walk through all three countries on the same day. I would traverse Switzerland, Germany, France, and Switzerland again, all in one go. After all, these three countries meet in one spot (in the middle of the Rhine) and all have open borders accessible by foot. I became determined to do it because I could. Three countries in less than thirty minutes. Bring it.

To start, I jumped the #8 tram to Germany, as if I was going to the Marktkauf. Instead of going all the way to Weil am Rhein, I got off at the last tram stop in Switzerland. From here, I would walk across the bridge that straddled the entry to the Port of Basel, and saunter on down to the border crossing. At least here, the Germans have put up a large colorful sign welcoming you to Baden-Württemberg. It's far more festive than crossing over into France, that's for sure. Even crossing into Switzerland is incredibly underwhelming. No matter where you cross over into Switzerland, it is always just a tiny little metal sign the size of an American license plate with just the Swiss flag painted on it. It's kind of laughable. The Swiss are like, "yeah, you are here, so what?".

Once across the border, I would pass the Marktkauf grocery store. On the north side of the store is another bridge that crosses the Rhine, called the Friendship Bridge. This will take you from Germany over to Huningue, France (a suburb of St Louis, which is a suburb of Basel). A quick check of my watch tells me that so far, I have spent all of fifteen minutes walking from Switzerland to Germany to France. My goal of three countries in thirty minutes was already completed, and in half the time!

In the very middle of the Friendship Bridge is a small metal sign with the French and German flags painted on it. Again, that's all she wrote. It's weird to an American, this lackadaisical welcome (or lack thereof). In the US, each state greets you with enormous twenty-foot-tall billboards with slogans like "Welcome to Utah, home of bees and Mormons!" or "Welcome to Illinois, home of Rampant Corruption!". Though I suppose loud patriotic banners aren't really a rage in Germany anymore…

The town of Huningue is odd. It's as if an American contractor was tasked with building the theme park version of a French city square. While it all looks kind of Gallic, you realize it's all new pre-fab construction with zero personality.

It's actually rather insulting. I've been in a mall food court *Au Bon Pain* that felt more genuinely French than the main square of Huningue, France. Had the French tri-color not been flying in the center of the square, I'd have been hard pressed to tell you which country I was standing in. My answer might well have been Epcot.

Now that I was on the other side of the Rhine, I would simply follow it upriver back to Basel, following the south bank promenade.

I followed the footpath along the river for about fifteen minutes or so until I come to a spot where a small tributary interrupted my way. Seeing a beautiful tree-lined river winding its way into town, I decide to follow it for a while, sure to find a bridge over to get me back on my way back to Basel. The Canal de Huningue quickly began to narrow and grow rocky and swift. Soon I found myself in the middle of a whitewater rafting training center and competition course. Teams of firefighters were practicing water rescues, and I sat and watched from the walkway above. Moving on, I came upon a four story tall rock climbing wall with children as young as four being taught how to scale the craggy face. A torrent of toddlers was being geared up and sent scrambling up the wall, all without an ounce of fear.

My wanderings led me to a beautiful manicured garden and a small footbridge over the canal where I was able to head back toward the Rhine. For as disappointed as I have been every time I've been across the border to France, this little slice of green and adventure took me by pleasant surprise. To be fair, subsequent journeys into St Louis and the French burbs never revealed any further hidden gems or pleasant surprises. This was the anomaly, and frankly it made me a little sad.

I really wanted to spend lots of time wandering around and exploring the French side of the border. It was so close and I truly thought it would reveal many splendid things. I imagined a cozy Old Town or sidewalk cafes or some fun architecture. Instead, I was met, on every turn, with what looked like an alternative future where the USSR had invaded France. Again, let me stress, once you got out of the French suburbs of Basel, France once again becomes France. But here, on the edge of the city, it was Francostan. A Gallic gulag, if you will.

Once back on the shore of the Rhine, it was time to head back to Switzerland. By now the sun was out in full force and there wasn't a single tree or slice of shade for the next two miles of my walk. I was sweating like a glassblower's ass. Almost all of the Rhine Promenade in Basel is wonderfully tree-lined, and I was expecting the same along this part of the river. Instead, I was in a cleared-out strip of land that left the riverbank barren. My view across the river was the industrial Port of Basel and all its barge-docked wonder. On this side of the river, I found myself walking along the fenced ramparts of the enormous BASF and Novartis manufacturing campuses. What shade I did find was in the tiny slivers of darkness cast by towering smokestacks. There wasn't a single breath of breeze. A French seagull shrugged laconically at me, too hot to fly, and took a drag from a discarded cigarette butt.

"C'est plus chaud que le cul d'une prostituée, no?"

By the time my own exhausted butt hit the typically sad sign signifying the border (again, just a small metal rectangle with the Swiss flag), I was too tired to celebrate achieving my goal. I thought at this point I would continue on down the river into the Old Town, following the promenade down to familiar climes, and grab a beer at the Farmers Market.

It was just too hot to go on.

Of course, immediately after crossing the border, there were now trees and benches and a friendliness to the river path. Though only another two kilometers to Old Town, I instead made a beeline for the closest tram stop and just about cried when I found it was ice cold from air conditioning. A quick check of the weather app on my phone told me it was now 97F. The next day, Basel would hit a record high of 104F.

Nevertheless, I had done it. I had walked from Switzerland to Germany to France and back to Switzerland!

Because I could.

I just love stupid shit like that. Of course, it all sounded cool, but I learned that in reality, it was far from cool.

It had actually kinda sucked. Still, it was a thing I could do, and I did it.

Booyah.

I have an odd relationship with France.

Years ago, when we were going to Paris, everyone told us how rude and snotty Parisians are. They would ignore us, talk down to us, spit in our faces. We would have a miserable time. Instead, we never once encountered a single aloof Parisian, were never treated as less, and never had to wipe a Gallic loogie off our Yankee mugs. On the contrary, everyone was beyond gracious, friendly, helpful, and kind.

By the fourth day of our trip, Lisa's feet had swollen to twice their normal size and none of her shoes fit anymore. We were desperate to find somewhere to buy her a pair of shoes for the remainder of our holiday. We were in the middle of the tony St Germain neighborhood, full of tony shops and tony boutiques. Finding the French equivalent of a Payless in this part of town was not going to happen. We'd have to suck it up and fork out a fuck-ton of Euros for some designer skips. Taking a deep breath, we ducked our heads into a nearby shop that had a few pairs of ladies' shoes in the window, next to a variety of luxe overcoats and fur hats.

"Bonjour!"

First lesson of surviving Paris: always announce yourself with a friendly hello when entering any establishment.

"Bonjour!"

The ethereal Jeanne Moreau look-a-like salesperson took one look at Lisa who was limping and leaning on the door frame and ran to her. She led Lisa to a chair and had her sit down, offering her water, and tut-tutted with genuine concern. I explained our predicament and she smiled.

"I think I might have something for you, *mon cher*"

She disappeared for a moment and came back holding a pair of shiny gold sneakers that would not be out of place in Harajuku, Tokyo or the MTV Music Awards. They were gaudy and cartoonish, and yet, incredibly, incredibly cool. I tried my best to be casual about looking at the price tag.

"Oh, *non, non, monsieur*, these are very affordable. Your wife is hurt and we need to get her on her way. I would not take advantage."

True to her word, these shoes were less than €100, and they fit perfectly. After ringing us up, she even offered to have Lisa's old shoes sent to our hotel so we wouldn't have to walk around with them, but we were staying at an Airbnb, so it wasn't possible. We were blown away by the kindness this woman showed to us. Where was this infamous Parisian meanness? Where was the disdain? We had yet to see it. On the contrary, we had some of the best customer service experiences in all our travels.

Part of it could be our attempts to speak as much French as we could, even if it was bad pidgin French. In our experience, just trying was the key to successful interactions. My French is deplorable, but I try. Lisa's is marginally better. Neither of us could carry on an actual conversation. But we do our best. It's the effort that counts. Follow social rules and norms, like always saying *"Bonjour!"* whenever you enter a store or restaurant, always saying goodbye when you leave, and not assuming that everyone speaks English, and you will be treated well.

On our last evening in Paris, we stopped at a cafe near our rented flat for dinner. Everything was absolutely singing. When it came time for dessert, I was excited to see that they had Bertillon ice cream on the menu (a gourmet luxury Paris institution, I had some at least three other times that week). Not only that, they had my favorite flavor: pear.

The waiter's face fell. Apparently, they were out. Not only did they not have pear, they had no ice cream at all. I shrugged and went for my second choice without another thought. When he returned with our treats, he had two flutes of champagne with him, which we didn't order. Our French language skills not the best, we thanked him, but tried to let him know we didn't order those. A helpful older gent at the next table leaned over with a smile.

"He is embarrassed that he ruined your meal, and would like to apologize with the drinks"

Visiting in the off-season helps, too.

So when I made my first forays into St Louis, I expected that following these simple rules would lead me to the same great experiences I had in Paris. My *"Bonjour!"* fell on indifferent ears. My vain attempt at ordering *"trois tartelettes au sucre, s'il vous plait"* at the *boulangerie* was met with blank stares.

The charm of Parisians was replaced with a deep Gallic melancholy. There were no fabulously dressed ingénues strutting down the boulevards. The dress code in St Louis was strictly Wal-Mart at 10pm on a Saturday. When the locals figured out you were from across the border in Basel, they became even more surly. There is a palatable disdain between the two cities. My guess stems from the wild economic disparity between the two. St Louis is strictly industrial. Many of the pharmaceuticals that are formulated in Basel are manufactured in St Louis - the labor is French; the profits are Swiss. Basel is one of the wealthiest cities in Switzerland (if not Europe), while St Louis is one of the poorest cities in France.

It took me a long time to get used to the coldness, especially at the grocery store. Shoppers at the Géant always looked so downtrodden, and the employees were dead-eyed. And yet, I kept going back, because the quality of meats and produce and pastry made it all worth it. No matter how sad this corner of France may be, they still revere food, and thank gods for that.

Once I deduced that St Louis was a shopping-only destination, I figured France had to be France again once we got away from Basel. The next biggest town was Mulhouse. This small city shares its namesake with Basel at the Basel-Mulhouse International Euro Airport. A *ville* of 100,000 people, it is home to the largest auto museum in Europe, and from day one, I was itching to see it.

I love car shows, car museums, car expositions. Do I know anything about cars? Mechanically, no. But I appreciate cars. I love the design of cars; especially European cars. I've seen every episode of Top Gear and The Grand Tour (for fans, Lisa is the Captain Slow to my Jezza). I would religiously go to the Chicago Auto Show every year. I was devastated when the Geneva Auto Show was cancelled due to Covid. Bugatti and Peugeot both have their headquarters less than thirty minutes from Basel, but Covid kept me from visiting those meccas, too. Our apartment was across the street from a Fiat and Alfa Romeo dealership and I loved watching all the new Alfa C4 sports coupes get unloaded from the car carrier parked right underneath our dining room windows. One of the best parts of my daily walks was seeing all the unusual and unfamiliar cars on the streets. So I was truly excited to visit this museum so close to home.

Lisa and I made plans to go spend a Saturday there. A quick thirty-minute train ride and we headed across the train platform to a bank of ticket kiosks and looked for the one that sold tickets for the tram. Not a single machine gave an option for instructions in English. Not a single machine gave an option for instructions in German, either. After hitting all of the machines and wasting over forty-five minutes trying to buy a stupid tram ticket, we decided to try at one of the customer service counters. Here we learned, from a nonplussed and sleepy-eyed clerk that the ticket machines were located outside near the bus stop.

"By the tram stop?"

"Bus stop"

"The tram tickets are at the bus stop, not the tram stop?"

"Oui"

Finally, we had our tickets and waited for the tram to arrive. Lisa started perusing online info about Mulhouse and discovered that the town "has no Old World charm after being decimated in the war and everything is modern and boring". Guess we weren't hanging around downtown Mulhouse today. The museum was on the opposite side of town, and as we made our way across the city, I could see that this was, indeed, not a place to linger unless you had to.

"I feel like I'm in French Peoria"

We exited the tram to a group of French gang-bangers beating the shit out of each other.

Thankfully, the museum was just across the street from the tram stop and we followed another family, quickly, to the entrance. At this point, I will tell you that all of the bullshit that is Mulhouse is worth it to visit this museum. The building itself is a fantastic modernist cube that is built over a small river. The sheer size of this place will astound you. Not only does it house the largest Bugatti and Duesenberg collections in the world, it is all located in one Astrodome-sized exposition area. You literally cannot see from one end of the space to the other. And it is packed with cars displayed shoulder to shoulder like a Safeway parking lot on the day before Thanksgiving. Wall to wall cars as far as the eye can see. And not a single non-European car among them. It's an absolute mecca for anyone who loves cars. I was in heaven. And we damned near had the whole place to ourselves. It took us three full hours to see it all. Lisa enjoys looking at cars, too, and declared it to be one of the best museums she's ever been to.

As we waited for the tram back to the depot we watched a group of shirtless Gallic hooligans throw glass bottles on the tracks while listening to French hip-hop. Lisa leaned her tired head on my shoulder.

"It's not even good hip hop"

Apparently, France only gets better if you are exponentially further afield from Basel.

Having enjoyed the marvels of Strasbourg on two occasions, I knew that "good" France was out there. The general consensus amongst Lisa's coworkers and our neighbors was to get ourselves to Colmar as soon as possible. Considered one of the most beautiful cities in France, we figured it had to be far enough away to avoid the taint of St Louis' bummer stank. Late spring is the time to visit, when all the flowers are in full bloom, but the humid heat of the Lorraine Valley hasn't settled in yet. So we picked a weekend in May and planned a day trip. Worst case scenario was if it sucked, we could just chug another twenty minutes north and spend the day in marvelous Strasbourg.

Right away, the journey started on a positive note.

Usually, French trains are a bit… French. They're always shabby, and not in a chic way. If you don't catch the very first train of the day, chances are you are sitting in a crumb-strewn seat with a sticky Fanta-coated floor and the lingering stink of *Gauloises* cigarette smoke (and, no, smoking is not allowed on French trains, so there you go). After the wonders of a Swiss train, all others are a disappointment, but French trains that much more so. Even the Deutschebahn can be a sad affair. Clean, but sad. French trains are both sad and dirty.

To be clear: Swiss trains > German trains > French trains

What makes Swiss trains so awesome? Beyond the near perfect punctuality, they are universally clean. Sure, by the end of the day, the bins may be full, but at least all the trash is in the bins and not on the floor and seats. Bathrooms on a Swiss train are immaculate. Many have floor to ceiling murals making it feel like you are pooping in a small farmhouse looking out over your cows grazing on the flower-strewn mountainside. The outlets at your seat work, as does the folding table. The windows can actually be seen out of. All of the digital stop displays work.

French trains have bathrooms, but you are safer trying to poop in the toilet from the movie *Trainspotting*. The outlets almost never work (and you must remember to bring your plug adaptors for trains!) and nine times out of ten, the tables haven't been wiped down since De Gaulle was President. The lights are usually flickering, if on at all, and the displays almost never work. I always get the feeling that I may or may not get to my destination depending on whether the engineer decides he wants to stop at the given stop, let alone decide to even make the train go at all. Would he decide to go on strike midway through the journey? One never knew. French trains are transportation roulette.

So we were shocked to find a well-appointed train waiting to speed us north. Instead of the drab white carriage with boring blue upholstery, this was a fantastic Art Deco affair, in muted dark greens, with velvet chairs and thick celery colored curtains in the window. All the lights were warm sconces and were working perfectly. The digital board was scrolling in fine order. Our table was clean and our feet didn't stick to a single surface. The outlet, too, fully charged my phone. The conductor even cracked a friendly smile! This was a prestigious start, indeed!

The journey is rather unremarkable, scenery-wise. The majority of the Alsace is flat farmland. To the west, however, you can just make out the ridge of the Vosges mountains. On a sunny day, it feels like traveling through the Central Valley of California. The farther away from Basel you get, the less civilization you speed through. As you get closer to Colmar, tiny villages spring up near the foothills in the distance, with their church spires glinting in the sun. You know that if you were to stop in one of these villages, you'd find genuine France, with charm, hospitality, and great food. The great Michelin-starred chef Hubert Keller is from one of these tiny villages just minutes from Colmar.

Our train pulled into the station and we had a short fifteen-minute walk through streets of row houses to get to the center of town. A small curved street leads you around a bend where suddenly, poured out before you, is the most storybook fairytale square you have ever laid eyes on outside of an animated Disney movie (in fact, Colmar served as the inspiration for Belle's village in the animated *Beauty and the Beast*). Crooked timber-framed cottages with flower boxes and ornately carved shutters lean over the cobbled square. Cafe tables under red umbrellas crowd the center of the plaza and the happy clinking of wine glasses fills the air. It's a strange feeling to be suddenly enveloped by a scene so technicolor and literally magical. It is impossible not to smile here. The whole vibe is one of warmth and charm and welcome. There simply aren't enough words in a thesaurus to describe how lovely this town is. Your jaw will get sore from constantly falling open in awe.

"Oooh, gelato!"

Lisa is a sucker for a good gelato. I mean, what kind of commie bastard isn't, right? So we step up to the counter and order two cones. I will always get amareno cherry, with its amaretto punch of booze. Lisa is more Quixotic and will grab whatever flavor strikes her fancy that day. On this occasion she chose rum raisin.

Or should I say RUM raisin.

"Jiminy Christmas!"

Her eyes were popping out of her head. She handed me her cone.

"Try this"

"Well now I'm scared"

This wasn't rum raisin. This was a shot of pure pirate rum that was masquerading as gelato. Even the raisins had been soaked in rum for what tasted like eighty years. After one bite, I felt like I already had a buzz. After three bites, Lisa was three sheets to the wind.

We decided it was time for some lunch, and found a table in a square opposite one of the many gothic churches in the town center. As we sat down, our eyes scanned the menu for the one thing we were both craving, and were delighted to find it there.

"Yes, we'd like two glasses of something pink, and two dozen escargots, to start"

"Two dozen?"

"Oh, oui en effet!" (Oh, yes indeed!)

She nodded wryly and scuttled off. As we scanned the crowd around us, we knew we were in for a treat. Not a single person at any table was speaking anything other than French. There were no tourists, save us, which meant that this was a place for locals. If you aren't sure if you're going to get authentic, good food when abroad, stand near the tables and listen. If you hear a lot of English and you aren't in an English-speaking country, it's probably a tourist trap. But if everyone is speaking the native language, you're most likely in for good, honest food

We literally wept as we ate our tasty, garlicy, perfect, amazing snails. Both of us, if we could, would sit all day and eat nothing but escargot until our stomachs burst. For me, it's one of the best French dishes and I will order it every single time it is on a menu. If you've never tried them, I encourage you to seek them out. Put aside any squeamishness you may have, close your eyes, and just try. They are a culinary religious experience.

My favorite French dish, however, is duck confit. This is my favorite dish in the entire world. Slow roasted leg and thigh of duck, basted in its own juices until the skin is crisp and crackling. Oh man oh man oh man. I have eaten at some of the finest and most famous restaurants in the world, but I still think the single best meal I ever had was at *Cafe Le Soufflot* in Paris. In the shadow of both the Sorbonne and the Pantheon, we sat down at this sidewalk cafe and had *escargot* (of course) and the most magical, succulent, perfect duck confit that ever existed. I dream about that meal. I want to go back to Paris, not for the museums and cathedrals and catacombs, but to eat that meal all over again. If I could, I would eat duck confit every single day until I bled duck fat.

So I was incredibly saddened to learn that this little cafe did not have duck confit on the menu. I had to settle for a boring steak and frites instead. Lisa had to stop me from just ordering two dozen more *escargot* for my main meal.

Americans think they know French fries. Americans know jack shit about French fries. Americans don't fry their potatoes in duck fat like the French do. Duck fat makes everything better. Everything! One of life's greatest pleasures is a cone of duck fat fries, or *frites*. All fries ever after pale in sad, limp comparison.

We wandered tipsily through town (three carafes of wine and a cone of boozy gelato will do that to you), admiring the beautiful canal that winds its way through the city streets, bedecked with colossal flower boxes and dripping ivy. There are so many boxes of flowers that the whole town smells like a florist's shop. Soon, though, we smelled the sweet burn of caramel, and followed our noses to a sweet shop. Barrels and barrels of caramels and Alsatian nougats greeted us. We grabbed a sack and started filling it up. Because of our buzz, we didn't care that we had just spent nearly 40€ on a bag of candy.

Next door, a sample of *spritz*-like butter cookies convinced me to buy two kilos of them. At this point we realized we might be making bad decisions and deftly avoided the *fromagerie*. Instead, we tooled past elaborately decorated shop windows and wound down tiny medieval alleys. We stumbled upon a courtyard with some stunning sculptures, only to find it to be the home of Frédéric Auguste Bartholdi, the creator of the Statue of Liberty. On a second trip to the city, we took note of the small brass triangles embedded in the streets to denote historic landmarks, all bearing the face of Lady Liberty. He is Colmar's most famous son.

Lisa and I would return to Colmar on many occasions. Most of the time, it was because we were simply craving snails.

"I want *escargot*"

"Let's go to Colmar!"

And so we would. We'd glide quickly through the village to our cafe, plonk ourselves down, and order a couple dozen pans of snails. Sometimes, that was all we had. We wouldn't linger over lunch or dinner. We'd just drink wine and eat *escargot*.

Until one afternoon we sat down and opened the menu (we were planning on having an actual lunch), and Lisa gasped.

"It's different!"

Indeed, the menu WAS different.

"Where the fuck is the *escargot*!?"

Our waitress saw our panicked faces.

"We have a new owner. We no longer serve *escargot*"

We thanked her and got up and left. This was our place, they made them perfectly, and now they went and screwed it all up.

God damn it, France!!!

For an hour we wandered from cafe to cafe, checking menus to find a place that made them. Finally, we found a spot and sat down. Our server brought us out two dozen and a carafe of pink wine. We both sighed sadly.

They were baked in pastry.

This is the inferior way to serve them. Now, I realize the French know pastry, but for me, when it comes to *escargot*, it dulls the flavor and inhibits the pure experience of the texture that makes them so unique. We were sadder now than an Adele album.

We never went back to Colmar again.

When I was in the eighth grade, I was given the opportunity to take a foreign language class at the high school down the street. We were all asked to rank our preferences between Spanish, French, German, and Latin. French was at the top of my list, but I ended up being placed in the German class. When the new semester started, our rag tag group of middle schoolers trundled across town to the high school first thing in the morning to attend our language course, five days a week. My teacher was a tall dark haired man who looked at lot like the Austrian singer Falco (of '80s Rock Me, Amadeus fame). Herr Mensing was charismatic and humorous and became one of my favorite teachers of all time. He was the first person who ever recognized my last name as being French. After introducing myself to the class, he exclaimed

"We have an Alsatian in our midst!"

When we would catch on to things or get a question right, he had a great quirk of clapping his hands and rubbing them together, declaring

"Now we're cooking with gas!"

When we arrived in Basel, I found I was required to take German language courses, or take a test to prove proficiency. This was to ensure that I, as a "trailing spouse" was able to function in society to a minimum degree of difficulty. I considered taking the test outright, but when I realized that the last time I was in a German class was back in 1988, I decided I should just take the free class.

The Canton paid for the accelerated learning course at one of the language schools in town. I would need to take the equivalent of two years of German language study over the course of eight weeks. This meant going to school for three hours each day, five days a week, for two months. The school I chose was in the very heart of Old Town and class began at 8am each morning. Joining me would be just two others: Thuy, a young restauranteur from Vietnam, and Fernanda, a veterinarian from Brazil. Together, we faced a tall, thin, bug-eyed American woman who whisper-spoke, making it nearly impossible to ever hear a word she said. There was no text book, but rather, mimeographed handouts. Prophetically, before we left the States, I had ordered a copy of my trusty old high school German language book *Unsere Freunde*. I found it insanely useful, even if it was only last updated in 1979.

After the first half of the course was complete, we took the A1 proficiency test, which we all passed. The second half of the course would be with a new teacher. Yasmin was a star player on the Basel Frauen football team (soccer for you Yanks) and was the teacher we wished we had the whole time. Not only did we hone our language skills with her, she taught us so many important things about Swiss culture and how to assimilate as foreigners. Most importantly, though, I struck up a lovely friendship with Fernanda. Our mutual love of cats led her to becoming our pet sitter when we traveled. Our little black panther, Tupac, still misses his "girlfriend". To this day we remain friends online.

I ended up taking three years of high school German. The only reason I stopped was because Herr Mensing left the school to move to Australia. In the time I spent with him, I developed a great fascination with Germany and its culture. This was back in the 1980s when the Berlin Wall was still up, so when we did learn about German culture and lifestyle, everything was divided up between East and West Germany. Just like my inherent curiosity about The Evil Empire of the Soviet Union, I had a deep desire to visit Berlin and see The Wall myself. Of all the places in Europe I wanted to go, Germany was number one on my list for years afterward. Though the USSR was technically the first European nation I ever visited, my first trip to Europe "proper" was to… Finland. Great Britain, France, and Switzerland all came before my primary goal of Germany.

It would be my tagging along on Lisa's work trip to Basel for me to finally be able to set foot in Germany. Not having a lot of time on that short trip, I chose the closest big city to Basel: Freiburg im Bresgau.

An hour north of Basel, Freiburg is technically larger than Basel, but it feels much smaller. A university town, it is one of the greenest (energy) cities in Europe. Tucked in a tight valley in the Black Forest, it is surrounded on all sides by deeply forested foothills. This gives the town a cozy feel. It somehow makes the city feel so much more intimate. I likened it to a German Portland. There is a bohemian feel to it; an artsy, care-free feel. There are dozens of microbreweries dotted around town, and the boutiques here cater more to the second-hand thrifty type. There is a pretty Old Town to wander, but the majority of it is post-War rebuild. Much of the surrounding area was built up in the '60s and '70s and has that distinct brick and frosted glass feeling of an American suburban shopping mall circa 1981. That's not a detracting descriptor, either. It actually works in terms of creating a sense of place. It is unique here. It's a town that feels comfortable with itself, and that comfort is felt as you wander around.

That comfort, though, momentarily fades as you notice the brass plaques in the ground in front of buildings, noting where Jews were expelled from their houses and taken away to concentration camps. You will find them all over town - a sober reminder of why the town had to be rebuilt in the first place. Traveling anywhere in Germany, you will find these markers. I admire the Germans for not shrinking from this part of their past, unlike the American South which still refuses to acknowledge their own savagery. At least the Germans have the good taste to not hold weddings at Birkenau like Americans hold debutante balls at Twelve Oaks.

The first time I encountered these plaques, I was taken aback. I wasn't expecting to see such a thing, and it hits you fast and hard when you do. Even the language of these plaques is meant to evoke absolute horror. The word *ermordet* is used, which means "murdered". These poor souls didn't die in Auschwitz or Birkenau; they were murdered there. Yes, they make you feel guilty about being a tourist, sightseeing in a place where something so horrible happened. You can only silently appreciate that modern Germans do not hide their past, own up to their role, and lay bare their evils for all to contemplate.

When you do move on, you'll notice another kind of street-inlaid notice. Back when literacy was reserved for the wealthy few, it was necessary to be able to communicate to the masses without the written word. To let the illiterate, know what shops sold what, or what services were provided, mosaics were inlaid in front of each building. The baker had a pretzel, the pub had a tankard, the banker had a bag of coins. Freiburg has one of the most extensive collections of mosaics and it makes for a very colorful walk. Newer businesses have also added their own mosaics, with a pet store having a black cat and an adult "establishment" having a red high heel. We had seen these mosaics in Strasbourg as well, but there, the pictures were at the end of a street, denoting a whole cache of like businesses could be found on that street. In Freiburg, each individual shop had its own mural, so there were dozens and dozens more of these unique pieces of art to admire.

Throughout the town are tiny canals. Called *bächle*, these foot-wide, 6" deep troughs once brought drinking water to the streets and people of Freiburg from the surrounding mountains. The citizenry kept them clean and free of debris and detritus. Now, they are purely decorative, and many shops sell rubber ducks to float in the canals. You do need to mind your step as every street in the Old Town has one. They're a charming quirk and make for some great photographs.

Lisa would have to travel to Freiburg for work, and once we were settled in Basel, one of the first outings we did was make the trip up there. We went on the weekend before she would have to go up for the day, giving her an opportunity to get familiar with the town. My first visit had been in the winter, so it was a lovely change of pace to visit in the late summer. Many of the small winding side streets now sported a canopy of wisteria and English ivy. The sun was blocked by the hundreds of vines that crisscrossed overhead, leaving the cobbles wonderfully dappled in sunlight. The town was even more lovely than I had remembered.

We stopped to have lunch in a *biergarten* in the center of town. To my delight, one of the menu offerings was *sauerbraten*, a wine-marinated roast beef (holy German-language high school banquet flashback, Batman!). For me, this was a real treat. My mother didn't really cook-cook, and she especially didn't care for the vinegary profile of most German food. Lisa was similar in her vinegar disdain. So I devoured that roast like it was my last meal. And it was divine. I thought I would have found this in Swiss restaurants, but I never did. It seemed to be a strictly German menu item.

I did get Lisa to appreciate German food, though. Not that she had much choice. Sausages were the cheapest things we could afford, meat-wise, at the store. Bratwurst became a weekly staple, and when it became warm enough to grill out on the patio, we'd get skewers of mini sausages (bratwurst, currywurst, and kalbswurst). Ready-to-fry schnitzels were also popular, and Lisa eventually mastered a crispy mustard-vinegar roasted potato side dish. Once we returned home, we realized just how crappy American bratwurst is, and it took us months to find a palatable brand. Missing our weekly schnitzel nights, I mastered Wolfgang Puck's recipe and now it's become one of my signature dishes. My mother, however, takes umbrage with how I prepare mine, which is the proper European way: finished with lemon and parsley. Being an American Midwestern momma, she prefers hers with onions and mustard, which makes my adopted Swiss head explode.

Food became one of the ways we assimilated the fastest. Still, I was surprised that German foods like sauerkraut and pumpernickel weren't more popular in Switzerland. So when we went to Germany for any reason, I took every opportunity to consume all the German things, and that usually meant *sauerbraten*.

I thought, based on my long suffering desire to visit Germany that I would have spent more time there than I did. Truth be told, there just wasn't much near Basel, on the German side of the border, worth popping over to see. The places I did want to see were far away big cities tied to Lisa's business trips. I didn't accompany her on the initial ones she took because we were still getting settled, she was adjusting to her new job, and then a bit later, I wasn't able to because I was recovering from surgery. Once we had decided to start arranging things for me to travel with her, the whole continent went on lockdown. Dreams of visiting Berlin, Munich, and Leipzig evaporated [snap] just like that.

My real dream was to visit Colditz Castle, used as a POW camp for Allied officers during World War II. Shortly after my grandmother passed away, my mother shared some letters my grandfather had written to her while he was fighting in Europe. At the time, in his writings, he had to be cagey about what his unit was doing.

But the dates of the letters, the area of Germany he was stationed (near Leipzig), and the nature of a "liberation" led me to the conclusion that he had participated in the capture of the famous prison. I had SO wanted to go to the castle and then FaceTime my mom so she could go on the tour with me to see exactly where her dad had been and what he had done. Alas, Covid buggered that idea.

Instead, my detours into Deutschland consisted of quick hops across the border to towns and villages along the Rhine. When I would take my walks along the Wiese River north of town, I always made it a point to hop back and forth across the border hidden in the pleasant woods so that my afternoon stroll could be classified as international. Germany did hold a few bright spots of interest, and they never left me feeling as downtrodden as my ventures into France. Instead, my journeys into Germany always felt strangely Midwestern. Things felt very… ordinary. Nothing felt particularly exotic. Things felt safe and middling. If anything, I found Germany to be extraordinarily vanilla, just like my home state of Illinois. I never got used to the fact that everything in Switzerland is so perfectly preserved and genuinely ancient, while everything just on the other side of the river was new, practical, and less than 60 years old. Switzerland is like walking around the attractions at Disneyland while Germany is the industrial buildings behind the pretty façades. Then again, Switzerland was one of the few places in Europe that escaped the utter destruction of World War II.

There were some tiny pockets of preservation. One lovely little example was the village of Laufenberg. There are actually two Laufenbergs, one Swiss and one German, lying just across the Rhine from each other. In this spot, about 30km east of Basel, the river narrows and a stone pedestrian bridge connects the two former walled Hapsburg cities. There are castle ruins to ramble (and bbq in) on both sides. The German side has an exquisite gothic church. The best part of exploring these pretty twins are the postcard views from the riverside parks. Both towns appear as colorful wedding cakes peeking up and over the forested edges of the Rhine. Every inch of public space is dedicated to flowers, and both towns feel more like arboretums than villages. Both are tiny, with less than 2000 people each, so getting the perfect Instagram shot is easy-peasy. Laufenberg is what most people think of when they picture a tiny little German hamlet in their heads. Though small, it is anything but disappointing.

I would spend hours poring over Google maps, looking for towns and sites to visit that were both within my train pass area and less than an hour away. Quick little exploratory jaunts. Everyone thinks getting to know a country is hitting the big cities or giant nature parks. I found that popping over to a tiny little burg on the river, or the ruins of a castle in the foothills, or just taking the long way to get to a particular destination revealed more to me than any capital or amusement park or mountaintop panorama. My favorite days were jumping on the train for about a half an hour, walking into a small town I had found on the map, and just perambulate at leisurely pace taking in the terroir.

For example, I once visited the town of Laufen in

Switzerland, just thirty minutes south, simply because it was the home of *Ricola* (the world-famous cough drops). It was small, but it had a wonderful main drag with 15th century towers on either end of the street. I didn't plan on it, but my feet ended up directing me on a walk through the herb fields where all the wonderful ingredients for *Ricola* are grown. I ended up with splendid views of the Jura foothills and it began to lightly snow while I was frolicking in the open farmland. It was magical. Just magical. To be fair, I was disappointed that the *Ricola* gift shop was closed due to Covid, but still, I had a wonderful walkabout in some tiny little farm village, all because I stumbled on the fact that a famous cough drop was made there

Likewise, I discovered that the incredibly boring town of Weil am Rhein had an art walk. I guess not totally surprising, as the Vitra Design Museum is there. This would end up being one of the best walks I would take in Germany. Stretching from the Design Museum in the western part of town, it would wind up into the foothills, through orchards and vineyards, affording insane views of the whole of Basel and the Rhine. For 7km I passed *Avant Gárde* metal sculptures hidden in copses of cherry and apple trees, hanging from spindly chestnut branches, poking out from endless rows of grapevines. Eventually, I ended up back at the German-Swiss border in the town of Riehen on the east side of Basel, where my walk ended at the Fondation Beyeler Art Museum. It strangely felt like a stroll through Napa Valley. I went in late fall when most of the leaves had fallen, but what remained were brilliant yellow and orange. Everything had a wonderful Robert Redford hazy glow. Weil am Rhein is such a dull little suburb so it was incredible to find something so beautiful within its confines. You gotta get out and just... explore.

Lörrach was the biggest of the German suburbs. My physical therapist lived there. When I asked her if it was a nice place to live, she just looked at me sideways and shrugged. Looking at a map of the town, you'd swear it was an

American suburb. It was all shopping centers, one after another. A closer inspection and you'd be surprised to learn that smack dab in the middle of all that commercialism is a 12th century castle. I had made it a mission to visit as many castles in the area as I could, and this would be my first German one. I hopped the train and in less than fifteen minutes, I was huffing and puffing up the lone mountain in the middle of town.

Sitting atop this hill was the best preserved castle I had visited yet. Burg Rötteln was massive. This was ten times bigger than anything I had visited yet. It was even pink, with the majority of the stone used to construct it being the same pink granite used to build both the Basel and Strasbourg Cathedrals. Began in the 1100s, it reached its pinnacle in the 1500s. The massive courtyard, of course, sported dozens and dozens of bbq pits and picnic tables. The keep was the most intact building and I climbed the six flights of stairs to reach the top. Wow, was it worth it! From here you could see all the way, over 100 miles, to the Bernese Alps. Standing tall above them all were the Mönch, Eiger, and Jungfrau, clear as crystal. If there wasn't a posted sign telling me that I was, really, seeing these mountains over such a long distance, I would have never believed it. Who'da thunk that I would be peering out over the Swiss Alps from atop a pink castle in the middle of a German shopping suburb?

We did, occasionally get out of Dodge and see some Europe.

Before I had my first surgery, Lisa offered to take me on a weekend getaway anywhere on the Continent I wanted to go. Let's see something cool before I was trapped in the house for weeks. We were scanning flight prices and were completely dumbfounded: Basel to Amsterdam for 40CHF (roundtrip), to Athens for 45CHF, to Venice or Barcelona for 70CHF. Prague was out of the question at a wallet-busting (cough, cough) 120CHF (roundtrip). Not only did Europeans get weeks and weeks of vacation, they could afford to take these vacations! Sure, these were budget airlines, but with flights only lasting an hour, two at most, who cared? We spent a few days trying to narrow it down. Every city was tempting, every city was alluring, every city was on our travel bucket list. It was becoming hard to choose. So I simply gave our top five choices numbers in my head, from one to five, and asked Lisa to pick a number.

Amsterdam it was, then.

We'd fly up for a long weekend, walk the canals, and see some art. It was February and the off-off season, so we anticipated no crowds. This was going to be our first extra-Switzerland trip in Europe together, and I was really looking forward to it. Lisa booked a swanky boutique hotel on one of the main canals within walking distance of all the museums. The trams ran all the way to the airport, so getting from Schiphol to the city would be a breeze.

Indeed, the Rijksmuseum is one of the greatest art museums in the world. All of the old Dutch masters in one grand display space was exhilarating. There was a Rembrandt, a van Dyke, or a Vermeer at every turn. I'm much more of an Impressionists-onward kind of guy, but I was still awestruck to see so many famous paintings in one place. The building, too, is a masterwork itself, featuring an amazing Victorian research library and a cavernous atrium blending old and new architecture in a seamless way. It reminded me of the glass canopy at the British Museum in London. I have a great fondness for the blending of old and new architecture (which London does so well).

Better still, and without a doubt, one of, if not the, greatest art museums I have ever had the privilege to visit, was the Van Gogh Museum. I've been to the Art Institute of Chicago, the

Museé D'Orsay in Paris, the Tretyakov Gallery in Moscow, the National Gallery in London. Nothing compared to this temple to history's greatest painter. Housed in a sleek super modern cube, it features all of his greatest hits and more. His easel and palette, his notebooks and letters. What I loved most is that everything is shown in chronological order, so that you can see the evolution of his style and subject matter. The last painting, he ever made is the last painting you see, which leaves that much greater an impact.

My best friend's mom, who was like a second mother to me, had a framed poster of Van Gogh's Bedroom in Arles. One of his most recognizable, it is simply a yellow bed in a blue bedroom. To see her favorite painting in person, with the knowledge that this one piece of art meant so much to someone I loved, made it all the more special to see in the flesh. It was one of the most personally moving museum experiences I've ever had.

Outside of the museums, however, I found disappointment.

Switzerland had spoiled us.

By American standards, the city was clean. By Swiss standards, Amsterdam was a sty. It was grimy and trash-strewn (though a New Yorker might find it "immaculate"). The sidewalks were un-walkable because they were buckled and pot-holed. They were also insanely narrow, allowing only single-file, and if you strayed off the curb, you would be obliterated by a bicycle. I don't know how the overly-high bud tourists don't trip into a canal at every step. You couldn't look at the city as you walked it because you had to mind your every step. I even became bored with the canals. It became impossible to differentiate any of them, any of the buildings, or any of the neighborhoods. It lost its charm because it was monotonous. In retrospect, the weather probably contributed to our doldrums, as it was grey and damp and cold, leaching out any color from our surroundings

After a day of stumbling around the city, we were hungry. Looking up, we realized we were at the Anne Frank House. You cannot actually see the house from the street because it is enclosed in a smoked glass atrium. The line snaked out the door and down the street. Next door to this dark monument was a brilliantly white and blue chalet. A pancake chalet. It was like someone had plunked an IHOP next to Ground Zero.

Of course we wanted pancakes.

Inside, the place was bright, sunny, and humming. Looking around, we noticed that the decor was all cheeky and vulgar. One shelf held a series of decorative plates featuring a flashing frog in a trench coat. Another series of plates featured penises as fighter jets. Every waitress was an *Agent Provocateur* model. After perusing a list of over one hundred different kinds of pancakes, we both ordered stacks with apples and calvados. She must have thought I was Ron Swanson because she brought me *all* the pancakes with apples and calvados. I could have climbed this stack of breakfast awesomeness and been able to touch the moon. Best god damned pancakes I have ever, or will ever, eat.

"This is too weird eating pancakes next to Anne Frank's house"

"It's not the pancakes that makes it weird; it's the penis plates"

"*Penis Plates and Pancakes* - that's the name of my band"

To top off our odd culinary sojourn, our waitress brought us cups of *advocaat*, an extremely boozy butterscotch pudding. This was a revelation. This was the voice of God in a glass. Lisa could see my saucer-plate eyes and offered me hers, which I greedily accepted without argument. This made *everything* better. This redeemed Amsterdam. This immediately made my list of Ten Greatest Things I Have

Ever Eaten (for the curious, the single best bite of my life was a roasted duck heart from Heston Blumenthal's *Dinner* in Hyde Park in London). It wasn't the art or the canals or Anne Frank pancakes that I would remember - it was this tiny cup of boozy manna.

To me, Amsterdam felt like European Vegas. If you wanted to party, you came to Amsterdam. I could see the madness of summertime when hordes of Euro-bros descended on the town to ogle prostitutes in windows and overindulge in coffee shops. The city felt tired. It felt like it was once a gleaming beacon of propriety and prosperity, but was now just another abused holiday town. It seems Amsterdam agrees, and is taking steps to prevent marijuana tourism by foreigners and sex tourism in the Red Light District. Amsterdam knows it has been used and abused and is finally trying to change things. I hope it does. Underneath it all, I can see how it was once a great and beautiful city. If I were a single man in my twenties, I think Amsterdam would be a place I'd come back to again and again. As a married man in his fifties, I just wanted to relax and wander, and this just wasn't the place to accommodate that

But we had checked it off our list, seen some wonderful art, ate pancakes, found God in a cup, and that wasn't too bad.

Summer descended on Switzerland and Lisa's boss insisted that she take some time off.

"Like a proper European"

It was August of 2020, and in Europe, the initial wave of the Corona pandemic had passed, but just barely. Borders were once again open and cities were begging for tourists to return and Spend! Spend! Spend! to kick-start stalled economies. The US was still in the midst of a viral clusterfuck, but because of the swift and stringent acts of European governments, the worst of it here was close to being over. Other than mask mandates and immunization checks, the continent was re-opening for business.

Once again, we perused the map to try and figure out where to go. Southern climes were out. All of Europe descended on Spain, Sicily, Corsica, Turkey, and Greece during the vacation month of August. Even with cautious travelers, we knew that the popular beach-y spots were still going to be packed. The less people the better. We began to think about the less popular spots in Europe. Places like Split in Croatia and Bratislava in the Czech Republic went to the top of our list. So, too, did Tallinn, Estonia, and Copenhagen and Berlin. We truly wanted to go to Edinburgh, but the UK was following the US's lead in screwing-the-pooch when it came to a consistent and effective Covid response. Besides, even if we wanted to, Switzerland wouldn't allow it; the UK was on their list of banned travel destinations.

Finally, we picked a spot and booked it.

What I knew of Budapest came from ads for Viking River Cruises. The Danube, the gothic Parliament building, Buda Castle on a bluff overlooking the city. Always shown in golden sunlight, these ads made it look like a fairytale. Flights were super cheap (the total for both of us to fly there and back ended up being 120CHF - not each, but total!). Lisa, the Travelocity Gnome of the family, found us an amazing room at the Hilton right on the river with stunning views of Buda Castle. The hotel was just fantastic. A former enclave for Communist party elites, it was now a luxury hotel housed in a Soviet-style brutalist tower. Redecorated for capitalist pig tourists, it was now a mid-century-modern masterpiece. The service was five star.

Our little trip got off to an inauspicious start when Lisa

twisted her ankle getting up from her seat on the plane. By the time we got to the hotel, it was badly swollen. The staff sprang into action, bringing buckets of ice and towels and a map for the closest place to purchase paracetamol. Without asking, we had a knock on our door every two hours, with a smiling member of the staff holding a fresh bucket of ice and clean towels to wrap her ankle in. I left Lisa in the sprawling window seat overlooking the Danube and went to find this drug store. On this short little walk through the nearby shopping district, I fell hard for this city. Not only was it Swiss-level clean, it was charming and warm and welcoming. This little neighborhood was full of baroque and rococo buildings from the age of the Austro-Hungarian Empire, all housing gleaming futuristic shops and restaurants. The streets were still lit by ornate gas lamps, and every cafe was ensconced within fanciful iron fencing, giving each a quaint and cozy feeling. Street musicians played violins and cellos. I felt like I was in the oldest of cities, and in the newest of cities. Had I not been on a mission, I could have lingered in these few blocks for hours and hours.

Once we got Lisa drugged up, and wrapped up in a new sports brace, she was okay enough to get out and explore.

The skyline of this city is a photographer's dream. There isn't an inch of the whole Danube waterfront that isn't a perfect postcard. On our first excursion of the day, we walked from the hotel, along the Danube, to the massive stone Széchenyi Chain Bridge. Resembling, to me at least, the Brooklyn Bridge, it was a majestic span with enormous bronze lions guarding each end. Once on the Buda side of the river, we could look back on the Pest side where our hotel lay, to view the sprawling city. The enormous St Stephen Cathedral and the famous Parliament building dominated the scape. Every angle of this town was awesome. I think I took over three hundred pictures just on the first day.

Our first full day was blazing hot. A record heat wave had settled over the whole of the continent, and we were facing cloudless skies with near 100F temperatures. We seemed to have a habit of taking vacations during weather anomalies.

One year we went to Cancun when a bomb cyclone hit the whole of North America. It was 80F on our first day, and 40F on our second. All of the hotel guests were huddled indoors with layers of towels wrapped around them. We even thought about booking a flight out to somewhere further south to escape the cold, but even as far south as Aruba, off the coast of Venezuela, was no warmer than 50F. On another occasion, we went to Universal Studios in Orlando and a freak weather system dropped the temperature from 75F to 35F. On the plus side, we learned that you can get hot Butterbeer in Harry Potter World (and it's delicious!).

So, of course, on this trip, we got to experience record high temps. Lisa already hates the heat; I love it (I am always cold). But even this was too stifling for me. Not only was Budapest broiling, it was humid as hell, making it that much worse.

On the plus side, all that sunshine made the city gleam.

Budapest is one of the friendliest places I have ever been. Keeping true to our desire to be as respectful as possible, we tried to learn some key phrases before we visited. This proved far more difficult than we imagined. Hungarian is unlike any other language in Europe, and is considered one of the hardest languages in the world to learn. In the end, we ended up learning only one word, which we thought was the most important: *köszönöm* (thank you). The delight on people's faces when we used it was magical. You literally see the appreciation in their eyes. We spoke for a short time with a gentleman at the large indoor Marketplace where we bought canisters of Hungarian paprika. He said Hungarians never expect foreigners to use any Hungarian words because they are so hard to learn, so he applauded us for learning one and pronouncing it correctly. He said it was a lovely gesture of friendship, and he genuinely meant it.

We took a sunset stroll around the über-gothic Parliament building. This is probably the most famous landmark in Budapest, and it is a remarkable thing to behold. At night, lit up like a fairytale castle, it is stunning. Our walk took us back along the Danube riverfront where we encountered a most sobering and somber scene. Strewn along the banks of the river are hundreds of bronze-cast shoes. This is the memorial to commemorate the slaughter of Budapest's Jews during WWII. Shoes were highly valuable, and in order to re-sell them, Jews
were forced to remove them before being shot on the river's edge, where the current of the river would sweep their bodies away. Americans tend not to realize how every corner of Europe was touched by Nazi atrocities.

Just a stone's throw away from the Parliament building is a bit of an oddball statue. To honor the man who "defeated communism", a life-size bronze statue of Ronald Reagan can be found "walking" through Freedom Square. Of all the faces I expected to see in Hungary, The Gipper wasn't even on the list.

I found Budapest to be one of the most beautiful cities I have ever visited. Lisa was not as enthralled, but we both agree her ankle and the heat clouded her view. This was a city I could have spent a month in, exploring all the nooks and crannies of Buda and Pest, taking enough pictures to wallpaper the Pentagon. I appreciate places, I like places, and I feel places – Budapest spoke to me. I felt at home there. I saw a cosmopolitan city that embraced its Empirical past, its communist past, and its shining technological future. Were it not for the idiotic xenophobia of Hungary's Viktor Orban, I think Hungary might well become one of the most prosperous and popular places in Europe. I would go back in a heartbeat.

Budapest? More like BudaBest!

Not having had a beach vacation in two years, Lisa was determined that we should have one. To avoid the August crush of tourists, we scheduled a getaway in May to celebrate our anniversary. As Americans, we were used to all-inclusive resorts, having frequented them in Mexico and Jamaica. Finding an all-inclusive in Europe is not as easy as one might think. The majority are located in Turkey and Egypt, and those book up incredibly fast by hordes of pasty Brits. After a little research, we ended up booking a week in Greece.

I have never been more appalled at the condition of a country than I was crossing the island of Rhodes. Just off the coast of Turkey, it was once home to the Colossus of Rhodes, one of the original Seven Wonders of the Ancient World. Our resort was on the opposite side of the island, and that meant an hour in a car. As soon as we left the vicinity of the third-world airport, the economic devastation that Greece had been suffering for a decade or more came swiftly into focus. It seemed like every other building was either completely abandoned or abandoned mid-construction. Concrete shells of villas and apartment blocks littered the countryside. Drought had burned every inch of vegetation and the whole of the landscape was dead and brown.

Strangely, the one thriving business on the island was the furrier. We passed at least two dozen fur merchants, all in gleaming new buildings with parking lots packed with Maseratis and Maybachs. Not sure who needs fur on an island where it never dips below 75F.

Exiled Russian oligarchs. It's exiled Russian oligarchs.

The resort itself was small but modern, and we had our own

swim-up pool outside the room. Built on a small hill, we looked out over the Aegean. Here was the main reason I wanted to come here: to swim in the Mediterranean.

"It's not the Mediterranean. It's the Aegean"

"The Aegean is part of the Mediterranean."

"Well the Gulf of Mexico is part of the Atlantic Ocean but you don't say you went swimming in the Atlantic, do you?"

"We need drinks"

I had developed a taste for Aperol, the bitter orange liqueur from Italy. Not wanting to waste prosecco making Aperol Spritzes at home, I mixed mine with Sprite instead. Besides, bubbly wine gives me a headache. So when I explained to the bartender what I wanted, he was confused.

"May I have an Aperol and lemon lime, please?"

"You want an Aperol Spritz with lemon lime?"

"Lemon-lime *instead* of prosecco"

"Then it is not an Aperol Spritz"

"Yes, I know. Aperol and lemon lime, no prosecco"

"This is all wrong"

But he made it, and because I was offending all of Europe with my beverage choice, he remembered me and my abomination of a tipple. He must have told all of his coworkers because no matter where we were at the resort, I didn't have to ask for a beverage, they just brought me my unusual cocktail. Sitting in one of the cocktail lounges one evening after dinner, my cocktail appeared before me with a hearty Greek wink without my ordering anything.

"I think he wants you"

"Dude, everyone wants me. I'm a tall drink of water"

Swimming in the Aegean was everything I had hoped for. I'm not a swim person. It's not that I can't, it just gets boring, fast. But on a vacation like this, I can float in a pool all day long, cocktail in one hand, book in the other. I desperately wanted to get my feet in the Mediterra... Aegean Sea. I have put my feet in the Pacific, Atlantic, and Arctic Oceans. This was another famous body of water I needed to experience and touch with my toes. The water was wonderfully warm and so incredibly clear. You could see six feet or more to the bottom. For once I think I was enjoying the beach as much as Lisa. I could see why all of Europe flocks to the shores of this glorious body of water.

The next morning, I awoke just before dawn. Annoyingly wide awake, I decided to put my shoes on and head down to the beach and get some pictures of the sunrise. I've seen hundreds of sunrises in my life, but feeling the sun hit your face as it creeps up over this ancient corner of the world, you are transported to a place of complete contentedness. The whole of the world washed away in that moment and I was alone in this best part of the day.

Would I go back? No, I wouldn't. The beach scene, without the tropic vibe, hits differently. The barrenness of the island bled into the periphery and it never quite felt like it was a place you could fully relax. The people were nice, but it felt as if they knew they *had* to be nice, and it wasn't quite genuine (unlike Mexico which just gushes with friendliness and cheer). It wasn't bad, it's just that I wouldn't do it again. I feel like I could have a better Mediterranean experience in Italy or France or Croatia. Again, not a bad experience - it was a very nice holiday getaway.

I just think Greece is tired, and it shows.

The coolest place I got to visit, ironically, was the most boring.

Well, not boring to me, but, still, kind of boring in the grand scheme of things to do there. It's not on anyone's vacation or holiday list, and every guide book out there will tell you there isn't a single reason to visit other than to say that you did. Which is exactly why I had to scratch the Principality of Liechtenstein off my travel bucket list: because I could.

The sixth smallest country in the world, Liechtenstein is tucked into a tiny corner of eastern Switzerland on the border with Austria. How small is small? There are less than 40,000 people in the whole of the country. The capital, Vaduz (which, I learned, is pronounced *vah-doots*) has a population of only 6,000 people (the neighboring "city" of Schaan is the largest with 6,300). The country is too small to be a member of the European Union (they apparently don't do microstates) so it shares its currency, the Swiss Franc, with Switzerland. It is, though, a member of Schengen, which allows freedom of movement between member states. Switzerland is a member of Schengen, which is why cross-border shopping is so easy.

Like their conservative Swiss neighbors, Liechtenstein was dragged into the twentieth century kicking and screaming – they were the last country in Europe to give women the right to vote (in 1984 – the Swiss didn't allow it until 1971, but Cantons had to approve it themselves, and the last Canton didn't give women the vote until 1991 (and it was those carrot-eaters in Appenzell who were the last to get on board)). Abortion is strictly forbidden in the country, and when it came up for referendum 2012, the ban was upheld by over 75% of the country's voters.

Liechtenstein is a Principality, meaning it has a Prince as a head of state, much like fellow microstate Monaco (which has Prince Albert (not in a can)). The current Prince of Liechtenstein is a bloke named Hans-Adam II, who just happens to be one of the richest heads of state in the world (even richer than British King Chuckles III). In fact, Liechtenstein is one of the richest nations in the world, in terms of personal purchasing power, and its citizens enjoy the fifth strongest standard of living in the world.

Weirdly, while a tax haven for bankers and the like (even more so than Switzerland), the country's riches comes from… refrigeration. Almost 90% of the world's refrigeration parts and components come from Liechtenstein. This highly specialized industry has made the country incredibly wealthy. The landscape, too, reflects this. Instead of picturesque chalets and cobbled streets, the majority of Liechtenstein's towns are immaculate business parks and warehouse districts. Even the center of Vaduz is basically an outdoor mini mall.

Still, the minute we learned we were going to be moving to Europe, I was determined to make a pilgrimage. I had even read that it was possible to walk the length of the country in a day. I figured the width was more doable. I could walk from Switzerland, across the whole of Liechtenstein, to Austria. I'd get to cross that country off my list, too. I knew this would be a bigger outing for me, so I took my time in planning when to go, how to get there. The more I read about it, the more I kept seeing the phrase "there is no reason to visit Liechtenstein". Well, now my curiosity was definitely piqued. Just like being told not to visit the Evil Empire of the USSR, now I had to go to Liechtenstein, the "Nothing Burger" of Europe.

In the pre-dawn of a summer morning, I set off from Basel. I would take a train to Zurich, where I would grab another to the border town of Sargans. The train ride itself was stunning. Once east of Zurich, we followed the shores of

Lake Zurich, and then the Walensee (another large alpine lake). The mountains here hugged the lakeshore, creating the feeling of a crater filled with water. This was the landscape of *The Sound of Music*, and it was stunning. It was also a lengthy journey, taking over three and a half hours. I was, after all, traversing the entire width of Switzerland.

In the valley town of Sargans, with soaring granite mountains on either side of the train station, I boarded a bus which would take me over the border to Liechtenstein. I had learned that the goal of walking the width of the country was impossible, as a massive mountain range lay in my path (which is why people walk the length of the country instead). My plans now simply consisted of visiting Vaduz, seeing its cliff-side castle, and getting my passport stamped. The ride to Vaduz would be a mere twenty minutes. Because the two countries share a transport network, I was able to buy my all-encompassing ticket to include all forms of transit between Basel and Vaduz, meaning I would not have to buy a separate bus ticket to travel inside Liechtenstein.

The whole of the area is visually stunning. Monolithic mountains surround a verdant green valley. As we approached the first town across the border, the view outside made me hop off the bus to explore. I was just blow away by the beauty here. To enjoy my day, I had left Basel at 4:45am. The golden morning sun was just starting to peek up from behind the mountain peaks, casting dreamlike rays down into the valley. Here, in the tiny town of Balzers, was an ancient castle on a hill, surrounded on all sides by vineyards, which in turn were surrounded by alps. Outside of Lauterbrunnen, there was no prettier spot in all my travels. The sun's rays were more golden than I have ever seen them, the valley so lush and vibrant.

And it was quiet.

So, so quiet.

Nothing but meadowlarks and chickadees and crickets. Not a soul was in sight. I had this entire fairytale scene to myself. I strolled up the path towards the castle, snapping photos every two feet. Every step revealed a new stunning angle. I was in photographer's heaven. While the castle was not yet open for the day, I sat on a bench on the top of that hill and enjoyed the single greatest morning I can ever recall. I could literally feel my heart swelling at this amazing scene. That this was a real place just boggled my mind. This was a spot where I could spend the rest of my days and be very content and happy, indeed.

Eventually I made my way back to the bus and headed into Vaduz. The drive was an odd one. Giant alps on either side told me I was in Europe, but the road was lined with gas stations, banks, banks, banks, gas stations, and banks. I was shocked at how mundane and utilitarian the whole area was. I had read that Vaduz was not a traditionally pretty town, but this was not what I was expecting. If not for the surrounding alps, and the über-cleanliness, I could have sworn I was in the States. In fact, I only realized I had reached my destination because the bus route ended at the city center. While I say city center, what I mean is the two blocks of shops that makes up the business district of Vaduz. The whole of the area is made up of a café, a Coop grocery store, seven banks, the ultra-modern Parliament building, and the tourist information kiosk.

After a quick breakfast of coffee and croissant, I made my way to the tourist office. This is where, for 5CHF, I could get my passport stamped. Because the country has no official border postings, crossings, or international airport, there are no customs officers to stamp passports. So to get this tiny country in your book, you need to pay for a stamp, which I happily did. There are only two questions that everyone asks at the office, so they have a large poster with the answers posted for you:

1. Follow the white signs to get to the castle (which is the private residence of the Prince and is not open to the general public)
2. Follow the yellow signs to reach the Austrian border – this is a 10km, or 2.5-hour walk

The castle would be my first stop. You could see it half way up the mountain that towered over the town. Afterwards, I would head to Austria. Realizing how close the border was from here, I knew I could make that walk, no problem, and catch the bus back. While it wasn't technically walking the whole length of the country (Vaduz was a third of the way already), I could at least walk to Austria.

I followed the white signs through town and headed up the dirt path towards the cliff side. The route quickly became steeper and steeper and as the sun rose in the sky, I began to huff and puff and sweat. Thankfully, there was plenty of shade on my way up. The view, too, of the whole valley, was incredible. At the top was a small meadow and the stout little castle. Here, the mountains took off vertically to my left, and to my right, was a view of the entire country of Liechtenstein. It was spectacular. Here, you could see the neat and precise rows of refrigeration plants and office parks. From this height, however, your eye was drawn to the incredible surround of mountains and snow-capped peaks. What Liechtenstein lacks in character, it makes up for in jaw-dropping natural beauty.

Once back down in town, it was nearly noon, and the heat of the day was already oppressive. My knees were not happy about my climb to the castle, and even less so about the descent. I wasn't quite sure I could make the walk to Austria without dying. At a decent pace, I wouldn't reach the border until after three, and I still had to get back to Switzerland and home. I also knew I wouldn't just walk – I'd be stopping every few minutes to take pictures, so I figured the trip would take at least three and a half hours. I reluctantly made the decision to forgo my walk to Austria.

Instead, I made my way across town to the Rhine River. Yes, the same river that flows through Basel has its start here, and forms the Swiss-Liechtenstein border. Here it is nothing more than a large stream. But because of the minerals in the rocks, the water is an iridescent milky blue. It gives the water a strange, surreal look. Stretching over the river is a 200-year-old wooden covered bridge. In the midpoint is the border, and I happily took a rare selfie there. Staying on the Swiss side of the river, I walked down to the water's edge and splashed my sunburnt face with ice cold water. Here at the riverbank, you could see the whole of Vaduz, with the old Prince's castle nestled on a ledge half way up the peak that loomed over the valley below. It's one hell of a vista.

I found the nearby bus stop and headed back to Sargans. On a cliff in the middle of town is Sargans Castle. Climbing to the top of the keep, I experienced the most insane view. Spread out before me was the entire nation of Liechtenstein. I mean, the whole, entire country is visible from this one parapet. You can see all the way to Austria from here. The sprawling valley is spread out before you with its surrounding cupola of snow-capped alps. You almost feel like a god looking down upon your very own Eden.

It was true, though, after all. There is no reason to visit Liechtenstein other than to say you visited Liechtenstein.

But now I could say it.

I visited Liechtenstein, the sixth smallest country in the world.

And it was fantastic.

Chapter Nine - And Then The Pandemic Set In

People always ask why we ever left Switzerland, if we loved it there so much. Pardon my vulgar, but justifiable, response:

Fucking Covid

On the one hand, thankfully, no one we knew died from the disease, and neither Lisa nor myself ever contracted it. On the other, its long reach into every aspect of life decimated our expat dream in ways we couldn't manage. I am bitter to this day about how this god damned pandemic upended our European dream, derailed the very opportunities for Lisa that brought us overseas in the first place, and kept us from enjoying our time in Switzerland to the fullest.

Fucking Covid

When we made the decision to move to Basel, it was with an understanding that we did so with zero intention of ever leaving. This was going to be permanent. Neither of us held any love or attachments to life in America. After the ordeal of making such an insanely expensive and stressful move, we affirmed our desire to stay in Europe the moment we arrived. In those naïve salad days, we had no inkling that some stupid bat meat in a faraway marketplace was going to royally fuck things up.

Thing is, Covid didn't crash over us like some sudden earth-shattering event, shaking us to our very foundations. It was a slow-rolling snowball of tidbits about some SARS-like infection in a far corner of the world that the West ignored, in hindsight, longer than it should have. We didn't watch a cataclysmic attack like 9/11 or witness some history-making moment like the bizarre night the Berlin Wall fell. There isn't a day or date that we associate with the start of the pandemic, but there hasn't really been a day since where we can't find a way in which it has affected us

And affect us it did.

Like everyone on the planet, it hit us big time. It may sound selfish to recount how this devastating disease upended our plans for a life in Europe, and truthfully, it is. So many suffered exponentially worse that we, and I am cognizant that, when all is said and done, we came out the other side far better than others. I am certainly not comparing our own experiences with others – I am simply recounting ours.

Life overseas was irrevocably changed, and it is impossible to talk about our experience without mentioning Covid and the impact it had on our lives. In the bubble that is our expat experience, Covid was a bitch, and this is the chapter where I tell you about how day to day life in Basel was upended, how it negatively sank our fortunes, and why it sent us packing. Not the most fun chapter for me to write, or, I'm sure, for you to read. Seems as if nothing in this world is free from the reach of Covid and the havoc it wreaked.

Everyone has their Covid story.

This is ours.

―――

January, 2020

While the pandemic started in China, its first real impact on the West was felt first in Europe. Like so many other health scares, if it wasn't in our backyards, we ignored it. We ignored Covid when it started because it was half a world away. The first time it entered the European consciousness was in January of 2020 when three cases of this mysterious new respiratory disease was reported in Bordeaux, France. Even then, it wasn't met with any semblance of panic. It wasn't until five deaths and over 200 infections suddenly exploded in next door Italy that Europe began to see that something dark was brewing. By the end of the month, the death rate in Italy was in the hundreds, and it became the first nation on the continent to issue lockdown orders. The news about this explosion of a new health threat was front and center in every news outlet in Europe, while it barely registered a mention in the US.

When the death rate jumped from the hundreds to the thousands within a week's time, panic immediately set in. Italy closed its borders. Switzerland, however, did not. The Swiss imagined that their neutrality extended to diseases, and if they pretended Covid did not exist, then Covid would pretend Switzerland didn't exist and pass it by.

Meanwhile, Italy was foundering like a drowning man. France, too, began to see a significant uptick in cases. Still, the Swiss carried on in a Trump-like manner: nothing to see here, move along, move along! The Swiss news outlets led us to believe that our neighbors were containing this tiny little outbreak and we had nothing to worry about.

February, 2020

Experiencing the Christmas Markets was one of the coolest things we could imagine. Our volume-challenged neighbors laughed and said we hadn't seen anything yet. The biggest event in the Basel calendar wasn't the *Herbstmesse* or the Christmas Market. No, the event of the year was the Swiss version of Carnival, known locally as *Fasnacht*.

When we were researching our move, we had seen many posts about this festival, but had no idea of just how important it was to Baselers until every person we met asked us how excited were we to experience it. One of Lisa's coworkers tried to put it into terms we could understand.

"It is bigger than *Eurovision*!"

[blank face from Lisa]

"You do not know *Eurovision*!?"

[blank face from Lisa]

"It is... it is... it is the World Cup of music!"

Now I had heard of *Eurovision* and was curious to experience it, but I had no idea just how big it is in Europe. After chatting with our friend Cass up in Scotland, she had asked if we were excited to watch our first *Eurovision*. After explaining the ins and outs of this weeklong song contest (and after watching the Will Ferrell movie *Eurovision Song Contest: The Story of Fire Saga*), we were pretty psyched to check this crazy thing out.

All of Europe drops everything for three things:

The World Cup
August holiday vacations
The *Eurovision Song Contest*

Nearly every country in Europe sends an act, be it a group or an individual, to perform one song, live. The general public and a jury of members of all participating nations vote to declare a winner. Past winners include ABBA and Celine Dion (who won representing Switzerland!). I cannot stress how huge this is in Europe. This particular year, Switzerland was a favorite to win (or at the very least place in the top five). Showmanship is a big part of the show, with many longshot entries resorting to outlandish costumes and set designs. When we finally were able to watch our first *Eurovision* on the BBC, with Graham Norton providing pithy and biting commentary, I downloaded the app so that I could vote (casting mine for a pre-war Ukraine). Italy ended up winning the first post-Covid *Eurovision*, not only because their act, Måneskin, was beyond fantastic, but also as a way to honor the European country hit hardest by the pandemic.

And it was truly one of the best cultural experiences of all time. I loved it! Lisa was highly entertained at my complete absorption into this phenomenon. I became an instant devotee, and have watched yearly since.

Eurovision is held in May, so we didn't have the chance to experience yet it to understand how big it was to adequately compare it to the excitement for *Fasnacht*.

There are hints, strewn throughout the city, at just how big *Fasnacht* is. The local Ueli beer features a *Fasnacht* clown as its logo. The symbol for the free *pissoirs* in the city is a *Fasnacht* clown letting loose a voluminous stream of urine (with a smile). Hundreds of shops throughout town have their clique's lanterns hanging above the door or in the window. Street art featuring costumed revelers can be found on nearly flat surface in the city. Even the river ferries are named for famous *Fasnacht* cliques.

So what is a *Fasnacht* clique, and what, actually, is *Fasnacht*?

Fasnacht is Carnival. This is the let-it-loose-and-party-hard-before-Lent festival, like Mardi Gras in New Orleans or Carnival in Rio de Janeiro. Unlike other celebrations of debauchery, there is a regimented schedule of events in Basel. I mean, the Swiss do love order and discipline.

Fasnacht begins on Shrove Monday, precisely at 4am. This is known as *Morgenstreich*, or the Morning March. At the appointed time, all of the lights in the city will be turned off. More specifically, the city will cut the power to the Old Town to ensure complete and total darkness. The bells of the churches will toll the hour and the procession of hundreds of cliques, or festival groups, will begin marching through the Old Town. They will all carry fantastically decorated lanterns held high on long poles. They will surround their clique's main lantern, quite like a parade float. This will be a larger version of the smaller lanterns. Cliques will choose a theme for their lanterns and costumes (they will be elaborately dressed in oversized *papier-maché* masks and fantastic costumes), most with ribald and raunchy humor directed at political or social issues. Along with the lanterns, clique members will play drums and fifes. All of the cliques play the same song, hundreds and hundreds of years old, creating the world's largest drum and fife corp. The music will echo throughout the whole of the city. The parade will wind out of the Old Town, across the Middle Bridge and into Kleinbasel, where it will end at the Messeplatz (festival hall).

You are not allowed to dress up for *Fasnacht*. You should dress as plainly as possible so that the parade cliques enjoy all the focus. You will actually be asked to leave if you should try to wear anything festive or outlandish. The normally passive Swiss will beat the ever-loving shit out of you should you show up to watch the parade in a mask.

The only adornment you may wear, and wear proudly, are your *Fasnacht* brooches. Sold by cliques to raise money for their costumes and lanterns, these are gold, silver, and bronze pins that depict the year and the theme of that year's festival. Immediately after the New Year, cliques will have representatives stationed in every square and busy tram stop in the city selling pins. The gold will cost you 30CHF, the silver 20CHF, and the bronze 10CHF. These pins are highly prized by Baselers, and on *Fasnacht*, you wear every single pin you have ever bought – the more pins you sport, the more patriotic and "blessed" you are.

When the *Morgenstreich* parade is over, the cliques will regroup inside the Messeplatz convention hall and have breakfast. Baselers will have a picnic breakfast along the parade route, too. No one leaves lest they lose their place. This is because after fueling up, the cliques begin their parade back along the same route to where they started. This time, in the daylight, they will dance and sing silly songs and throw candy and treats to the children along the way. Instead of the solemn pre-dawn orchestrated procession, this parade is one of joviality and dance and humor and celebration.

Once the parade is over, Baselers retreat to their favorite bars, pubs and restaurants, where they will camp out for the remainder of the day. The cliques will disperse to these eateries and drinkeries, as these are the places that sponsor them. Each clique calls a particular establishment home, and will spend the day there singing raunchy songs, reciting raunchy poems, acting out raunchy pantomimes, and telling raunchy jokes. Everyone gets completely shitfaced.
Revelers in the streets throw bags of confetti everywhere and kiosks and carts are set up all over town selling beer and brooches (for a month before *Fasnacht*, grocery stores sell 60 liter bags of colored confetti, and the streets of Basel are inches deep with the stuff).

This will go on for the next twenty-four hours.

Then, just as suddenly as it began, it stops. The bells toll throughout town, and *Fasnacht* comes to an abrupt and solemn end. Lent begins and the oldest Carnival celebration in the world (first mentioned as occurring in 1376) comes to a close.

Of course, this is all second hand information because on February 28th, 2020, the City of Basel cancelled that year's *Fasnacht* activities.

Fucking Covid

By the time March 2nd rolled around, and what would have been *Morgenstreich*, the city was devastated. The local paper reported that diagnoses of clinical depression in the Canton had tripled since the beginning of the new year, and most of it was linked not just to restrictions on gatherings, but specifically to the cancellation of *Fasnacht*. The festival is so ingrained in the DNA of Basel, that the city felt like one of its limbs had been lopped off. You could literally see dazed and confused locals out on the streets looking as if their dog had been shot. The depression was palatable and contagious. I've never experienced a collective gloom fall over a place like it did in Basel the first year Fasnacht was cancelled.

Even though grocery stores still sold their enormous bags of colorful confetti, Baselers did not toss it around like a coked-up Rip Torn hosting the *$1.98 Beauty Pageant*, but instead gravely scattered it around the city like the ashes of a murdered *Fasnacht* clown.

At least we would have next year when all this was over.

[cue bitter, sarcastic laughter]

Of course it was cancelled the following year, too. We never got to experience the greatest festival in all of Europe.

Fucking Covid

March, 2020

Looking back years later, the whole of the pandemic seems a blur of confinement, masks, and petulant bitching. Well, at least from the US and UK. Give credit where credit is due: Europeans, on the whole, grabbed their masks and dutifully wore them without complaint. There were no massive anti-mask demonstrations or entire "news" networks decrying masks as an "attack on freedom". Then again, there is a big difference between the thought process of Europeans, who believe in the collective good, and Americans who are taught all about the value of the individual from the moment they are born. To be clear, I am firmly in the "socialism is good" camp. The whole concept is rooted in the term "society", which is just another term for "everyone". I appreciate the notion of people and governments looking out for everyone, equally. I don't cotton to the notion of the American ideal of "me, me, me." Ask an American what is so great about America, and everything will be couched in terms of "me" or "my"; ask a European what's so great about their country and you'll hear them talk about "we" or "our".

Collective vs individual.

When it came to the pandemic, you can easily see where the crisis was dealt with in a "me, me, me" attitude in the States, and a "we, we, we" attitude in Europe. An American would ask "why should I wear a mask?"; a European would ask "why are you harming us by not wearing a mask?"

Call me biased, because I am.

When the pandemic finally hit the States, the American reaction, especially and specifically from Trump, was one of abject ineptitude. Europeans had already seen tens of thousands die, even in the face of the most stringent precautions. To see absolutely none being taken by the American government was confounding and rage-inducing to most Continentals.

Even the head-in-the-sand Swiss were quick to realize that this course of action was wrong. To be sure, they took their sweet-ass time pulling their head out of the sand (and their own ass), but they came around. And when they acted, the people listened. Dutifully, the community rallied around any and all measures meted out by the government. They didn't question, they complied, because they inherently knew that whatever measures the government was taking was in the name of containing a health crisis, and not, conspiratorially, to "take away personal freedoms."

[heavy sigh]

Jiminy Fucking Christmas

By March 13, schools were shuttered for the next thirty days and all public gatherings were cancelled. It wasn't much, but it was a start. Confoundingly, however, the Swiss decided that the border with Italy would remain open, but with restrictions. Italians seeking medical treatment would be refused entry, but cross-border workers would be allowed to continue to move back and forth.

Foreseeing an economic impact, based on the quickly collapsing Italian economy, the government set aside CHF 10 billion aimed at keeping major businesses afloat, and another CHF 8 billion was set aside for hardship loans. It was easy to see, based on the goings on in neighboring Italy, that businesses were quickly going to shut their doors and send their workers home, and Switzerland began to make moves in the event the pandemic crept across the border. These figures were significant considering the entire 2020 Swiss federal budget was CHF 75 billion. But again, here was an action based on protecting society as a whole. Also,

Switzerland was going to protect its bedrock economic supremacy at all cost.

The main issue Switzerland faced was the autonomy of the Cantons. Like the US, how the Cantons dealt with the pandemic was largely up to them and not the federal government. In Switzerland's case, however, the heads of all 26 Cantons met in Bern to discuss measures meant to combat the inevitable crisis in a cohesive and cooperative manner. An agreement was made that any measures enacted by the federal government, in regards to containing Covid, would be followed by the Cantons (though time would test that when it came to Zurich).

By this point in March, authorities in all Cantons had urged people to avoid public transport if possible (which is a huge ask in one of the most public transport-dependent nations in Europe), and to not go out to eat. Restaurants were not closed yet, but people were discouraged from visiting them and Basel-Stadt set a limit of no more than 50 people in a food service establishment, bar, or disco at a time.

Masks in public were not yet required, but simply encouraged.

Within three days, all that changed.

On March 16th, the federal government stepped in and shut the whole country down.

Schools, shops, restaurants, cafes, bars, museums, sports facilities, gyms, salons, cinemas, concert venues, theaters, libraries, swimming pools, and ski facilities were shut down completely.

Grocery stores, petrol stations, hospitals, banks, post offices, take-aways and delivery services, pharmacies, and train stations would remain open, with limited capacity and access.

All non-emergency medical treatments, therapies, and surgeries would be indefinitely postponed.

The federal government dictated that all workers should continue to be paid or go on paid leave.

The next day, I posted this to my Facebook page:

> *Watching from the epicenter of the pandemic, I am just gob smacked that the US is SOOOO far behind in taking definitive measures. Are you learning NOTHING from what is going on over here in Europe!? Close ALL businesses except grocery stores, pet stores, pharmacies, and banks! The longer you wait the less effect it will have towards flattening the curve. And for the love of Christ, STOP GOING OUT!!!!*
>
> *Now that we're in a lockdown, it's a bit eerie here. The trams and busses are running but are completely empty. The main drag in our neighborhood, which runs in front of the train station, is completely empty- and usually it's one of the busiest streets in Basel. Had to go to the store today to see what we could find, and was surprised to see that the Swiss are not "hamstering", and the shelves are at least 75% stocked. There were no lines, no crowds. Everyone did, however, deliberately give each other wide physical berth. I was not the only one wearing rubber gloves.*
>
> *Lisa continues to work from home as her office building is being disinfected - there were confirmed cases in her office, but they have not been seriously ill.*
> *Life is about to get a lot different here, but I take comfort in knowing we're not in the US and dealing with the dumbfuckery there. For now, even though we are in a very hot spot, contagion-wise, we're*

doing A-Okay

At this point, Lisa had been working from home for about two weeks, so thankfully it had limited her exposure to others. Because she has lupus, I was adamant that she stayed the fuck at home and let me be the one to go out when necessary, to minimize her infection risk. When I did venture out to the Coop, I wore a mask and surgical gloves. Sanitizer stations appeared everywhere overnight. Plastic barriers also went up at cashier check-outs and counters, at bank teller windows, and at the pharmacy. I have never washed my hands so often or vigorously. Every possible place a person could stand was plastered with distancing decals.

The Swiss are not ones to be kept indoors. It is not in their nature. Sundays especially are days for long walks and frolicking in the park. Figuring that it was safe to be outside instead of in an enclosed space, the Swiss flocked to the many public parks in town. This immediately became a huge problem as these spaces became more crowded than ever before since no one had anywhere else to go.

The *polizei* began to patrol the parks and public places breaking up groups of more than three people. Within a few weeks, they would be authorized to fine people up to 100CHF, per person, for gathering in groups of more than three. Large placards were placed in all public parks and plazas warning people against gathering. Playground equipment was roped off. In Lucerne, the entire waterfront promenade, stretching for over 5km along the lakefront, was cordoned off. In Basel, instead of roping off the Rhine Promenade, the *polizei* increased their presence and simply moved people along who stopped to sit.

The following week, I had made a trip to the Coop to stock up on food supplies and was on my way home with my fully laden cart. Just two blocks from home, I was stopped by two *polizisten* who asked me what I was doing out. I showed them my cart, my receipt, and my ID, telling them my address, which was just over there, officers.

"You will go straight home now!"

"Well, yeah, that's what I'm doing"

"Good. Then do that!"

"Okay, I will"

"Go, then!"

"I'm going!"

"Good, go!"

At this point, Baselers, unlike toilet paper-hoarding Americans, were not "hamstering" anything. Sure, there were shortages in the stores, but it wasn't nearly as apocalyptic as I imagined it would be. Baking supplies, chocolate, cheese, bread, and pasta, though, were wiped out. Potatoes, a major Swiss food staple, were well stocked. And there was plenty of toilet paper.

On the 19th, Italy went on full and total lockdown. Italians in the north scrambled to get across the border to avoid being shut in, assuming that things would be better on the other side of the fence. Many hoped to escape to Austria to ride out the Covid storm, or to bypass the Italian-Swiss border by scooting through Austria to Liechtenstein to Switzerland. The Swiss completely closed the entire nation's border in response. Infections had soared exponentially and the Swiss, now in a bit of a rightful panic, were finally realizing that the majority of cases were coming from their Italian neighbors to the south. To really bring home the seriousness of the situation, Italy forbade holding funerals. The most Catholic nation on earth forbade holding funerals.

The Pope even cancelled Easter! What other sign does one need that this is some serious, serious shit?

The morning of the 20th, news outlets all over the world showed scenes from across Italy where every city looked post-apocalyptic, without a single person on a sidewalk or a car on a street. Basel, too, was a virtual ghost town. It was creepy and eerie and unnerving. I sat looking out our front window and an hour passed without seeing a single car drive by. What I did notice were the sirens. It seemed like the *neener-neener* of rushing ambulances was constant now. The Basel-Land Hospital was just two kilometers away from us and had set up one of the largest Covid response centers in this part of the country. It seemed like an ambulance soared past our front windows every fifteen minutes.

On March 20th, the numbers jumped, and so did the nation. Panic began to set in. The number of infections increased by nearly a thousand in less than 24 hours. Almost 50 people had died in Switzerland from Covid by now.

The federal government sprang into action, and would finally be working in a proactive manner. They immediately suspended the waiting period to collect social insurance benefits. Self-employed persons were entitled to 80% of their salary in benefits. Part-time workers who would not ordinarily qualify for social insurance benefits were now allowed to collect 90% of their wages. Banks were authorized to issue loans to businesses up to 500,000CHF with no conditions and fully guaranteed by the government. The VAT (value added tax) was suspended from all goods and services indefinitely (as a cost-saving measure for consumers). All internet and cellular companies were directed to provide full capabilities to all customers at no additional cost (to accommodate everyone now working from home). *Die Post* would increase deliveries to seven days a week to accommodate online shopping demands. All train and bus tickets were now fully refundable and there would be a suspension of all ticket takers on public transport. Monthly recurring charges for transportation passes would be suspended and all public transport would effectively be free (though discouraged from use).

Meanwhile, in Norway, they, too, were readying a bailout package for business. The caveat to qualify was that no executives could take a bonus or collect dividends for at least two years (imagine that happening in the US!). All laid-off employees were entitled to full pay from the government for at least 20 days. Moves like this, taken in the whole of society's interest, is why I find myself firmly in the "socialism is good" column.

And finally, the border was completely closed (with exceptions being made for healthcare workers who lived in Germany or France and worked in Switzerland). Cross-border workers from Italy were now forbidden from entering the country.

Just like that, Switzerland went from hemming and hawing to taking rapid, concrete steps to stem the tide of rising infection rates. It worked hard, too, to buoy the economy and keep its citizens getting paid.

More importantly, instead of complaining or whining or bitching or protesting, the Swiss sighed a collective, relieved thank you.

What did the US do? They lowered interest rates.

To be fair, the largest grocery chain in Chicago asked people to keep the 7-9pm hours on Tuesdays and Thursdays for the elderly in order to minimize risk to the aging and infirm. It lasted a week before Americans got too impatient at having their "freedoms impinged".

This was also the middle of Spring Break for American college kids, who flocked like a plague of drunken starlings to every beach on the Gulf coast. Without strict state or federal laws preventing travel or public gatherings, the US's infection rate nearly tripled overnight. My Facebook feed was clogged with videos of news outlets interviewing shirtless idiots in Panama City Beach and South Padre Island who claimed "it's not a big deal and it's ruining my Spring Break", "everyone is blowing this way out of proportion", "I'm young, I don't get sick."

It was during this week that I found myself reading *The Splendid and the Vile* by Erik Larson about the London Blitz. The passages about the enormous sacrifices of Londoners just made the petulance of those who refused to stay home or wear a mask boil my blood.

That night, following the lead of the UK, all of Switzerland took a moment at 7pm to gather on balconies and in back yards to bang pots and pans, clap and yell thanks to all the healthcare workers putting their lives at risk to help others.

Three days later, on March 23, Switzerland's infection rate nearly doubled, from 4500 cases to 7800. The death rate, too, had gone from 43 to 98. A thousand new cases were reported in less than 24 hours. This was the thick of it.

Basel had been experiencing the 4th worst infection rate of any Canton up to this point, but after imposing all of the measures of the past few days, they had dropped to 7th. Zurich, on the other hand, was getting worse and worse, and it came down to the Canton's über-rich ignoring federal decrees because those things were for the poor people (rich people don't get sick, right?). A local news outlet excoriated Zurichers, claiming they are "privileged, snobbish, above-it-all". Indeed, Zurich had still not shut down their ski resorts and idiot Brits were still lingering in the resorts, refusing to go home. The SBB national rail service cut all service into and out of Zurich by 90% to keep the city as isolated as possible. Graffiti began to pop up all over Zurich proclaiming *money can't protect you*.

Across the border in Italy, the government increased penalties for people violating Covid lockdown restrictions. Violators now faced increased fines of €400-3000 and prison terms of one to five years. Yes, prison for violating lockdown. Shit was serious in Italy. In terms of cases to population, it was the hardest hit nation in Europe, and the second most hard hit in the world.

Meanwhile in Texas, the dumb-as-fuck Lt Governor put out the following statement: *Let's get back to work, let's get back to living, let's be smart about it, and those of us who are 70-plus, we'll take care of ourselves. But don't sacrifice the country.*

Spoken like a true 'Murican.

Basel's newspaper, *die Zeitung*, published this op-ed on March 30th:

> *Why Corona Strikes America So Devastatingly*
>
> *The United States has become the hotspot of the global corona crisis because it is particularly poorly equipped to deal with epidemics. Three reasons for the misery.*
> *If the number of people who died because of Covid-19 remained around 100,000, "we would all have done a good job together," said Donald Trump on Sunday. A death toll of this level would be significantly higher per million people than in European countries with comparable health care.*
>
> *Why? Three American peculiarities provide an answer: the health status of minorities and poor people is significantly poorer in comparison, the number of homeless and prison inmates is high, and health care in poorer neighborhoods and rural areas was already poor before the outbreak of the epidemic.*

1. Pre-existing diseases endanger African Americans
According to the latest information, 42 percent of Americans are obese, two in three adults are overweight. The unhealthy diet of poorer sections in particular contributes to widespread cardiovascular diseases, high blood pressure and diabetes. The analysis of data from Wuhan has shown that contagion with the virus can be particularly dangerous due to such previous illnesses.

African Americans in cities such as Chicago, Detroit, Baltimore, Milwaukee, St. Louis and Memphis would be particularly affected. The African American community in his state is a "crisis in crisis," says Wisconsin's democratic governor Tony Evers. Medical care for poor people in the inner city was problematic before the Corona crisis, but it could now be catastrophic.

The pathogen also poses special risks for socially disadvantaged Latino communities in California, along the US border with Mexico in Texas and in major cities such as New York and Houston. Many Latinos and African-Americans from the lower classes continue to work whenever possible despite the epidemic. In New York, for example, poor people in particular are now using the subway and are thus exposed to an increased risk of infection.

2. Millions homeless or in prison
The nationwide high number of homeless people - around 50,000 in the Los Angeles area alone - should make the fight against the disease even more difficult. Meanwhile, a total of 2.2 million people are imprisoned in federal and state prisons, more than in any other country in the world. Because they fear an outbreak with devastating consequences for the inmates, doctors and social workers are pushing for

> the early release of as many detainees as possible.
>
> *3. Too few beds and ventilators*
> Deficiencies in the American healthcare system could also contribute to a comparatively high number of coronavirus deaths. In the United States there are fewer hospital beds per 100,000 inhabitants than in Italy, and the hospitals would hardly be able to cope with a surge of Corona patients.
>
> "We will no longer have enough ventilators this week," feared William Nungesser, the Republican Vice Governor of Louisiana, where the pathogen is currently spreading rapidly. The state had requested 12,000 ventilators, but received only 192 by Monday. The situation is no better elsewhere, as there is a lack of respirators and respirators nationwide.

Europe was watching the goings-on across The Pond with both great interest and great horror. Watching Trump lambast Dr. Fauci, refuse to issue a mask mandate, refuse to shut down business or schools, and let states willy-nilly their way through a raging epidemic was simply unbelievable (though, in fairness, it was also up to the individual Cantons, in most cases, in Switzerland). Everyone asked us if we were thankful we weren't back home (of course, our response was "*this* is our home"). But, yes, absolutely, yes, yes, yes, we were very thankful we weren't back in the US. Especially since our last address was in the shit-storm of Texas, where masks were verboten and Covid was nothing more than a conspiracy theory.

Though my physical therapy sessions had been cancelled, Dr. Schwamborn still wanted to see me to check on how my shoulder was healing.

"Donald Trump is a stupid, evil man. He is killing his own people and no one seems to care. I am glad you are here in Switzerland, my friend."

April, 2020

April 1st was when the Swiss government realized that the projected date of the 15th to end the lockdown was not going to happen. Lockdown was not going to end *anytime* soon. In just a week, there were now over 17,000 cases nationwide, an increase of 10,000 in seven days. Testing had now become commonplace and it was determined that 15% of the population had Covid (which is significant when you consider the whole population of Switzerland is 8 million people).

Meanwhile in the US, over 90,000 people had now died from the disease, and people were still taking Carnival cruises.

On April 19th, the Swiss National Yodeling Festival was cancelled (well, shit), as was the Montreux Jazz Festival. Art Basel was pushed back from June until September (which was laughably optimistic), and the Swiss answer to Coachella, called Paleo, was axed as well (Celine Dion was scheduled to headline). The Basel Zoo announced their intentions to reopen on May 1st (spoiler, it did not).

Also on April 19th, the *Boston Globe* printed 15 pages of Covid-related obituaries.

April became a dark time for us personally as well. With so many companies foundering due to the massive economic impact of the lockdown, Lisa was told she would have to have her pay cut by 10%. Their reasoning was that it would enable the company to keep people on the payroll and not resort to layoffs. Being a team player, and not having any other choice, Lisa agreed.

But it hurt. We were already learning that while her pay in

the US was a comfortable salary by any means, in Switzerland, it meant living frugally and economically. Having it reduced by such a chunk would result in a real hit to our finances. At the time, we may have been saving money by not going out, not travelling, not shopping. But utilities and rent and insurance were still as expensive as ever. Not being able to shop in France or Germany, too, hit the pocketbook hard. Going across the border usually saved me upwards of 30% on our grocery bill. Now, I was forced to pay Swiss prices with less money in the bank.

Lisa's office had continued to fund her lunch card and encouraged her to use it to order delivery. This would keep people physically out of restaurants while simultaneously keeping them in business. A protocol emerged with Uber Eats drivers, where they would ring the buzzer, confirm the delivery, and place your food on the bottom of the stairs in the lobby for you to come down and collect after they left.

More depressingly, the pandemic meant that plans for Lisa to head up a new international team was indefinitely postponed. The reason we came in the first place, the reason she took the promotion in Basel, was now looking like it might not happen. Covid had already cast a pall over everyday life, but this made the gloom that much darker. All the plans we had made for me to accompany her on business trips were scuttled. All the plans for her to climb the corporate ladder were stymied. No one was going anywhere.

May, 2020

Gods damn it, *Eurovision* has been cancelled!

June, 2020

By the end of May, the worst of it seemed to be over. Infection rates were dropping and the government felt as if it could begin to ease some restrictions. They set up end dates for closures and set about trying to rebuild society.

By June 1st, groups of up to 30 people could once again gather. On the 6th, all businesses were allowed to re-open. Restaurants could not, however, seat more than 4 people to a table, and everyone must leave their contact information when they dined so that people could be contacted should an outbreak be linked to that particular establishment.

June 15th saw the border re-open with Germany. The French border, in Basel only, had remained open to cross-border workers, and never fully closed. When the German border did finally open, border guards on both sides continued, however, to turn away cross-border shoppers. Given the economic headache, I began to resume my shopping in France at this point, as there are almost zero border controls on the way to the Géant. Was it irresponsible to go back to shopping in France? Probably. But economics, especially with Lisa's reduction in pay, meant I had to save as much money as possible, and that simply wasn't possible by hitting the Coop down the street.

The border with Italy, though, would remain closed until July.

The Basel Zoo, as promised, managed to re-open, albeit it a month later than they anticipated. Because we lived just blocks away, we had bought yearly passes. Due to the unexpected closure due to Covid, the Zoo extended our passes for five months to compensate for the lost time. Though you could visit the Zoo, all of the indoor enclosures were closed to the public, and the restaurant remained shuttered, with only the ice cream kiosks offering food in the park.

July, 2020

But of course, all Swiss National Day festivities, including the fireworks, have been cancelled. So, too, have all Bastille Day celebrations across the border (a favorite holiday of mine, I was looking forward to spending my

first one in France, even if it was St Louis). To celebrate, we ate schnitzel on Swiss Day and snails on French Day.

At home.

Yay.

August, 2020

There was a semblance of normalcy now, although social distancing and mask wearing were now considered a part of everyday life. At this point, Baselers were used to waiting in lines to enter stores and shops, having their temperatures taken and being asked to wear a mask in all public places. I watched a tram driver refuse to embark until a passenger put on a mask. When the idiot refused, the tram driver announced that the tram would not leave until they put it on or got off the tram. This stalemate lasted for almost five minutes until the *polizei* were called and forcibly removed the miscreant from the tram. The whole front section of trams and buses were taped off to keep the drivers distanced and safe. I still avoided using public transport as much as possible (I had no choice but to take the tram to France to shop). I enjoyed the walk. I was increasing my steps and my ass had never looked more firm and shapely. I was racking up between 60-70 miles walked a month. Not renewing my monthly tram pass also saved us a good chunk of change.

I had to go to the Apple Store as my phone was having some battery issues and I needed someone to take a look at it. First, I had to make an appointment. There were no walk-ins allowed. Arriving on my scheduled day, I was made to wait in line outside where my temperature was taken, my appointment confirmed, and I was issued a fresh mask and a pair of latex gloves. There were two alp-sized bouncers manning the door, who were both super friendly, but coldly menacing to those who tried to sweet-talk their way past them. No more than 10 people were allowed in the store at one time. After I left, I noticed every business up and down Freiestrasse had bouncers stationed outside with lines snaking down the sidewalk.

It did piss me off, though, to see the longest line formed at the Louis Vuitton store. Idiocy knows no boundaries.

September, 2020

After enjoying a gradual easing of restrictions, the government announced on the 15th that reported cases were beginning to rise again, and that the country should be prepared for a return of some gathering restrictions should the trend continue. At the same time, they allowed public sporting events to be held, but at two-thirds capacity. For the first time, real arguments began to spring up in Bern about the easing of restrictions, with many health experts saying it was too much too soon and that the rebound of cases was evidence of that. The government, keen to kick start the economy, was eager get as many facets of life back to normal as possible.

I think we all know where this is headed.

October, 2020

Sure enough, on the 16th, the #8 tram to Weil am Rhein was standing room only as rumors quickly spread that the border was going to be closed again due to the spike in Covid cases across Europe. Local news reported the line to get into the Marktkauf stretched all the way back into Switzerland, and the wait was up to two hours to get in. This is why I shopped in France.

The next day, the border was closed and both Switzerland and Germany went into a second lockdown.

Restaurants were once again shuttered. Salons, clubs, bars, sport venues, and schools were all closed. For two weeks, Basel was once again lifeless.

By the 30th, Paris, France experienced the largest traffic jam in European history, with cars jammed in a stand-still for *438 miles* as people tried to flee the city before it went on total lockdown. Fights broke out over café tables as restaurants were set to close at midnight and Parisians were determined to get one last meal in before being locked indoors. The Covid rate in France had skyrocketed and hospitals were now overflowing. At the current rate of infection, it was estimated that almost 10,000 people would be in French intensive care units, which was miles over capacity. The French were locking down hard to prevent that from happening. Still, the border in the Basel area was allowed to remain open (St Louis had one of the lowest infection rates in all of France).

In all my times crossing the French border once Covid hit, I never once saw a single gendarme stopping people or cars. No Swiss *grenzsoldat* appeared, either. They were all, apparently, on the Swiss-German border, which hadn't been this fortified since the end of World War II.

To the horror of Baselers, the *Herbstmesse* (Autumn Fair) was cancelled. In 550 years, it had never been cancelled.

Not once.

Not for war, not for the Black Plague, not for either World War.

This would be the first time *ever*. And Basel was sunk. A deep depression hung over the city. On the other hand, it helped reinforce, at least to some, just how serious and deadly this pandemic was. To keep Baselers from committing mass *hari kari*, the city decided to at least put the Ferris Wheel up (thank goodness the tower of the Münster was permanently closed because even in the best of times, Baselers seem to love to jump from there).. The number of riders was strictly limited, but it was something to keep the streak going. With the wheel up in the Münsterplatz, technically, the *Herbstmesse* officially celebrated it 551st year.

No brats and *glühwein* for us. My heart, too, was sunk. I was settling, uncomfortably, into an angry depression. Lisa, too, was in a dark mood. Between the loss in pay and her stalled career, she was in a deep funk. Our only way to exorcise our cabin fever demons was to take daily walks in the nearby park or around the neighborhood. Even being outdoors, we still felt like we were under house arrest. We knew it was necessary, but it still got to us.

November, 2020

People were getting sick of this shit, and the edges were beginning to fray. Fights were beginning to break out over people not wearing masks or gathering in large groups in the public squares. Local governments were getting frustrated and took their case to the federal government.

From *The Local*, a Swiss online daily:

> *Switzerland's Federal Council has just made it easier for police to fine someone for failing to wear a mask.*
>
> *In its session on Wednesday, Switzerland's Federal Council made a number of decisions related to the ongoing coronavirus pandemic.*
>
> *In addition to making more funds available for businesses hit hard by the pandemic, the government also submitted changes to the Epidemics Act to make it easier for police to issue fines for minor violations of Switzerland's mask requirement.*
>
> *Previously, while there was the scope to issue fines, this would require court action. As a result, minor violations - such as the refusal of an individual to wear a mask - were not punished, the major focus on businesses who failed to enforce the mask requirement.*
>
> *According to Swiss news outlet Watson: "Minor violations of the Epidemics Act such as violations of the obligation to wear a face mask should now be punishable with fines."*
>
> *In a press conference after the decision, Federal Council spokesman André Simonazzi said the goal was not to hand out thousands more fines. "We had this possibility in spring (to issue fines), now we have created it again. But it is not the goal to issue many fines."*
>
> *Ueli Maurer added that making it easier to levy fines "helps" in the fight against the virus. "We have to realize that things will only get better soon if we all*

*stick to the measures. You can also fine people for demonstrations against the measures," he said.
"You can protest and complain, but if we don't bring the numbers down, it won't work. Sometimes a fine can help."*

*How much I be fined for not wearing a mask?
The government did not comment on the amount someone has to pay for so-called "minor" violations of the mask requirement.
Technically speaking, breaching the mask requirement can lead to a fine of up to CHF10,000 under the Epidemics Act*

In Basel, the *polizei* took this to heart and began to issue tickets in earnest in an effort to get people to comply with the mask mandate (and keep infections down). Once the local paper started posting about the number of tickets issued in one week along the Promenade and in the city parks, and apocryphal stories were shared among neighbors, the public began to take the hint and refrained from grouping in public. The playground equipment in the parks was taped off, and *polizei* patrols were the norm in Margarethenpark.

The anti-mask movements in the US, UK, and Canada were beginning to bleed into Europe, especially among expats and right wing parties. Rallies were now being held in major cities across Europe demanding the end of mask mandates and social distancing rules. While no large marches hit the streets of Basel, Zurich was the scene of a 10,000 strong march that ended in street fights and police firing rubber bullets. As frustrating as it was to see this kind of thing in Europe, it was nothing compared to the sheer lunacy going on back home in the States. Dr. Schwamborn was beside himself.

"My family would always take a Florida vacation, every year. It was a tradition. Twenty years we did this. We would go to Disney World and the beach. Now, we are never, ever going back to the US. Ever."

December, 2020

Of course, the Christmas Markets were cancelled.

Christmas across the Continent was cancelled. In place of the market stalls and children's *Märchenwald* village, the city kept the Ferris Wheel up through the New Year as a consolation. It was one of the most depressing Christmases in recent memory. It made shopping for presents especially challenging (as did our reduced income). The most magical time of year was anything but. Economies that were struggling to rebound had been counting on the tourism dollars of Christmastime. That rebound was not in the Christmas Cards (which are expensive as hell in Basel – the only place I found them was at the bookstore for about 15CHF a card).

The city still put up their lights and decorations in the Old Town, and many restaurants set up grab-n-go *glühwein* kiosks. Lisa and I bundled up the week before Christmas and headed down to Barfüsserplatz to have a mug of mulled wine and take in the festive window displays. We were relieved to see that there were no large groups; just couples huddling together enjoying what they could. Everyone kept a respectful distance, and we made sure that when we lifted our masks to drink our tasty beverage, we weren't near anyone else. Still, seeing the city try and be festive just amplified the sadness of the markets being cancelled.

Fucking Covid

Switzerland also had to specifically ban travelers from the UK, who were sneaking past lockdown restrictions and taking holidays at Swiss ski resorts. The resorts had reopened in limited capacity to help rural communities make it through the season. Switzerland was not yet open for tourist business, and let the resorts open for Swiss locals to compensate for the limited offerings at Christmas. Brits snuck into the country and had to be forcibly removed. Americans, too, were banned from the country due to the absolute lack of coherence in their Covid response.

January, 2021

The lockdowns were over by the end of the month and the vaccine had *finally* hit the market – albeit not in Switzerland. It would be months before the shot, which was ironically manufactured in Basel, would be available to the Swiss. We sat in furious anger as Americans, who scoffed at everything Europe did to battle the virus, were the first to get the vaccine (that most considered a hoax or poison or a vehicle for a 5G microchip). It was a slap in the face to Europeans. Italy had borne the brunt of the virus, had taken every precaution imaginable, been militant about containing the spread of the virus, and here were the cavalier Americans, who flaunted masks and social distancing, and even the truth on the news, getting the shot before anyone else.

Europe was *pissed*.

February, 2021

Once again, the Basel Zoo extended our passes to compensate for time lost during the second lockdown.

Once again, *Fasnacht* was cancelled.

Fucking Covid

This time, the cliques decided to celebrate the festival anyway, just in a slightly different way. They crafted their lanterns and floats and costumes as they normally would, but this year, they would create virtual parades throughout town. This meant taking a main or busy street and hanging their clique lanterns above every doorway and displaying their masks in every window. One could walk down St Albanstrasse and look at a hundred different *Fasnacht* lanterns, at your leisure. Instead of these lanterns whizzing by you in the pre-dawn darkness, you could linger and admire the artwork. In the Cathedral Square, large two-story tall towers stood, made of mosaics of clique lanterns that lit up at night. Drum and fife corps would stage guerilla performances randomly throughout town for short ten minute bursts. This year, the confetti was thrown with slightly more enthusiasm.

March, 2021

Lisa's office was finally allowing people to come back to work, but offered those working from home the option to remain doing so. Those who chose to go in had to have their temperature taken at the door and randomly throughout the day. Color-coded badges were issued to help track any infections that might spring up. Within a month, the building would be shut down again as an outbreak hit the office. Lisa wisely remained at home and only went to the office on two occasions to retrieve personal items and necessary equipment. Those would be the last times she would set foot in her office.

Europe was still ticked that the Swiss-made vaccines were not yet available for distribution on the continent. A Norwegian travel agency began offering vaccinations in Moscow. For €1499, you could fly to Russia two times (and fly right back, same day) to get the Sputnik V shot (administered at the airport). For €1999, you could go twice, but be put up in a hotel and get your shot administered in a hospital. Neither option required the standard visa, which was being waived by the Russian government in a bid to legitimize their vaccine.

For an honest to God moment, Lisa and I both considered it.

April, 2021

Finally, we could get vaccinated.

Because we both have autoimmune disorders, we were bumped to the front of the line. The majority of Swiss would not receive their first shot until June. By the end of April, it was reported that almost 200 Swiss had taken the Russians up on their Sputnik V offer.

The vaccination center was in Kleinbasel in one of the large convention centers. Again, bouncers were at the door checking your name against the appointment calendar. Once inside, you went down a set of escalators and were deposited in the most *Logan's Run*-looking 1970s sci-fi scene. Soft tubular New Age music floated ever so softly on the air. As you descended, you could see the entire set up: a waiting area of precisely separated chairs, a bank of kiosks at the end of the chair garden, and an endless maze of small cubicles. Everything was white. The kiosks, the cubicles, the workers' uniforms. It felt strangely dystopian. You know those movies where the clueless masses gather to be given their ration of *Soylent Green* or shots of *Soma*, all dispensed by smiling white-clad representatives of The State? It definitely felt like that. It was a weird combination of comforting and unnerving.

I had my temperature taken and was told to wait in the last chair in a middle row. When the person in front of me moved up one chair, so would I, until I reached the kiosk at the front. There was no cell signal in this area, so you just sat there, with this Brian Eno space jazz on the overhead, watching everyone else looking around nervously. Once at the kiosk, I was checked in and issued a vaccination passport. A small yellow book that looks exactly like a normal passport, this would be the paper documentation of my vaccination and I should carry it with me at all times. The Swiss are issued these passports at birth when they get their first vaccinations (and were instructed to bring theirs with), but as a foreigner, this was my first opportunity to get one.

After sitting for a short spell in a second seating area, I was called back to a cubicle to get my shot. In a thoughtful gesture, the Swiss had decorated the maze of hallways around these cubicles with palm trees and tropical plants. A gentleman with a thick French accent led me into his small cubicle where I took a seat, got my shot, and had my passport "stamped". His serene manner, his pristine uniform, his robotic "I've done this a thousand times" movements kind of made the hairs on the back of my neck stand on end.

I was made to wait in a third seating area for fifteen minutes to ensure I had no bad reaction to the shot (I got the Moderna version, Lisa got Pfizer). The entire room was facing the enormous clock on the far wall, watching intently for their time to expire. When mine was up, feeling perfectly fine, I hopped the escalator back to the surface. The sudden rush of grey skies, rain, traffic, and noise was a bit of a slap. I felt like I was coming out of a trance. I guess they actually had succeeded in relaxing me down there.

The next day, my arm was throbbing. I could barely move it. My temperature spiked and I got a severe migraine (I don't get headaches; I get migraines).

That night on British television, the featured movie was *Outbreak*.

I was feeling myself again the very next day (though my arm ached for another three). Lisa had a far more severe reaction to her shot and spent two days in bed.

Shortly after we received our second shot, Switzerland rolled out an electronic vaccination card. We would have to show our QR code whenever we went out to eat (restaurants were still tracking customers and this new app made things so much easier). Even doctors' offices demanded to see your vaccination certificate when checking in.

I cannot stress how relieved we were to finally get our shots. Again, Europe was angry and resentful that the rollout of the vaccine, manufactured in Europe, went overseas first. On top of that, the rollout in places like Switzerland were far slower than in other parts of Europe. Nearly all of Italy had been given their first shot before Switzerland began administering their initial shots to the elderly and infirm (though, to be fair, they were the hardest hit of any European nation and deserved it first). My parents back in Illinois had already received both of their shots *three months* before we got our first.

Now that the country (and the continent) was getting vaccinated, life finally started to return to some semblance of normal. The last travel restrictions were lifted in June when Switzerland finally allowed travel to and from the United States and Great Britain. By this time, Boris Johnson was as much a laughingstock and pariah as was Trump. Neither would ever be thought of without bitter disdain by continental Europeans. Though the rollout was slow in Switzerland, I was very glad to be thousands of miles away from the disastrous discombobulation of a Covid response in the States.

May, 2021

Lisa had had enough.

The new international division she was supposed to head (and the reason we came to Switzerland to begin with) had been officially scrapped. The company had no plans to return her salary to its original level, and bonuses had been cancelled. With our reduced income and job prospects fucked, she decided it was time to look for something new. Finding a job in Europe was going to be extremely difficult (in a post-Covid economy without any connection to the EU or visa sponsorship of any kind), so she expanded her search for opportunities back in the States. When she landed a position with a company in Denver, Colorado, we agreed she should take it. The cost of living alone dictated our decision to fall back and regroup.

Per Swiss law, Lisa had to give a three-month notice, which meant we would be looking to leave Basel in August. We would be leaving almost two years to the day we arrived.

To add insult to injury, when we went to book a moving company, we learned that shipping rates had literally doubled what they had been two years prior. The exact same shipping container, with the exact same moving company, had been $12,000 on the way to Europe, but would now cost $24,000 to take our stuff back. Tail between legs, Lisa had to go back to her new employers and ask for an increase in the relocation fund to cover the cost (which they graciously agreed to).

This was how our expat adventure was to end: in ignominy.

Fucking Covid

Chapter Ten – Repatriation

It was less than twenty-four hours since we had arrived in Denver before I watched a homeless man stand in the middle of a busy downtown sidewalk, whip out his dick, and piss all over a light pole.

"We are not in Kansas anymore"

Until we could find a place to live, Lisa's new employers were putting us up in an Airbnb in the downtown Capitol Hill neighborhood. The area was a mix of vagrants, meth heads, tech bros, and wealthy gentrification poseurs. Other than the occasional bahnhof miscreant, we had not seen a single homeless person in two years. Now, one camped next to the garbage bins behind our rented flat. I expected some reverse-culture shock moving back, but not so suddenly, not so soon.

As we walked the business district of Denver, scoping out our new surroundings, I was both excited and mortified.

It was good to see skyscrapers again. I love a good, towering skyline. Having grown up in Chicago, I loved heavily-built up cities, soaring towers of glass and steel, and buildings that fought each other to be the tallest. Skyscrapers aren't really a European thing. Sure, some cities have their fair share of tall buildings (Frankfurt and London come to mind), but most European metropolises build out instead of up.

I was shocked, however, at how dirty, polluted, garbage-strewn, and smelly this city was. Having lived in pristine, Lysol-level cleanliness for two years, the visual neglect was hard to take in. It was an odd to feel disconcertingly un-safe. In fact, I had become so used to having my guard down that Lisa had to remind me secure my wallet and not make eye contact with anyone. The more I looked past the modern, gleaming buildings above me, I saw nothing but neglect at eye level. We seemed to be the only non-itinerant people on the street. A crazed shirtless man literally howled at a passing bus. Another tried to karate-chop every passer-by. Bodies lay sleeping in more doorways than I could count.

This was not the Denver I imagined we'd be moving to. It was supposed to be a granola-crunching, IPA-swigging hipster paradise. Instead, it felt like Detroit in the 80s.

After living in an urban environment for so long, I was hoping to do the same once we got to Colorado. I had become accustomed to a car-free existence. I was used to walking to shops. I was planning out a continuation of that kind of city life for us. Plus, Lisa's office was smack dab in the middle of downtown, so the closer to the city center, the better.

Then we started exploring downtown Denver.

Every neighborhood near the center of town was this jumble of homeless tent encampments and ultra-modern, soulless apartment complexes. Further away from the business district, and you entered wealthy bungalow enclaves where houses felt like they weren't bought, but passed down from Muffy to Buffy to Kip to Skip. Of course, I'm a bit of a secret Preppy and would have loved to find a house in one of these gentrified neighborhoods, but rentals were hard to find, and priced well above what we wanted to spend.

Yes, we wanted to find a place to rent because, given our history of moving, we didn't want to get stuck with home ownership should a better opportunity befall us in the future. Plus, how do you buy a house in a city you've never been to before, and have no familiarity with? How could you possibly make such a huge purchase without knowing which area is the best for your needs? I don't know that we'll ever own our own place, and I'm okay with that. It allows us a sense of freedom. In many respects, it keeps us from feeling shackled.

Our immediate excursions around Denver proper confirmed that finding the perfect part of town to settle in was going to be a challenge.

One of the first things I noticed was how much of Denver is a food desert. Even the wealthy, tree-lined enclaves of Craftsman bungalows were completely free of grocery stores, bodegas, or markets. We began to cross houses off our list simply because of their lack of proximity to a grocery store. I was still in "I'll be walking to the store" mode, which I quickly came to realize was not going to be a thing for me, ever again. I had forgotten how car-centric America is, and it kind of crushed me to know that no matter where we lived, be it downtown or out in the burbs, we were going to need to buy a car, and that there was nothing within walking distance, anywhere. Even if we ended up with a condo in the city, I was afraid if I did find a grocery store within walking distance, I couldn't guarantee I'd make it home without being mugged or robbed.

For the first time in years, I was intimidated by my surroundings.

When we realized that living in the city just wasn't going to be an option for us, we set our search upon the suburbs. I kind of dread the suburbs. There is a monotony that is homogenous across American suburbia. Strip malls, chain restaurants, and track houses. I found that not being around this corporate beige-ness had awakened my spirits. Living in the thriving, unique, colorful surrounds of Basel had gotten me off my butt, made me active, piqued my curiosity, and made me feel like I was living a real life. The reality of being back in the US was that city living was for either the wealthy twenty-somethings or the itinerant and homeless. Suburbia was for everybody else. Lisa, realizing that I was crestfallen, tried pointing out how we'd be better off out of the city.

"You can have a yard, and that mean you can have a proper garden. You can putter with your plants and flowers and vegetables. You can put out bird and squirrel feeders. We can put up a pool for the summer. You can go all Clark Griswold at Christmas. And it would put us closer to the mountains and nature."

She made some excellent points. Even if she did make me sound middle-aged and white (which, technically, I guess I am).

I really wanted to have a proper vegetable garden. I had missed spending my days tending to all my plants and flowers and backyard critters. We were forbidden from having bird feeders on our back balcony in Basel. The rugby park next door was inundated with thousands of crows, and if we started putting food out, it would create a Hitchcock-ian nightmare in our courtyard. Feeding and attracting birds brings me great peace and joy, and I had missed that greatly. I would pack little baggies of bird food to take with me to the Merian Gärtens to feed the ducks and blue tits and chickadees. It would be nice to watch fluttering birds on feeders as I sat and had my morning coffee. It really is a perfect way to start a day.

"There won't be trams making noise every two minutes"

Lisa hated the trams passing under our front windows, especially in the summer time. With the windows open, it was impossible to hear the TV, or each other, when one lumbered by. The quiet would be nice. My only fear was that the suburbs were full of [shudders] families.

That meant children.

I couldn't deal with screaming children again. Then again, the wildest of mountain banshees could never out-do the Hieronymus Bosch nightmares that lived below us. Still, I was weary of summertime in the 'burbs because... children.

Being closer to the mountains would definitely be a plus. One of the things that brings me the greatest sense of peace is forest bathing. Whenever I get tense or depressed or bored, a walk in the woods soothes my soul more than anything else in the world. Denver itself is out in the flat, dry, brown plains of Colorado (no, it's not in the mountains, but rather, next to them). If I wanted to be able to disappear into a forest, it would have to be in the elevations to the west. Knowing that nature was now a car ride away (instead of a hop on a tram or train), making that car ride as short as possible was paramount.

Once we started looking at houses away from the city, we realized just how much more house we got for the money, especially compared to what we got in Basel for the same price. We wouldn't be paying utilities on communal areas. We wouldn't be paying a TV license. We wouldn't have to pay three month's rent as a security deposit. We would not only get 1000 square feet more house for the same price, but also that much area in private yard space, too.

I could do laundry whenever I pleased. Mow my yard whenever I pleased (but didn't because I hired a lawn guy, because I'm getting too old for that shit). Run the vacuum cleaner whenever I pleased (but let Lisa do it instead because vacuuming is a Zen-inducing activity for her). We could grocery shop on a Sunday (but didn't because Monday's are quieter). We could have Amazon deliveries again!

It took months, however, before I did laundry on a Sunday, or went shopping on a Sunday, or went out to eat on a Sunday, or ran the dishwasher after dark. These habits had become so ingrained that we both had to consciously remind ourselves that, oh, yeah, the store is open today if we need to grab some milk or eggs. Oh, yeah, we can do some spring cleaning on a Sunday because we don't have neighbors above or below us. We had assimilated into daily Swiss life more than we had realized.

We eventually found a place in a far western 'burb just a mile or so from the foothills of the Rocky Mountains. Only one of our neighbors had children, and they seemed to actually parent their kids, who were wonderfully quiet. It was odd at first having neighbors who stopped to chat with you, and who spoke English!

It took me forever to stop using German.

A simple thank you was the hardest adjustment. *"Danke vielmals"* had naturally flown off the tongue for so long that I kept thanking people in German for over six months post-Switzerland. My new barber (Vietnamese, not, sadly, Turkish) kept admonishing me when I'd slip up.

"No, no, you're not in Europe anymore! Use your English!"

A year later, I'm still finding myself thanking people in German, or sometimes French.

Lisa and I still use a mix of German and English at home. We almost never use "please", "thank you" or "you're welcome" in English anymore. *Bitte* is quite common in our house. When clearing plates after dinner, it is never, "are you finished", but rather *"fertig?"*. When playing board games, colors and numbers are German. Days of the week, too, are almost always German, too. While not fluent, we integrated linguistically more than we realized.

At the CVS, I gave my date of birth backwards when verifying my identity.

"Sorry, I gave it to you in European!"

Our new house had a flag pole installed on the wall near the garage. One of the first things I did was buy and display the Swiss flag (showing where my national pride actually lies). This last Halloween, a gentleman came to the door with his two young daughters.

"Are you Swiss?"

"No, but we just moved from there. We lived in Switzerland for the past couple of years"

"Where in Switzerland did you live? I am Swiss! I'm from Chur and seeing your flag when I take my morning run makes me happy"

"We lived in Basel!"

Small world, no?

Having a previous address in Switzerland provided challenges, too. Government forms here are not set up for foreign addresses. Drop down menus for online forms are not set up for foreign addresses. Getting our drivers licenses meant listing our old Texas address. On the plus side, I only had to hand in my Texas license when I got my Colorado one and got to keep my Swiss one.

Yes, I got a driver's license in Basel.

Lucky for us, as Americans, we had the option of simply paying a 300CHF fee, with proof of a current, valid license issued by a US State, and we could have a Swiss license without having to take any tests. Oddly enough, licenses in Basel are issued by the *polizei* and not a DMV. In fact, Lisa ended up swiping a Basel

Polizei pen during her visit to their office. While I never anticipated driving in Switzerland, should we have ever rented a car or had an emergency where I had to get behind the wheel, we were set. Lisa enjoyed renting a car when she had to go to Munich for work, so it was better that she had a European license. I still have mine, and it's valid for another eight years, so if I ever go back...

We had kept our American bank account open the whole time we lived in Switzerland, to pay on our American credit card bills and the like. Lisa's favorite part about moving back was banking. No more card readers, no more month-long clearance periods, no more peach-colored payment slips. On the other hand, the lack of security made us feel like absolutely nothing in our accounts was safe and we nervously laughed at the lackadaisical nature of American bank security.

Man, I forgot how ugly American greenbacks are. I used to think that all the colorful European bank notes were like funny money, or Monopoly money. But now, American dollars feel so antiquated, so boring, so last century. I look at a $20 bill and think, America is stuck, America isn't moving forward, America isn't as modern as it thinks it is. I laugh at how the US Treasury says it would take up to 10 years to put Harriet Tubman on the $20 bill, but Europe, with their plastic-paper hybrid bills manage to change their images every other year without issue. They also don't feature slave owners on their money, nor do the stubbornly refuse to put women and people of color on their currency.

American money makes me kind of sad.

I had also forgotten about sales tax not being included in the price. Being extremely budget conscious in Basel, I would tally up my grocery total as I went, and without having to figure in tax, I could be within a franc in my estimate by the time I got to the register.

Not so in America.

Having forgotten about this, my first trip to the Kroger was shocking. I thought I was saving so much more than I actually did, because I forgot to figure in sales tax. Again, this is one area of Americana that absolutely confounds and frustrates Europeans, and I am firmly in the Europeans' camp on this.

Same goes for yearly taxes. In Switzerland, the government sends you a yearly tax bill, and that is what you pay. In the US, you are coyly asked "so, what do you think you owe us? Go on, take a guess. If you're wrong, we'll fuck up your life, but go on, go ahead and guess for us!" It's weird and cruel and unnecessary. On the plus side, after our first year in Denver, we no longer had to pay double income tax.

I was reminded of the sneaky duplicity of government in America in another way. Shortly after buying our little silver Subaru (or Subie, as the locals call them – and, yes, I think it's a law that you have to own a Subaru in Colorado), I was pulled over by a cop in an unmarked cruiser. I was doing six over the limit (to be fair, I was still getting used to driving again), but I was momentarily shocked to remember that the police in the US will obfuscate their identity with the use of unmarked vehicles. This is anathema to the European mindset, where the *polizei* drive well marked, fluorescent-checkered cars with blue rooftop lights. Anathema to Americans, cops in most European countries do not need probable cause to pull you over and search your car. But they also do not abuse that privilege, either. I was tempted to hand him my Swiss license, but was afraid there might be legal repercussions of driving a car I now owned without local identity papers. I suppose it was ironic that after not driving for two years, and begrudgingly taking up the wheel again, I'd immediately get a god damned ticket.

The most frustrating part of life back in America is the car culture. I really, truly was, happiest not driving. I used to love to drive, but when I first started, there were half the number of cars on the road as compared to now. Cell phones didn't exist back then. Satnav didn't exist, either. Drivers weren't distracted, and they were actually taught how to drive while in school. It was a far more pleasant experience back in the day (dear lord, my old man is showing).

In Europe, the mentality is that driving is a privilege. In the US, it's considered a right. The process for earning a license in Switzerland will cost you thousands and thousands of dollars, which is intended to act as a deterrent. In the European mindset, the less cars on the road, the better. Three months of driving classes, costing upwards of 1000CHF, are all out of pocket expenses. You have to pay to take the tests (practical and written). Should you fail, you don't just get to take the test again – you have to go back to driving school, which is another 1000CHF out of pocket. If you fail three times, you are required to take a psychological exam and must be cleared by a therapist to continue on. After taking the tests again, at cost, finally passing, you need to fork over another 300CHF for the license. To register your car, the fee can be as much as the total cost of the car. Insurance can run thousands of francs a month.

You need to be wealthy as Bill Gates to own a car in Switzerland.

Speeding tickets are based on a percentage of your net worth (not a flat fee), so the richer you are, the more you will pay. All of this is designed to minimize the number of cars on the road, and it is quite effective. That being said, it creates an incredibly safety-conscious driving culture, where if you don't pay attention, it could bankrupt you.

I don't understand how Coloradans can drive distractedly because I find I need to keep my focus on the roads at all times in order to avoid the Grand Canyon-sized pot holes every three feet. The quality of roads might be one of the biggest areas where Switzerland had spoiled us, and we didn't even drive there. Potholes simply do not exist in Switzerland.

It's true, they don't.

I never saw a single pot hole in two years. Then again, it could be that Switzerland uses tax dollars to maintain infrastructure instead of spending two-thirds of it on the military-industrial complex.

I'm just sayin'...

So that I had access to the car during the day, I started taking Lisa to the commuter train in the morning. It would get her into the city center in 20 minutes, and then it was just a short hop on the free bus to her office. Of course, this wasn't like taking the train in Switzerland. The train was almost never, ever on time. There were times when I'd wait in the parking lot to pick her up and the train, that only ran once an hour, would be up to ten minutes late. The adopted Baseler in my head exploded. Stories abounded in Denver online groups about buses never arriving at stops at all. We waited for a bus once (when in our temp place downtown) to take us across town. Twenty minutes past the appointed stop time, we gave up. Both of us were aghast. Even to an American sensibility, this was egregious and unforgivable. Americans think of public transport as a last resort and as a symbol of poverty; in Europe, it is seen as the superior option for travel. The contempt for public transport in the US is a two-way street, with commuters finding buses and trains unreliable, and public transport authorities finding reliability, cleanliness, and safety to be overrated virtues. It is no wonder that public transport is so shitty in America, and that makes me very sad, indeed.

Eventually, we realized that it wasn't safe for her to take the train anyway, because Union Station, where she would disembark, was overrun with violent crack heads and hooligans. The city actually closed the facility for almost a month to try and clear the criminal element out. Stabbings, robberies, and assaults had become commonplace, and no matter the steps the city and police were taking, it wasn't worth the risk sending her on the train anymore.

In short order, it wouldn't be a problem any longer, as a sudden uptick in Covid cases, this time as a new and virulent variant, closed the office and she was ordered to work from home. While this outbreak was quickly contained, Lisa remained working from home permanently, so the sketchy train was no longer an issue. If she did have to venture into Denver for meetings or what-have-you, she'd drive, as it was so much safer. It broke my little Swiss heart to see the train as the bad option, and the car as the good.

Not walking everywhere began to take its toll on me.

Mentally, I couldn't let go of my anger when I drove. Why was everything so far away, and why was everyone in my way a colossal twat?

Physically, I lost my finely shaped and prized toned butt and began to grow a well-appointed middle aged man gut. This made me quite sad. I had never had a visible butt before.

I was becoming far more sedentary. A quick check of my fitness app told me that compared to the 71 miles of walking I did the previous March, this first one in Denver I had only done 20. I lost the color on my face from being outdoors so often (though I would quickly learn that the Colorado sun, hovering a mile closer to my face, caused a nasty sunburn in just a matter of minutes).

Adjusting to the altitude, to be fair, did limit how much I exerted myself. Most people think that Switzerland, being so mountainous, is also high-elevation living. Basel sits a mere 856 feet above sea level. My Colorado home sits at 5,414 feet. That's a huge difference, and your lungs will be the first to tell you that. While I never experienced altitude sickness, I did get short of breath quite quickly when performing any kind of physical activity. Even in the Alps, the altitude is not an issue like it is in Denver. The Matterhorn is not as high above sea level as the suburb I now live in (in fact, the summit is 140 feet lower). Here, just Swiffering the floors on cleaning day can leave you winded and gasping for breath.

For the record, the Swiss version of the Swiffer has much better smelling cleaning fluid. American Swiffer liquid smells like computer-generated cartoon flowers; the Swiss version smelled like freshly harvested Alpine-meadow honey. And it left a better shine. To be fair, it was also woefully more expensive. American cleaning products are half the cost of their European counterparts.

We were, thankfully, saving quite a bit of money at the store. Groceries were a third of the cost now, and it was far easier to make one large trip to the store once a week instead of going multiple times. We could actually stock our freezer. We could afford ice cream again (but man is the quality sucktastic here in comparison – milk, too, tastes so… flat). For a while, going to the Kroger was one of the things I enjoyed most about being back.

For a while.

Soon, I was missing the Géant more than I could have imagined. Sure, Pop Tarts weren't €8 a box, but cereal was cheaper in France. Pastries were cheaper in France. Granola and yogurt were cheaper in France. The yogurt here in the US now tasted so overly sweet to me. The quality of the breakfast bakery items was limited. No one seemed to understand what brioche was.

I ruined our first dozen eggs by not refrigerating them.

The produce section made me feel like I was going color blind. Tomatoes and strawberries weren't red, but a dull shade of mud. Fresh herbs like rosemary, thyme, or basil were brown and wilted. Potatoes weren't sold in color-coded bags! Most shocking of all was the price of flour and sugar. In Basel, at the expensive-ass Coop, I could get 2kg of flour for 1.20CHF and 2kg of sugar for .50CHF. In the US, I was now paying $3.25 for the same amount of flour and $2.50 for sugar. What the hell, man!?

I have yet to find a store that sells veal. Or duck.

One of the great conveniences of European markets is the ability to buy lardons (basically cubes of uncooked bacon). I use these often in cooking, and I spent a good thirty minutes searching for them in the meat section and the deli section on one of my first trips to the local King Soopers grocery store. Finally I asked someone.

"Oh, bacon bits are over there"

They pointed to a jar of pre-cooked crispy bits of bacon-like crumbs.

"Oh, no, no, no, you misunderstand"

"I guess I don't understand at all"

Eventually, I went to the butcher counter and bought two strips of bacon.

"You just want two strips?"

"Yep"

"You know we sell full packages of bacon over there in the case, right?"

"But I don't need that much bacon"

It took me forever to get used to the American notion of everything being packaged for a family of four. Everything was bigger. There weren't small options for anything. America seems to forget that singles and couples shop just as much as nuclear families do. I don't need a 6lb rump roast. I don't need 4lbs of deli turkey (but I do need more than two slices!). The economy of American prices meant nothing if things would spoil before I could use them all.

The corn syrup hit me hardest. It took nearly a year for my digestive system to come to terms with all of my food having some form of corn in it. Think about it. Almost every single thing you eat in the US has corn in it. How whack is that? I have suffered from irritable bowel syndrome for twenty years. Within weeks of moving to Basel, my system settled down and I only had one or two mild flare ups the entire time we lived there. Not having corn syrup in everything was a huge contributing factor to my healthier gut. It could also be why I started to grow a significant Buddha belly once we started eating American processed foods again. Foods tasted flatter, especially fruits and vegetables. I missed my orange-sherbet German soda *Sinalco* (the single greatest soda pop in the universe). I missed buying wine for less than $5. And good wine, at that.

Most of all, I missed European cashiers.

Nothing vexes me more than waiting in line at the cash register in an American grocery store. First of all, there is way too much idle chit chat. Second, I've seen blind, pregnant snails move faster than an American register worker. Things back-up even more as they have to weigh everything for you. In the meantime, instead of packing up their own groceries, the mouth-breather in front of you will just stand there, arms folded, and wait for the cashier to do it for them. Some stores have baggers (which blows the European mind – my neighbor Judith thought I was pulling her leg when I told her this was an actual job) who will inevitably move slow enough that less than half of a bag has been filled by the time the checker is done scanning everything, and will have stacked the 2lb bag of potatoes on top of your carton of eggs. While this sloth-fest meanders on, the mouth-breather will sigh heavily and complain about everything taking so long. To top it off, they will then decide that the pin pad is technology too far beyond them, so writing a god damned paper check is the way to go.

Like a cartoon, steam can literally be seen shooting out of my ears and nostrils.

Finally, the bagger will haphazardly pile your bags back into your cart, smashing the potato chips and bread that they invariably put on the bottom.

If there is a bagger at the end of the counter now when I arrive, I will politely tell them that someone else at a different register probably needs their help more, I'm good, I got this, thanks.

Shoo, shoo, shoo, useless one!

The cashier will inevitable remark how fast I am at bagging my items and they can't keep up with me. Mentally, I tell them they'd be murdered by small German grandmothers for going so slow and for talking so much.

They'll ask me if I found everything okay, and I will bite my tongue because, no, I most certainly did not. I have already, in one trip to the Kroger, spoken more to this one cashier than I have to all cashiers I encountered in Europe, over two years, combined. I understand, now, the European aversion to small talk.

On the plus side, I don't have to wait 15 minutes for the next tram.

I feel this dread towards constant chit chat when we go out to eat. Now, I feel like my server is constantly hovering, buzzing in my ear like a pesky mosquito. Let me eat in peace. And, hey, where are you going with my debit card!?

Lisa, on the other hand, is happy never having to ask for ice, ever again.

Lisa struggled with the decision to move back State-side. She knew how in love I was with Basel, with Switzerland, and with life in Europe. She said in the twenty years she had known me, she had never seen me happier. It is true; I have never been happier in my life than during our two years in Basel. To this day, she feels guilty for "ripping you away from your happy place".

Honestly, the adjustment to life back in the US, after trying so diligently to integrate into Swiss life, was difficult for me. I tried to channel my energies into being excited about exploring and learning a new place to live, as I always have whenever we moved. This time, though, it was much more difficult. This wasn't comparing one American town to another; this was comparing one continent to another; one culture to another. I sat down and Googled "repatriation syndrome". It seems, for many expats, it can take upwards of *one to two years* to fully come to terms with your change in culture. A year in Denver and I am still having a hard time letting routines and opinions go. It does get easier, but it is still a slow process. At least for me.

Lisa was the one who, I think, looked forward to moving back to the US. This is not to say that she didn't like our life in Europe. Strictly from an economic perspective, though, she was pretty done with Switzerland. There is no amount of research that can prepare you for just how *insanely* expensive it is to live there. Had we not lived on the border, and been stuck in a centralized location like Zurich, we'd have been sunk, and fast. The lack of conveniences of life in America bothered her more, like early closing times, the lack of department stores in the vein of a Target, and the lack of delivery services like Amazon. Not to paint her as a commercialist, but as the one who usually managed supply logistics for the household, it became frustrating for her. It became frustrating to me. Knowing you couldn't just order a required thing on Amazon, but had to go physically find and buy it without great knowledge about who carried what made shopping for non-grocery items a pain in the ass in Switzerland.

To be fair, the thing that turned her off of Switzerland the most was the misogyny. You may recall, I mentioned that Switzerland was the last country in Europe to give women the right to vote (with one Canton holding out until 1991). Unlike other progressive states in Europe, the attitude towards women in Switzerland is still pretty antiquated. Remember, school children are not served lunch at school, and are sent home for an hour in the middle of the day. It is expected that mothers be able to arrange their schedules to be home to feed their kids. Many sacrifice their own lunch hours to tend to family matters instead. Not being able to join coworkers for meals limits their ability to network, build relationships, or be in tune to office gossip and goings on. For Lisa, opportunities to move up had her passed over for male colleagues, many without the same experience or skills. Part of that was also rooted in her being a foreigner. The Swiss are great xenophobes, and can be very American in their "Swiss First" attitudes.

The climate in her office space became cold and unwelcoming. While she was in no danger of losing her position (it is next to impossible to get fired in Switzerland), she knew that she would never escape her position, move up, or be celebrated. She was stuck.

The one opportunity she had, of heading the new international division, had been quashed by Covid (*fucking Covid*), and that was that. With no reinstatement of her full salary in the foreseeable future, she was mentally done. We both knew that staying in Basel was simply untenable. It was impossible to put any money away for a rainy day. While Lisa made six figures, we were living paycheck to paycheck. The smart option was to celebrate our two years as a major accomplishment and make plans to head back home.

Switzerland did, however, reward us right before we left.

After informing the Canton that we were leaving the country, we learned that her Swiss pension would then pay her out. Even as a foreigner, as a Swiss *resident*, she was given the option of paying into the Swiss social insurance program. On her last day of employment, she would immediately be paid her Pillar I social insurance in full, which amounted to a five figure check. Even better, as a resident, she had paid into the Second Pillar of social insurance, so when she turns 60, she will be paid out once again for her retirement. Given the astronomical increase in shipping costs, her payout meant we could afford not only to get home, but cover all of our deposits for housing and a down payment on a new car.

Thanks, Switzerland!

———

One week before we were scheduled to leave, I awoke to a pile of messages on my phone. All of my friends had called to tell me, before I read the news on Facebook that morning, that my best friend in the world, Aaron, had suddenly and unexpectedly passed away. He was 51 years old and had died in his sleep. I had last seen him two weeks before we moved to Basel. I was in Austin, and he lived in a small farm town outside of Texarkana. We decided to meet up at the Dallas Museum of Art for the day and say our goodbyes. It was just like old times. In our teen years, we would go to the Art Institute of Chicago and stand in the middle of a gallery room and go around the room pointing to the paintings.

"Crap, crap, crap, love it, crap, love it, love it, crap!"

It was a tonic to be able to do that with him one more time.

In the summer before we went off to college, we were inseparable. No summer will ever top it. We wrote an absurdist play, painted his bedroom (cornflower blue), and listened to The Smiths. We took endless midnight walks and dreamt of our post-college lives when we would both be glamorous European writers. He would be Hemingway; I would be Fitzgerald. He was the brother I never had.

In the weeks leading up to our return to the US, we made plans to once again meet up. If anything, we'd finally be in the same time zone and could chat on the phone or online whenever the mood struck us. He demanded that I would write about my life as an expat in Switzerland, and he would be my editor (after all, he worked as a writer for the *Texarkana Gazette*!). He encouraged me to do the thing I had always talked about: be an expat and write about it. So I was already churning ideas around in my noggin' when I got the devastating news.

For the longest time, I couldn't bear to think about writing this book. Soon, though, I realized that it was the best way I could honor him. Outside of my family, Aaron was my biggest cheerleader, and took great interest in our adventures.

And what an adventure it was.

I am one of the luckiest people on earth. I got to move across an ocean, to a new continent, a new country, a new culture. I did this with the woman I love more than life. I did this with the constant support and interest from our friends and family. I learned more about myself in those two years than in all the other 48 before.

I found my *happy place.*

Basel is truly a fabulous city. Switzerland is a confoundingly wonderful country. It has beauty I will never find anywhere else on earth. Perhaps it is with rose-colored glasses that I say this, but I feel as if our enterprise had far more ups than downs. I know that I was more at peace with life and I came out the other side of our experience a better person. I'm much more worldly, I can tell you that! I realized just how different attitudes and lifestyles are across The Pond, and I found just about everything European spoke to me in a way that America never has. I felt more at home there than I ever have in any of the places I called home in The States. If anything, living abroad only heightened my disdain for America and all of its ills. Having experienced so many ups in Europe, they only served to exacerbate the downs back home for me. Maybe it's the Repatriation Syndrome speaking, but I know I will only fully recover until I'm back on the other side of the Atlantic.

I have not given up on finding a permanent home in Europe. I know that, unless I win the Lotto, it won't be Switzerland. For all its natural wonder, convenience of transport, and central location, it's just too damned expensive. But in my heart, I will ever after consider myself Swiss. If we do end up back on The Continent, I will most certainly go back to see Basel one more time. Like a Harry Potter *horcrux*, it holds part of my soul.

Of course, absolutely none of this was possible without Lisa.

My rock. My love. My Boo.

We always manage to make a home wherever we land, and we are certainly not afraid of uprooting and trying somewhere new. Together, we have moved over 17,990 miles, lived in 6 different states, three different countries and on two different continents. In the grand scheme of things, I feel like all of that is just the beginning.

So, my friends, as the Swiss might say:

Ciao, ciao, adieu, ciao, tschüss!

Made in the USA
Las Vegas, NV
15 April 2023

70622509R00193